Phonics for Pupils Special Educational Needs

Book 7: Multisyllable Magic

Phonics for Pupils with Special Educational Needs is a complete, structured, multisensory programme for teaching reading and spelling, making it fun and accessible for all. This fantastic seven-part resource offers a refreshingly simple approach to the teaching of phonics, alongside activities to develop auditory and visual perceptual skills. Specifically designed to meet the needs of pupils of any age with special educational needs, the books break down phonics into manageable core elements and provide a huge wealth of resources to support teachers in teaching reading and spelling.

Book 7: Multisyllable Magic focuses on revising the main complex sounds from previous books and working on words with 2, 3 and 4 syllables. It also explores words with key suffixes (-tion/ -sion/ -ture/ -sure/ -cious/ -cial). Each chapter contains 10 engaging activities, including syllable jigsaw, sounds like a syllable, syllable trap and spelling challenge, plus handy highlighted word cards. Thorough guidance is provided on how to deliver each activity, as well as a lesson planner template to support learning.

Each book in the series gradually builds on children's understanding of sounds and letters and provides scaffolded support for children to learn about every sound in the English language. Offering tried and tested material which can be photocopied for each use, this is an invaluable resource to simplify phonics teaching for teachers and teaching assistants and provide fun new ways of learning phonics for all children.

Ann Sullivan is an educational consultant and trainer. Having gained experience of teaching in mainstream primary classrooms and in secondary learning support departments, she went on to become a high school SENCO. The move to specialist education seemed natural and for nine years she worked as an outreach/advisory teacher based at a specialist support school, providing advice, support and training to staff in mainstream schools to enable them to meet the needs of their pupils with SEND. She became a Specialist Leader in Education in 2017. Ann has made it her career's work to explore the best ways of teaching young people to read, spell and write effectively, leading her to develop these resources, which she has tested in a variety of mainstream and special schools.

Phonics for Pupils with Special Educational Needs

This fantastic seven-part resource offers an innovative and refreshingly simple approach to the teaching of phonics that is specifically designed to meet the needs of pupils with special educational needs. The books strip phonics down into manageable core elements and provide a wealth of resources to support teachers in teaching reading and spelling. They systematically take the pupil through incremental steps and help them to learn about and thoroughly understand all of the sounds in the English language.

Other resources in *Phonics for Pupils with Special Educational Needs*

Book 1: Building Basics	**Introducing Sounds and Letters**	
Book 2: Building Words	**Working on Word Structure with Basic Sounds**	
Book 3: Sound by Sound Part 1	**Discovering the Sounds**	
Book 4: Sound by Sound Part 2	**Investigating the Sounds**	
Book 5: Sound by Sound Part 3	**Exploring the Sounds**	
Book 6: Sound by Sound Part 4	**Surveying the Sounds**	
Book 7: Multisyllable Magic	**Revising the Main Sounds and Working on 2, 3 and 4 Syllable Words**	

Phonics for Pupils with Special Educational Needs

Book 7: Multisyllable Magic

Revising the Main Sounds and Working on 2, 3 and 4 Syllable Words

Ann Sullivan

Routledge
Taylor & Francis Group

LONDON AND NEW YORK

First published 2019
by Routledge
2 Park Square, Milton Park, Abingdon, Oxon OX14 4RN

and by Routledge
711 Third Avenue, New York, NY 10017

Routledge is an imprint of the Taylor & Francis Group, an informa business

British Library Cataloguing-in-Publication Data
A catalogue record for this book is available from the British Library

Library of Congress Cataloging-in-Publication Data
Names: Sullivan, Ann (Educational consultant) author.
Title: Phonics for pupils with special educational needs / Ann Sullivan.
Description: Abingdon, Oxon ; New York, NY : Routledge, 2019–
Identifiers: LCCN 2018015561 (print) | LCCN 2018033657 (ebook) | ISBN 9781351040303 (ebook) |
    ISBN 9781138488373 (book1) | ISBN 9781351040303 (book1 : ebk) | ISBN 9781138488434 (book3)
    | ISBN 9781351040181 (book 3 : ebk) | ISBN 9781138313583 (book 5) | ISBN 9780429457555
    (book 5 : ebk) | ISBN 9781138313637 (book 6) | ISBN 9780429457517 (book 6 : ebk) | ISBN
    9781138313682 (book 7) | ISBN 9780429457487 (book 7 : ebk)
Subjects: LCSH: Reading—Phonetic method. | Reading disability. | Special education.
Classification: LCC LB1573.3 (ebook) | LCC LB1573.3 .S85 2019 (print) | DDC 372.46/5—dc23
LC record available at https://lccn.loc.gov/2018015561

ISBN: 978-1-138-31368-2 (pbk)
ISBN: 978-0-429-45748-7 (ebk)

Typeset in VAG Rounded
by Apex CoVantage, LLC

To Matthew, Ruth and Tom

Contents

Introduction

Phonics is the established method for teaching reading and spelling in schools, but many pupils with special educational needs find conventional phonics programmes and schemes difficult to access and so struggle to find success.

Pupils with special educational needs require a clear and consistent, multisensory approach to phonics and the teaching of reading and spelling. A programme should give them the opportunity to systematically and thoroughly explore all sounds and letters, gradually building up their understanding and knowledge of how the written English language works so that they are able to apply these when reading and spelling words. They also require specific instructional techniques to develop and master key reading and spelling skills and be given the opportunity to work at a pace appropriate to their individual needs.

Phonics for Pupils with Special Educational Needs is a complete programme, made up of seven books, which simplifies the way written language is presented to the child, demystifying phonics to make it accessible and fun. The programme is multisensory, systematic, logical, thorough and cumulative in its approach, taking the child from their first encounter with sounds and letters through to managing and using multisyllable words.

Many pupils with special educational needs have underlying difficulties with auditory and visual perception and processing, which often goes unrecognised. Difficulties processing auditory and visual information will have a direct impact on reading and spelling acquisition, as written English is essentially a cipher or code that converts speech sounds into visual figures for spelling and vice versa for reading. The cipher is dependent on an individual being able to work with and interpret sounds and symbols; yet processing auditory and visual information may be the very things that a pupil finds difficult to do. Pupils with perceptual difficulties require access to materials that work to develop and improve these auditory and visual skills in the context of the sounds and letters they are learning. Built into the *Phonics for Pupils with Special Educational Needs* programme are worksheets, resources and activities which support the development of underlying auditory and visual skills.

Difficulties with visual perception and processing will also impact on the child's ability to easily access teaching materials presented to them. For this reason, the worksheets, resources and activities in *Phonics for Pupils with Special Educational Needs* are simple in format, uncluttered and with a simple to follow linear progression.

Book 7 Multisyllable Magic

Multisyllable Magic deals with all the sounds (speech sounds or phonemes) in words and how to manage these in 2, 3 and 4 syllable words, with a focus on revising key sounds and sound spellings. Book 7 also introduces some key suffixes.

In Book 7, the pupil:

- consolidates their understanding of the important concepts or ideas about the English language; that letters are **symbols** or **pictures** that **represent** speech sounds in spoken words; that some of the symbols are made up of one letter but some have two, three or even four letters; that some sounds are represented by more than one symbol and some symbols themselves represent more than one sound;

- revises the key complex sounds and all the sound spellings that represent them;

- learns to manage these sounds in 2 syllable words when reading and spelling;

- learns to manage sounds in 3 and 4 syllable words when reading and spelling;

- learns some key suffixes;

- continues to practise and develop the key reading and spelling skills of blending, segmenting and phoneme manipulation, if appropriate (dependent on pupil's skill level);

- experiences reading and spelling words at single word and sentence level and

- experiences reading at text level.

Book 1 introduced the pupil to the basic sounds and the single letters that represent them. Book 2 developed the pupil's ability to work with these sounds in words with a more complex structure: VCC, CVCC, CCVC and CCVCC+ words. Books 3–6 introduced and systematically explored the more complex sounds in the English language.

Working through the programme

It is strongly recommended that anyone delivering the programme reads through the teaching notes in the 'Working through the programme' section of this book, where the programme is explained in detail and specific techniques are described and explained.

Teaching materials

Most of the resources in the programme have instructions on delivery of the activity or worksheet on the sheet itself to provide a helpful prompt for teachers and teaching assistants. A few activities only have instructions written in the 'Working through the programme' section of this book and teachers and teaching assistants should make themselves familiar with the details of these.

All the resources in the programme are designed to have a simple format and presentation to support access for pupils with visual perceptual difficulties. As a result, they are age neutral and so are suitable for pupils of a wide age range; primary, secondary and post 16.

Phonics for Pupils with Special Educational Needs is suitable for pupils in mainstream and specialist school settings.

Planning and delivery

A simple to use planning sheet enables teachers and teaching assistants to plan teaching sessions by selecting from the menu of available programme activities, ensuring an overall even and complete coverage of skills, concepts and knowledge. The planning sheet also enables staff to track pupil progression thorough the programme.

A child or group of children can work through the programme at a pace that is appropriate for them or their peer group.

Working through the programme

Starting out

Before beginning to work through the programme with a child or a group of children, it is important for teachers and teaching assistants to read through this introductory section to familiarise themselves with the programme's structure and how it works, as well as the specific instructional techniques, resources and activities.

It is assumed that a child starting on the activities in Book 7 has worked through Books 1–6, the Building Basics and Sound by Sound books, or that the child has knowledge of the sounds and letters (sound spellings), key skills and concepts equivalent to having worked through Books 1–6.

This section covers **the things you need to know about and understand before you start**:

- the ideas or concepts which underpin the structure of written English;
- the skills that children need to master to be able to work with sounds and letters / letter combinations (sound spellings): blending, segmenting and phoneme manipulation;
- the body of knowledge children need to know, remember and recall and
- how words are split into syllables.

It covers **how to teach the programme** at Book 7 level:

- the teaching order of sounds and suffixes,
- understanding how words are made up of syllables,
- revising sounds and letters / letter combinations (sound spellings),
- reinforcing the child's knowledge of sounds and letters / letter combinations (sound spellings),
- managing syllables when reading and spelling,
- working in a multisensory way.

It also covers **how to organise delivery of the programme**:

- structuring a teaching session and
- planning and progression.

*Note that in the explanations which follow, sounds are always written in speech marks, e.g. 's' 'l' 'ch',
and letters / letter combinations (sound spellings) are always written in bold, **e.g. s l ch tch** etc.*

The written English language – an overview

Written language developed many years ago because people realised they needed to fix information in a form that remained constant over time. In this way information could be passed on easily, without people having to speak directly to each other. Writing developed as a way of storing information, carrying messages and sharing news and stories.

Experiments in drawing pictures to represent information proved ineffective as pictures can be interpreted in so many ways and are open to an individual's interpretation. However, people soon realised that there is one characteristic of the spoken word that could be exploited to create a fixed visual representation of the information.

The spoken word is made up of speech sounds (or phonemes). When we say any word, we must be consistent with the sounds we use and the order we say them for us to convey the intended meaning.

If I say the sounds 'c' 'a' 't' together to make a word, then you think of a furry pet. If I change the first sound to 'h' then the meaning changes and you think of something quite different.

Written English capitalises on this consistency and uses letters as **symbols** to, one by one, represent individual speech **sounds**. In other words, letters are a written form of spoken sounds.

This is the first of four ideas or concepts that children need to understand to be able to read and spell but there are three more; all are explained below.

The concepts – how the written word is put together

1. **Letters represent sounds**

    In the written word the letters represent the speech sounds of the spoken word.

    For example, the word dog has three sounds in it, 'd' 'o' 'g', which are represented by the three letters:

    d o g.

    This concept is explored from Book 1 onwards in the programme.

    In *Phonics for Pupils with Special Educational Needs*, letters are referred to as *'sound spellings'*. This label describes letters in terms of their function. In other words, a **sound** is represented in a written form when we **spell** / write words. It gives the teacher a simple term that describes single letters and, more importantly, also describes combinations of letters, which appear in this part of the programme. This term also reinforces the sound to symbol relationship, *'sound >* **spelling'** and the term is easy for children to understand and remember.

2. **Sound spellings can be one letter or more**

   Some of the sound spellings we use are made up of just one letter, like those in dog, but many are made up of several letters which, in combination, act as a single unit within the word, together representing one sound.

   For example, **sh** is the sound spelling for the sound 'sh' in the word **sh**op and **th** is the sound spelling for the sound 'th' in the word mo**th**. **sh** and **th** are sound spellings that are made up two letters, but some sound spellings are made up of three or even four letters, e.g. **igh** representing 'i-e' and **ough** representing 'o-e'.

   This concept is explored from Book 3 onwards in the programme.

3. **Sounds can be represented by more than just one sound spelling**

   Many sounds can be represented in more than just one way, i.e. by more than one sound spelling.

   For example: b**oa**t   t**oe**   s**o**   gr**ow**   c**o**d**e**   th**ough**

   These all have an 'o-e' sound, but it is written differently in each word, using the sound spellings:

   oa, oe, o, ow, o-e and **ough**, respectively.

   This concept is touched upon in Book 1, but is fully explored from Book 3 onwards in the programme.

   Phonics for Pupils with Special Educational Needs focuses on working on only **one sound at a time** and enabling the child to discover **all** the ways of representing it. Time is given to experience and explore all the sound spellings at word and sentence level before moving on to the next sound.

4. **Some sound spellings can represent more than one sound**

   Certain sound spellings can be used to represent one sound in one word but a different sound in another word.

   For example: gr**ow**   br**ow**n

   The sound spelling **ow** is in both words, but in the first it represents an 'o-e' sound and in the second it represents an 'ow' sound.

   This concept is explored from Book 4 onwards in the programme.

   Phonics for Pupils with Special Educational Needs addresses this at appropriate points in the programme for key sound spellings, giving the child the opportunity to explore all the sounds that these sound spellings can represent.

To be able to read and spell effectively, children need to understand these four concepts. *Phonics for Pupils with Special Educational Needs* presents children with the opportunity to explore them for each sound in English over the seven books in the series.

At this point it is important to understand that the child's understanding of these concepts will be implicit rather than explicit. This means that they will have processed their experiences of sounds, sound spellings and words and reached an unconscious understanding about the concepts. The programme does not demand that the child talks about or explains the concepts but instead they demonstrate their understanding by the way they respond to sounds, sounds spellings and words during teaching sessions and whenever they are reading and writing.

The skills – what we do with the sounds and sound spellings

As well as understanding these four concepts, children also need to be able to **work with** the sounds and sound spellings to read or spell words. Like all skills, these need to be taught and practised to achieve mastery. The skills needed to be able to read and spell are:

1. **Blending** – to be able to push speech sounds together to make a meaningful word. This skill relates directly to reading.

2. **Segmenting** – to be able to break up words into all the separate speech sounds that make up that word, in the right order. This skill relates directly to spelling.

3. **Phoneme manipulation** – to be able to slide speech sounds in and out of words. This skill relates to both reading and spelling.

Developing an understanding of how the English language is put together and practising these important skills starts on day one of the programme and continues right the way through to mastery.

The knowledge – what we need to know, remember and recall

Skills and concepts are not the only things children need to learn to be able to read and spell effectively. They also need a good working knowledge of the sounds and sound spellings. Specifically, they need to know the relationship between the two and this is something that is gradually and cumulatively built up as the child works through this programme.

There are around 140 sound spellings representing the 40 *or so* sounds we use (*regional differences influence exactly how many sounds we perceive in words with variation from 40–42*). At the end of this section there are two posters that show all the sounds and their main sound spellings which you may find helpful.

Step by step and sound by sound, *Phonics for Pupils with Special Educational Needs* works through all the sounds and all their sound spellings, guides the child to understand how written language is put together and supports them to master the skills needed to become fluent readers and spellers.

Automaticity

At first, reading may be a slow process of working through a word, sound spelling by sound spelling, but with experience, repetition and practice the child achieves 'automaticity'. Automaticity happens when all the things the child has experienced and learned come together to enable them to look at a written word, process it rapidly and without apparent effort simply say the word. As competent adult readers we have achieved this automaticity and can no longer remember just how we learned to read.

The activities and techniques in *Phonics for Pupils with Special Educational Needs* are designed to provide the child with this experience, repetition and practice with the aim of children achieving reading and spelling automaticity.

Syllabification

So far in the programme the child has encountered words containing a relatively small number of sounds which can be managed easily. The child has been taught to dynamically blend sounds and listen for a word forming. At the end of this blending process the child is rewarded by hearing a meaningful word and this is a signal that they have successfully read the word. The child has also been taught a sequential segmenting strategy for spelling.

Having built up a good working knowledge of the sounds and their sound spellings in 1 syllable words, the child is ready to deal with longer and more complex words which generally contain more sounds.

Splitting words up into smaller groups of sounds or syllables is called syllabification. There are many ways that teachers, academics and linguists view this. In dictionaries words are split into syllables according to etymology (the origin and meaning of words) and morphology (the structure of words in terms of roots, affixes and suffixes). However, it is far more useful for beginner readers and spellers to view syllabification in terms of phonology (the sounds in words). Even taking this route there conventionally exists a complex picture of syllabification, with a multitude of syllable types identified by linguists and rules constructed by teachers to describe how to interpret them for reading and spelling. This approach is bewildering for pupils with special educational needs who benefit from a far simpler and pragmatic approach that provides a tool for decoding and encoding (reading and spelling) these more difficult words.

An easy way to describe syllables to the child is that when longer words contain lots of sounds or sounds in an awkward combination it is difficult to 'speak' them all in one breath or mouthful. We tend to say words in a rhythmic way, collecting sounds within the word into groups as we go. Doing this makes it easier for us to say long words or words containing sounds in awkward combinations.

For example, the word fantastic has nine sounds and it is very difficult to 'say them all in one breath' without rushing the sounds, making it impossible to understand. Instead we collect the sounds together into three groups of sounds and say the three groups one at a time in order with a natural rhythm. Thinking back to the word fantastic, we say, 'fan' 'tas' 'tic'. These groups of sounds are syllables and splitting the word up like this can help us when reading and spelling and well as speaking.

By thinking of syllables in this simple way, with the child encouraged to think about how they say the word and naturally group sounds together, it is possible to present simple strategies for reading and spelling words (described later in this section).

Stressed and unstressed syllables

As well as naturally splitting words into syllables as we speak, by rhythmically grouping together sounds within a word, we also tend to emphasise one syllable and we can identify this as the dominant or stressed syllable (the other syllable/s being unstressed). A more child friendly way of thinking about this is to describe some syllables as being 'louder' and some being 'quieter' than others. If a child has accurately dynamically blended the syllables when reading, stressing the wrong syllable when finalising the word can impact on the child's success.

For example, a child is reading the word **rapid** and has correctly split the word into two syllables by dynamically blending the sounds, as follows: 'ra' 'pid'. When saying the word, the stress is on the first syllable: '**ra**' 'pid'. If the second syllable is stressed then the word sounds very different: 'ra' '**pid**' and the child will struggle to finalise a meaningful word.

To support the child when this happens, they should be guided to switch which syllable is the loudest and then search for a meaningful word.

There are no specific activities in the programme to address this as this is a subtle matter that can be better dealt with by skilful guidance and teaching in the context of reading. It is important that as a practitioner you are aware of this issue in order to be able to support the child when necessary.

Split it how you say it

When as children we learn to speak we are influenced by a variety of sources around us, including how our parents/carers speak, how our peers speak, the regional accent around us and the media we are frequently exposed to. As a result, we don't all pronounce all words in exactly the same way.

Since in this programme we are teaching the child to always refer to the sounds they can hear in words, they will hear those sounds in their own voice. How they say those sounds will impact on reading and spelling, especially when working at the multisyllable level.

An example used earlier was the word **fantastic** split into three syllables 'fan' 'tas' 'tic'. However, some people might split the word differently, as follows: 'fan' 'ta' 'stic'.

It is very important that the child is encouraged to listen to and follow how they personally say the word, as this is their guide for reading and spelling. How they split the word may differ from the way you, as the teacher, or this book splits it. Some of the materials in the book may need to be subtly modified to reflect the child's way of speaking and splitting words into syllables so be prepared to be flexible in where those syllable splits occur.

The schwa

Now that the child is working with multisyllable words, they will encounter a new phenomenon called the *schwa*. A schwa is a neutral vowel sound in an unstressed syllable. An easy way of describing the schwa sound to a child it that it is a 'sloppy or lazy sound' in a syllable. For example, when we say the word **button** the 'o' sound in the second syllable is not a clear and precise 'o' sound but an 'untidy' sound that is 'somewhere between' an 'o' and a 'u' and more like an 'uh'.

It is important to stress that we *all* speak in this 'untidy' way (using schwas) as is helps us to speed up our speech so we can get the information out more quickly. Being able to understand the schwa and identify it in words is helpful for the child when reading and spelling. This is explored further later in this section and in the worksheets within the programme.

Suffixes

The programme's approach so far has remained faithful to the simple relationships between sounds and sound spellings (the symbol > sound reading strategy and the sound > symbol spelling strategy) which, when coupled with practising the key skills of blending, segmenting and phoneme manipulation, is all the child needs. There has been no need to artificially group sounds or sound spellings together and teach them as distinct units such as consonant blends, onset and rime, word families or word endings. This would be confusing and add additional layers of complexity for the child.

However, at this stage in the programme the child has now had lots of experience, repetition and practise of applying their knowledge of sounds and sound spellings to reading and spelling and should be close to mastery of the three key skills.

In some multisyllable words there are much more obvious patterns of sounds that could be said to make up 'word endings' in multisyllable words and there is some benefit to breaking with principle and teaching some suffixes (word endings) to aid fluency and speed. The programme does not teach a wide range of suffixes, as the basic principle still holds that if the child is able to look at a word, identify all the sounds from the sound spellings and blend, then they can read the word (and vice versa for spelling). Instead the programme works on a few of the more complex suffixes, as given in Table 2.

Book 7 Managing Multisyllable Words

Book 7 is divided into two parts, each with its own planning sheet:

- Part 1 covers revision of the main complex sounds and their sound spelling with a focus on 2 syllable words and a brief introduction to reading and spelling 3 syllable words.
- Part 2 covers reading and spelling 3 and 4 syllable words and words ending in common suffixes.

The teaching order of sounds is shown in Table 1.

Table 1 The teaching order of sounds in *Phonics for Pupils with Special Educational Needs*

Phonics for Pupils with Special Educational Needs teaching order			
Book	**Sounds**	**Word structure**	**Skills**
1 Building Basics: Introducing Sounds and Letters Focus: basic sounds and their relationship with letters	s a t p i n m d g o c k e u r h b f l j v w x y z	VC and CVC words	Blending, segmenting & phoneme manipulation
2 Building Words: Working on Word Structure with Basic Sounds Focus: increasingly complex word structure	All the sounds from Book 1	VCC words CVCC words CCVC words CCVCC+ words CAPITALS	Teaching to mastery
3 Sound by Sound Part 1: Discovering the Sounds Focus: complex sounds and their relationship with letters and letter combinations	sh th ch k qu ng f l s	Mixed VC CVC VCC CVCC CCVC CCVCC+ words	
4 Sound by Sound Part 2: Investigating the Sounds Focus: complex sounds and their relationship with letters and letter combinations	o-e z ee a-e er e ow		
5 Sound by Sound Part 3: Exploring the Sounds Focus: complex sounds and their relationship with letters and letter combinations	oy oo u i-e aw air ar		
6 Sound by Sound Part 4: Surveying the Sounds Focus: complex sounds and their relationship with letters and letter combinations	s (advanced) l (advanced) b and d (advanced) o i u-e Miscellaneous consonants		

Phonics for Pupils with Special Educational Needs teaching order			
Book	**Sounds**	**Word structure**	**Skills**
7 Multisyllable Magic: Revising the Main Sounds and Working on 2, 3 and 4 Syllable Words Focus: reading and spelling 2 syllable words and revising the main sounds. Reading and spelling 3 and 4 syllable words and words with key suffixes.	Revision of o-e	2 syllable words ↓ 3 and 4 syllable words	
	Revision of ee		
	Revision of a-e		
	Revision of er		
	Revision of e		
	Revision of ow		
	Revision of oy		
	Revision of oo		
	Revision of u		
	Revision of i-e		
	Revision of aw		
	Revision of air		
	Revision of ar		
	Revision of o		
	Revision of i		
	Revision of u-e		
	Suffixes		

Table 2 The teaching order of sounds and suffixes in *Phonics for Pupils with Special Educational Needs* Book 7

Book 7	Revision of sound / introduction of suffix	Number of syllables
Part 1	oe	2
	ee	2
	ae	2
	er	2
	e	2
	ow	2
	oy	2
	oo	2
	u	2
	i-e	2
	aw	2
	air	2
	ar	2
	o	2
	u-e	2

Book 7	Revision of sound / introduction of suffix	Number of syllables
	Mixed sounds	3
	Mixed sounds	4
	tion/cian/sion/ssion/shion/cion	2, 3 & 4
Part 2	sion	2, 3 & 4
	ture	2, 3 & 4
	sure/zure	2, 3 & 4
	cious/scious/tious	2, 3 & 4
	cial/tial	2, 3 & 4

Working with sounds

When working with a child on any reading and spelling activity it is important to be aware of the need to be careful about our personal articulation of the sounds as we are modelling our pronunciation for the child to copy and learn. When we say individual sounds to children it is easy to fall into the trap of saying them inaccurately or 'untidily'. Indeed, many of us were taught to say the sound that way when we were at school; but things have changed.

For example, the sound 'm' is often mispronounced as a 'muh' sound rather than a pure 'mmm'. This is unhelpful for the child who needs to hear the precise sound in order to be able to deal with it when reading and spelling words. The apparent addition of an 'uh' sound after the 'm' can easily result in confusion and lead to reading and spelling errors. So, we must make a conscious effort to say the sounds clearly and accurately. We also need to support the child to always say 'tidy' sounds themselves and gently correct them if necessary.

Be aware that we are not trying to change the way pupils speak. We are giving them as good a chance as possible to hear and access sounds in words (whatever their natural regional variations are) to increase their success with reading and spelling.

Table 3, below, goes some way to explain some of the pitfalls encountered when working with sounds, but it may be helpful to access an audio or video file of correct 'phonics' pronunciation, many of which are readily available on the internet.

Table 3 Simple speech sounds and strategies for accurate articulation

Sounds	Strategy	Difficulties
b c/k d g j t ch	Be aware of the need to *gently* 'clip' these sounds when speaking and avoid the 'uh' on the end. When reading a word, it is more difficult to blend from these sounds into the next so make sure you encourage the child to say the sound and rapidly move on the next sound.	Short, clipped sounds – very easy to add an untidy 'uh' sound at the end e.g. 'buh' rather than 'b'.

Sounds	Strategy	Difficulties
f l m n r s v z sh th ng	Wonderful sounds that can go on for a long time, e.g. 'mmmmmmmmmm'. Make the most of these sounds when playing the blending games with the child.	
h p	Practise saying these sounds in a breathy way rather than 'huh' and 'puh'.	Breathy sounds – very easy to add an untidy 'uh' sound at the end, e.g. 'huh' rather than 'h'.
a e i o u a-e ee i-e o-e u-e er ow oy oo aw air ar	These are vowel sounds and are quite flexible and can be spoken for an extended time for emphasis.	If overextended, these can become distorted e.g. with the sound 'ee' there is a tendency to add a 'y' sound at the end.
y z	Practise saying them clearly. A good strategy is to start to say a word containing the sound, e.g. yes. Start to say it but stop without saying the 'e' 's' part of the word. In this way you say the pure 'y' sound.	Treat very carefully. These are always followed by another sound in words, e.g. yes, wet. When we say them on their own we tend to say 'yuh' and 'wuh'.

Describing and working with sound spellings

During a teaching session it is helpful to focus on the sound spellings as a whole, without describing them by using letter names.

Using a sequence of letter names to describe a sound spelling, e.g. referring to **oa** as 'o-e' 'a-e', places an additional cognitive burden on the child. They have to learn and then recall the letter name and convert that to a visual symbol, requiring the brain to carry out an additional processing task. Additionally, using letter names confuses the child, as letter names do not actually have a part to play in the relationship between sound and symbol, a relationship which we are trying to teach and strengthen. To avoid saying a list of letter names when talking about a sound spelling it is helpful to have the sound spelling cards from the programme available as a visual reference to use during teaching sessions. For example, if the child is spelling the word **toast** we can say, "In this word we use this sound spelling (showing the card that matches - **oa**) for the 'o-e' sound". Alternatively have a whiteboard handy and when talking about a specific sound spelling write it on the board so that you can show it to the child as you are talking about it and simply refer to it as 'this way of writing the sound…'.

It is also not advisable to describe sound spellings by basic sounds associated with their component letters, e.g. **oa** as 'o' 'a'. Once again this is confusing for the child and actively works against what you are trying to teach, as the focus should be the relationship between the sound 'o-e' and the sound spelling **oa**. Having the sound spelling cards or a whiteboard handy, used as described above, supports the child's understanding of the sound to symbol relationship whilst also giving you a way to talk about individual sound spellings.

Dynamic blending for reading – syllable by syllable

If you have worked through Books 1–6 with a child or group of children then you will be familiar with the blending technique used in *Phonics for Pupils with Special Educational Needs*, although a refresher is always helpful. If you are starting the child at this point in the programme, then it is important that you read this section.

Blending is the ability to push sounds together to make a word and is a key skill in reading. It is important that blending is taught as an active or ***dynamic*** process – pushing the sounds together as the child moves through the word and listening for the word forming.

The dynamic blending technique

- When the child is reading a word, ask them to say the sounds as you simultaneously move your pen or finger underneath the word so that you are indicating which sound spellings to think about.

- Have the child say the sounds in a ***dynamic*** blended fashion (connecting the sounds and pushing them together).

  So rather than the child saying separate sounds quickly one after the other, e.g. 'm' 'a' 'n', have the child actively push the sounds into each other without a gap, e.g. 'mmaaann'.

  In this way the child simply has to listen and then say the word they heard forming. It may be helpful to point out to the child that it sounds like we are saying the word very slowly and ask them what the word would be if we speeded it up.

  Be aware of the need to say the sounds clearly and purely. Some sounds are more difficult to blend as they are clipped, e.g. 'b', 'p', 't', 'd' etc. When reading words with these sounds, you will have to make sure the child says the sound and very rapidly moves on to the next sound. This avoids the child distorting the clipped sound; if it takes too long they are forced to artificially stretch it out before blending it into the next.

- Model this dynamic blending technique for the child.

- When working on any task with the child be aware of the need to gently correct their blending technique and encourage them to push the sounds together, modelling the technique if necessary.

The dynamic blending – syllable by syllable reading strategy

When the child encounters a long word or a word with sounds in an awkward combination in a text, it is a signal that they are likely to have to think about looking for groups of sounds that make up a syllable within the word.

The child is encouraged to:

- Dynamically blend through the word from the beginning until they have said a group of sounds which 'sit comfortably together'; adding any more sounds to this syllable would make it difficult to say 'in the same breath'.

  This requires the child to have an intuitive sense of the general patterns of sounds which occur in the English language which they will have developed by working through the programme so far.

  e.g.   **fantastic**   **f a n**   **t a s t i c**

                  'f'>'a'>'n'   'fan'

- Then set aside that first comfortable group of sounds (syllable) and continue on through the word, blending and listening for the next comfortable group of sounds.

  e.g.   **fantastic**   **fan**   **t a s**   **t i c**

                  'fan'   't' 'a' 's'   'tas'

- Next, set aside that second comfortable syllable with the first and continue on through the word, blending and listening for the next comfortable group of sounds.

  e.g.   **fantastic**   **fan**   **tas**   **t i c**

                  'fan'   'tas'   't' 'i' 'c'   'tic'

- Finally the child recalls all the syllables and blends them together.

  e.g.   **fantastic**

                  'fan'>'tas'>'tic'   'fantastic'

Even this simplified approach to reading multisyllable words requires the child to carry out some additional cognitive tasks which teachers and teaching assistants need to be aware of.

So far the child has learnt to blend dynamically and listen to the word forming with the reward of meaning signally reading success. Now the child is required to deal with a sequence of syllables, many of which hold no meaning or reward.

e.g.   'fan'   - has meaning but the child is aware that this is not the complete word

         'tas'   - no meaning

         'tic'   - has meaning but is not the whole word

Only when combining these syllables does the child gain the reward of meaning in the context of the text they are working on.

The child is reliant on auditory memory skills to recall the sequence of separate syllables and then blend those together.

Reading multisyllable words represents a significant leap in cognitive processing for the child with special educational needs and for this reason many of the activities in Book 7 focus on the child understanding, practising and overlearning this reading strategy.

Schwas and reading

Being aware of schwas in words is useful for the child when reading multisyllable words.

When using the dynamic blending – syllable by syllable reading strategy the child will naturally say clear sounds in words and dynamically blend these. The word that the child may say at the end of this process may be accurate and precise but not reflective of how we actually say the word in every day speech.

e.g.   **button** has a schwa sound at the **o** sound spelling – the **o** is not spoken as an accurate 'o' sound but the 'uh' schwa sound instead

Being aware of the schwa means that the child can listen for the word forming as they blend but understand that they may need to look for a more natural way to say the word when finalising what it is.

Sequential segmenting for spelling – syllable by syllable

Segmenting is the ability to split words up into their component sounds in sequence and is a key skill in spelling. The child needs to isolate each sound and match a sound spelling to that sound to successfully spell a word. It is important that the child is taught to segment sequentially through the word as this is how to access sounds in words to be able to spell them effectively.

The sequential segmenting technique

When supporting a child to spell a word it is helpful to provide visual prompts to indicate where to listen for a sound, e.g. draw lines on a whiteboard or piece of paper.

- Say the word in a dynamic blended style and at the same time move your finger across the board across all the lines. Your finger should be pointing to the line that corresponds to the sound in the word as you say it.

- Pointing to the first line, ask the child, "What sound can you hear *here* in the word.......?" Repeat and emphasise the sound, if necessary, until the child is able to identify it. Then ask the child to write the matching sound spelling on the appropriate line.
- Once the child has identified the 'initial' sound and written the sound spelling, move onto the 'middle' sound using the same technique and then the 'final' sound. By working sequentially through the word, the child has identified the sounds and can then match sounds spellings and so successfully spell the word. This simple technique can be used to spell any word.

The sequential segmenting – syllable by syllable spelling strategy

When the child is required to write a long word or a word with sounds in an awkward combination, it is a signal that they are likely to have to think about how they say the word and how they naturally split it into groups of sounds or syllables.

The child is encouraged to:

- Identify the first syllable they say in the word. Then, thinking about just this syllable, encourage the pupil to sequentially segment it to access all of the sounds in order. The child then matches a sound spelling for each sound.

  e.g.　　　'fantastic'　　*says*　'fan'　　　　'f'>'a'>'n'　　　*writes*　**fan**

- Then set aside that first syllable and continue on through the word, listening for the next syllable they say. Then, thinking about just this syllable, encourage the child to sequentially segment it to access all of the sounds in order. The child then matches a sound spelling for each sound.

e.g.	'fantastic'	(says	'fan'	'f'>'a'>'n'	writes	**fan**)
		says	'tas'	't'>'a'>'s'	writes	**tas**

- Next, set aside that second syllable with the first and continue on through the word, listening for the next syllable they say. Then, thinking about just this syllable, encourage the child to sequentially segment it to access all of the sounds in order. The child them matches a sound spelling for each sound.

e.g.	'fantastic'	(says	'fan'	'f'>'a'>'n'	writes	**fan**)
		(says	'tas'	't'>'a'>'s'	writes	**tas**)
		says	'tic'	't'>'i'>'c'	writes	**tic**

- Finally, encourage the child to proof read what they have written, look back over the word and think if it ' looks right' or 'feels right', making changes if necessary.

Schwas and spelling

Being aware of and able to identify schwas in words is useful for the child when spelling multisyllable words.

It is helpful for the child to be encouraged to try to remember what the 'perfect' (produced by strictly accurate dynamic blending) version of the word should be and use that to then think about the sounds and match sound spellings.

e.g.   **button** has a schwa sound at the **o** sound spelling

Remembering and recalling the perfect word in this example means that the child remembers that there is a clear '**o**' sound before the 'n'. In this way it is much easier to match the correct sound spelling and so spell the word.

Spelling, spelling choices and the accepted spelling

In Books 1 and 2 of the programme the majority of the sounds investigated were represented by one sound spelling made up of one letter. The child learned a simple sequential segmenting strategy for identifying the sounds and then matching a sound spelling to spell the word. At this level this is an easy strategy which brings a high level of success for the child.

In Books 3–6 the child learned that the relationships between sounds and their sound spellings are more complex than previously discovered.

Despite this the sequential segmenting spelling strategy can still be used by children when writing with some additions, as follows:

- For some sounds there may be a choice of sound spellings which could be used.

- For these sounds encourage the child to try a sound spelling and write it.

- On finishing the word, encourage the child to look over it and think whether it 'looks right' or 'feels right'. The trickiest part of the word will be where there is a number of possible sound spellings for a sound.

- If the child doesn't think it looks right, ask them to try a different sound spelling and then reflect on the word again.

For example: The child wants to write the word **rabbit** which is made up of two syllables, five sounds and five sound spellings:

2 syllables		'ra'	'bbit'		
5 sounds	'r'	'a'	'b'	'i'	't'
5 sound spellings	r	a	b / bb / bu	i	t

There are three possible sound spellings for the 'b' sound.

b, **bb** and **bu** *all* represent the sound 'b' so any one of them is ***technically correct***.

If the child writes **rabit** or **rabuit** then they have written a 'correct' spelling for the word brown.

If the child has previously struggled with spelling, then this is a really encouraging discovery; they might not be as be wrong as they thought they were!

The key point to make is that unfortunately it isn't helpful for us all to spell words with any 'correct' sound spelling we fancy. Everyone would get very mixed up and it would take much longer to work things out and read messages and stories.

Dictionaries list words and their meanings, but their writers also choose one sound spelling when writing the word and this was set in print. Over time these have become set as the 'agreed' or 'accepted' sound spellings to use in the word. So, when writing the word brown as broun or broughn, the child is correct but hasn't written the 'accepted spelling' and will need to make some changes.

When supporting a child with spelling always have this in mind and support them to use this strategy.

Part 1: Revising the main sounds and their sound spellings in 2 syllable words

Activity 1 only appears in the first three chapters of this book as it serves to introduce the child to the the dynamic blending – syllable by syllable strategy, the sequential segmenting – syllable by syllable strategy and the schwa. All have instructions written at the top of the worksheet.

Thinking about the sound (Activity 2) enables the child to revise the main sounds in 2 syllable words.

There are instructions on how to explore a sound at the top of the Activity 2 worksheet. In brief, the child encounters a list of words, all of which contain the focus sound, and reads through them. They then identify how the focus sound is represented in each word (find the matching sound spelling) and sort the words into groups or lists, which all have the same sound spelling for the focus sound.

Sorting word cards (Activity 3) requires the child to read through word cards and sort them into groups based on what sound spelling is used to represent the focus sound. This is an alternative way of identifying and revising the sound spellings.

The learning objectives for these activities are as follows:

Activity	Learning objectives
1 Introducing the reading strategy	Use the dynamic blending – syllable by syllable strategy to read words.
1 Introducing the spelling strategy	Use the sequential segmenting – syllable by syllable strategy to spell words.
1 Introducing the schwa	Identify the schwa in the word.
2 Thinking about the sound	Identify all the sound spellings that represent the target sound.
3 Sorting word cards	

Part 1: Reading and spelling activities

From Activity 4 onwards the activities are designed to give the child the opportunity to overlearn the relationships between sounds and sound spellings and gain experience of applying their skills, knowledge and understanding of sounds and sound spellings to read and spell single 2 syllable words and 2 syllable words in the context of sentences. The programme also incorporates reading at text level by sharing an appropriate book, usually at the end of a teaching session.

Activities 4–14 Reading 2 syllable words, Syllable split, Join the syllables, Match to a picture, Two syllable word tech, Syllable trap, Sounds like a syllable, Two syllable anagrams, Syllable jigsaw, Spelling challenge, Writing challenge focus on reading and spelling 2 syllable words with a target sound. **Activity 15 Reading or spelling 3 syllable words** introduces the child to working on 3 syllable words. All have instructions written at the top of the worksheet.

Spelling challenge (Activity 13)

The spelling challenge sheets provide the child with a structured method for practising and learning to spell the high and medium frequency words. Work with the child through the sheets in this way:

indeed   i n | d ee d   _ _*_ _ _   _ _ _*_ _ _ _   _ _ _ _ _ _ _ _

- Encourage the child to read the word on the left then look at the same word in the middle.

- Encourage the child to notice where the word is split into two syllables, indicated by the line, e.g. i n|d ee d.

- Encourage the child to notice the sound spellings that represent each of the sounds, e.g. 'i ' 'n' 'd' 'ee' 'd' are represented by the sound spellings **i n d ee d** – the sound spellings are spread out to make this clear and the focus sound's sound spelling is highlighted in colour.

- Next, notice that there are three sets of lines, one made up of a number of small lines, one made up of two lines and the other a solid line.

- The small lines in the first set correspond to the individual sounds in the word and the point at which the word is split into syllables is indicated by an asterisk.

- On the first set of lines, ask the child to write the sound spellings one by one on the small lines in the first syllable, saying the corresponding sound at the same time as writing each sound spelling,

    e.g.   *writes* **i n** *says* 'i' 'n' *and then says the syllable* 'in';

    then repeat for the second syllable,

    e.g.   *writes* **d ee d** *says* 'd' 'ee' 'd' *and then says the syllable* 'deed'

    and finally say the word, blending the two syllables together, 'indeed'.

- The two lines in the second set correspond to the two syllables in the word and the point at which the word is split into syllables is indicated by an asterisk.

- On the second set of lines, ask the child to write the word, syllable by syllable, on the two lines, once again saying the corresponding sound at the same time as writing each sound spelling.

- On the third set, ask the child to write the word, syllable by syllable, on the solid line, once again saying the corresponding sound at the same time as writing each sound spelling.

The child has now written the word three times and has made important connections between the syllables, sounds and the sound spellings we write. Next time the child wants to write that word they can use the syllables and sounds (which they can access from the spoken word) as a prompt to write the sound spellings in the right order and so spell the word.

To make the activity more challenging you could cover the words so that the child does not have a visual cue when writing the word on the lines. The child could then check their own work.

The learning objectives for these activities are as follows:

Activity	Learning objectives
4 Reading 2 syllable words	Use the dynamic blending – syllable by syllable strategy to read words.
5 Syllable split	Identify all the syllables in the word.
6 Join the syllables	Use the sequential segmenting – syllable by syllable strategy to spell words with the aid of visual prompts.
7 Match to a picture	Use the sequential segmenting – syllable by syllable strategy to spell words with the aid of visual prompts.
8 Two syllable word tech	Identify all the syllables in the word. Identify all the sounds in the word. Identify all the sound spellings in the word.
9 Syllable trap	Identify all the syllables in the word. Identify all the sounds in the word. Identify all the sound spellings in the word.
10 Sounds like a syllable	Identify all the syllables in the word. Identify all the sounds in the word. Identify all the sound spellings in the word. Use the sequential segmenting – syllable by syllable strategy to spell words.
11 Two syllable anagrams	Use the sequential segmenting – syllable by syllable strategy to spell words with the aid of visual prompts.
12 Syllable jigsaw	Use the sequential segmenting – syllable by syllable strategy to spell words with the aid of visual prompts.
13 Spelling challenge	Use the sequential segmenting – syllable by syllable strategy to spell words with the aid of visual prompts. Develop automaticity of spelling high frequency words.
14 Writing challenge	Read sentences closely matched to phonic knowledge with fluency and accuracy. Remember and verbally recall a sequence of words read. Recall and write a sequence of words. Use the sequential segmenting – syllable by syllable strategy to spell words. Spell words containing the target sound represented by all possible sound spellings.
15 Reading 3 syllable words	Use the dynamic blending – syllable by syllable strategy to read words.
15 Spelling 3 syllable words	Use the sequential segmenting – syllable by syllable strategy to spell words with the aid of visual prompts.

Overview of activities

Table 4 shows all the activities in Book 7 Part 1.

Note that some of the activities, indicated by an asterisk, do not require a corresponding worksheet and these are described and explained in this introductory section. Not all activities are applicable to all sections of the programme and for these worksheets and resources are not available, as indicated by a cross.

Table 4 Overview of *Phonics for Pupils with Special Educational Needs* activities and resources Book 7 Part 1

Book 7 Part 1	o-e	ee	a-e	er	e	ow	oy	oo	u	i-e	aw	air	ar	o	i	u-e
1. Introducing reading / spelling strategy and schwa	✓	✓	✓	✗	✗	✗	✗	✗	✗	✗	✗	✗	✗	✗	✗	✗
2. Thinking about the sound	✓	✓	✓	✓	✓	✓	✓	✓	✓	✓	✓	✓	✓	✓	✓	✓
3 Sorting word cards	✓	✓	✓	✓	✓	✓	✓	✓	✓	✓	✓	✓	✓	✓	✓	✓
4 Reading 2 syllable words	✓	✓	✓	✓	✓	✓	✓	✓	✓	✓	✓	✓	✓	✓	✓	✓
5. Syllable split	✓	✓	✓	✓	✓	✓	✓	✓	✓	✓	✓	✓	✓	✓	✓	✓
6. Join the syllables	✓	✓	✓	✓	✓	✓	✓	✓	✓	✓	✓	✓	✓	✓	✓	✓
7. Match to a picture	✓	✓	✓	✓	✓	✓	✓	✓	✓	✓	✓	✓	✓	✓	✓	✓
8. Two syllable word tech	✓	✓	✓	✓	✓	✓	✓	✓	✓	✓	✓	✓	✓	✓	✓	✓
9. Syllable trap	✓	✓	✓	✓	✓	✓	✓	✓	✓	✓	✓	✓	✓	✓	✓	✓
10. Sounds like a syllable	✓	✓	✓	✓	✓	✓	✓	✓	✓	✓	✓	✓	✓	✓	✓	✓
11. Two syllable anagrams	✓	✓	✓	✓	✓	✓	✓	✓	✓	✓	✓	✓	✓	✓	✓	✓
12. Syllable jigsaw	✓	✓	✓	✓	✓	✓	✓	✓	✓	✓	✓	✓	✓	✓	✓	✓
13. Spelling challenge	✓	✓	✓	✓	✓	✓	✓	✓	✓	✓	✓	✓	✓	✓	✓	✓
14. Writing challenge	✓	✓	✓	✓	✓	✓	✓	✓	✓	✓	✓	✓	✓	✓	✓	✓
15. Reading / spelling 3 syllable words	✗	✗	✓	✓	✓	✓	✓	✓	✓	✓	✓	✓	✓	✓	✓	✓
16. Reading text* (covered in this section)																

Part 2: Reading and spelling 3 and 4 syllable words and suffixes

The second part of this book focuses on the child applying their knowledge, skills and understanding to read and spell 3 and 4 syllable words.

The child is gently introduced to increasingly complex words in the following sequence:

Set 1   3 syllable words – basic sound to sound spelling relationship – no schwa

Set 2   3 syllable words – basic sound to sound spelling relationship – with schwa

Set 3   3 syllable words – complex sound to sound spelling relationship – with schwa

Set 4   4 syllable words – complex sound to sound spelling relationship – with schwa

Note the 'basic' relationship refers to the simple 1:1 correspondence discovered in Book 1 and where simple sounds are represented by single letters. The 'complex' relationship refers to sounds represented by more than one sound spelling and where the sound spellings may contain more than one letter.

The final six chapters of the programme cover words containing the following suffixes:

* tion, cian, ssion, sion, shion, cion   'shun'

* sion   'zjun'

* ture   'cher'

* sure, zure   'zjer'

* cious, scious, tious   'shus'

* cial, tial   'shul'

Reading word cards (Activity 1) requires the child to read the words on cards using the dynamic blending – syllable by syllable strategy for reading. There are two sets of cards available. One has the syllable splits highlighted by an asterisk to aid reading and the other set does not.

Activities 2–10 Syllable split, Advanced word tech, Word strings, Speeding fine, Syllable trap Nonsense word fun, Syllable jigsaw, Meaning and spelling and Spelling challenge give the child experience of reading and spelling 3 and 4 syllable words and words containing a suffix. There are instructions at the top of worksheets and learning objectives, as follows:

Activity	Learning objectives
1 Reading word cards	Use the dynamic blending – syllable by syllable strategy to read words.
2 Syllable split	Identify all the syllables in the word.
3 Advanced word tech	Identify all the syllables in the word. Identify all the sounds in the word. Identify all the sound spellings in the word.
4 Word strings	Use the dynamic blending – syllable by syllable strategy to read words.
5 Speeding fine	Develop fluency and speed when reading. Develop automaticity of spelling high frequency words.
6 Syllable trap	Identify all the syllables in the word. Identify all the sounds in the word. Identify all the sound spellings in the word.
7 Nonsense word fun	Use the dynamic blending – syllable by syllable strategy to read words. Demonstrate awareness of the orthographic tendencies in English (common patterns of sounds).
8 Syllable jigsaw	Use the syllable by syllable / sound by sound strategy to spell words with the aid of visual prompts.
9 Meaning and spelling	Use the dynamic blending – syllable by syllable strategy to read words. Identify the appropriate definition for a word read.
10 Spelling challenge	Use the sequential segmenting – syllable by syllable strategy to spell words with the aid of visual prompts. Develop automaticity of spelling high frequency words.

Overview of activities

Table 5 shows all the activities in Book 7 Part 2.

Note that some of the activities, indicated by an asterisk, do not require a corresponding worksheet and these are described and explained in this introductory section. Not all activities are applicable to all sections of the programme and for these worksheets and resources are not available, as indicated by a cross.

Table 5 Overview of *Phonics for Pupils with Special Educational Needs* activities and resources Book 7 Part 2

Book 7 Part 2	Set 1 Mixed 3 syllable words – basic sounds – without schwas	Set 2 Mixed 3 syllable words – basic sounds – with schwa	Set 3 Mixed 3 syllable words – advanced sounds – with schwa	Set 4 Mixed 4 syllable words – advanced sounds – with schwa	Suffixes (word endings)					
					shun	zjun	cher	zjer	shus	shul
1. Reading word cards with syllable highlighting	✓	✓	✓	✓	✓	✓	✓	✓	✓	✓
1. Reading word cards without highlighting	✓	✓	✓	✓	✓	✓	✓	✓	✓	✓
2. Syllable split	✓	✓	✓	✓	✓	✓	✓	✓	✓	✓
3. Advanced word tech	✓	✓	✓	✓	✓	✓	✓	✓	✓	✓
4. Word strings	✓	✓	✓	✓	✓	✓	✓	✓	✓	✓
5. Speeding fine	✓	✓	✓	✓	✓	✓	✓	✓	✓	✓
6. Syllable trap	✓	✓	✓	✓	✗	✗	✗	✗	✗	✗
7. Nonsense word fun	✓	✓	✓	✓	✗	✗	✗	✗	✗	✗
8. Syllable jigsaw	✓	✓	✓	✓	✓	✓	✓	✓	✓	✓
9. Meaning and spelling	✓	✓	✓	✓	✓	✓	✓	✓	✓	✓
10. Spelling challenge	✓	✓	✓	✓	✓	✓	✓	✓	✓	✓
11. Reading text* (covered in this section)										

Listening to a child read

Teaching a child to efficiently decode words is only one part of reading. Alongside this, children need to understand what they have read, which includes the ability to 'read between the lines and beyond the text', and develop an interest and enthusiasm for stories, poetry and writing. All teachers strive to generate in their pupils a 'love of books'.

Although this programme does not address the specifics of reading comprehension it does set a place for developing an interest and enthusiasm for reading at all levels by encouraging pupil and teacher to share a book and talk about what they have read.

Activity 15 (Part 1) or Activity 11 (Part 2) Reading book

The last **quarter** of any teaching session should be devoted to reading a book with the child, supporting them to apply their increasing knowledge, skills and understanding to read the text.

This gives you an opportunity to gently correct errors as they read, by highlighting sound spellings, referencing sounds, providing information about sounds they have not yet covered, correcting them when they use the wrong sound, pointing out where they have missed out or added sounds and by supporting and modelling a good dynamic blending technique.

During this activity also take time to enjoy sharing a book with the child and stimulate their interest in the story, poem or text by talking about it. The content of this discussion and the depth to which texts can be explored will depend on the child's age and cognitive abilities but some suggestions about areas of questioning and discussion are given below:

- Identify the general 'topic' of the text

- Identify where a story takes place

- Identify the main character(s)

- Identify what is happening and be aware of the sequence of events

- Identify characters, places and objects in illustrations and pictures

- Be aware of the importance of key events in the text

- Make connections between the text and personal experiences

- Draw conclusions about events in the text

- Make predictions about what might happen next

- Identify cause, effect and consequences within the text

- Make connections between the text and the child's prior knowledge or experience

- Describe the main character

- Express opinions about a character's actions or speech
- Express opinions about their enjoyment of the story or otherwise
- Identify different genres of writing and express preferences

Choosing the right book

There are several book series that take a phonics approach to writing and produce books that focus on a key sound or groups of sounds and in some cases on multisyllable words. These books are really useful if they match the sound that the child is working on from this programme, as the child is likely to experience a higher level of success when reading these, which is a great confidence boost. Be aware that the language in these books can be a little unnatural or stilted as the writers are restricted by which words are available for them to use to write the story.

Other books that do not take this phonics approach are just as accessible, but the child is likely to require much more adult support. The child is also more likely to encounter high frequency words (refer to section on high frequency words) that they have not yet worked on within the programme. Since a higher level of adult support may be required, the child may feel less successful when reading these books.

No type of book is better than another. A mixture of books is preferable to balance the child's diet of reading material to make it as rich and interesting as possible whilst allowing the child to experience success and independence.

Pace

When sharing a book with emerging readers the flow and pace of reading may be stalled if the child has to be supported to decode several words in a sentence. This may mean that the child will lose track of the meaning of what they have been reading. If this is the case, at the end of each sentence stop and re-read it for the child so that they can focus on language and meaning. This is a good opportunity to talk about the story, characters and events.

A few more considerations

By now you should have a good overview of the programme, how it works and how to begin to deliver it, but there are a few other aspects that are worth taking time to consider and reflect on which will help you when working with a child or a group of children.

Regional variations

Earlier in this chapter there was reference to the number of sounds in spoken English and the fact that this varies according to regional differences associated with accent and pronunciation.

For example, in most of the UK the words **book, cook** and **look** are pronounced with a 'u' sound in the middle but in some areas an 'oo' sound is used. There is a subtle difference in the pronunciation of the 'u' sound in words like **bus** and **run** in different parts of the UK and of course there is the classic 'castle' and 'bath' debate where the **a** sound spelling represents the sound 'ar' for some people but 'a' for others.

When creating the content of the programme every effort was made to reduce the impact of these differences by careful selection of example words. However, it is important for you as a practitioner to be selective about the words presented to your child or group of children and **always** follow your local pronunciations. In the rare event of you finding in the programme a word is out of place then just avoid it and remember to deal with it in a section appropriate to you and the child.

Terminology

Many phonics programmes use terminology that children with special educational needs find difficult to understand, remember and use. In *Phonics for Pupils with Special Educational Needs* this terminology is kept to a minimum and is made as child friendly as possible. Labels such as phoneme, grapheme, short vowel, long vowel, digraphs, trigraphs, dipthong and spilt-vowel digraph are not used in this programme. In Book 7 the terms syllable and schwa are introduced.

Knowing these terms does not have a direct impact on a child's reading and spelling accuracy and performance. Instead accessible terms such as sound, sound spelling and split sound spelling are used.

Tricky words

Phonics for Pupils with Special Educational Needs' view of written language means that nearly all words can be decoded and there are very few 'common exception' or 'tricky' words. Please refer to the list of high frequency words which also shows how these common words are coded.

There are some words that do appear to be truly 'tricky' and difficult to decode. Investigation of their origins and history can be quite revealing. Encountering these words in the course of their reading presents an opportunity to talk about this with the child at a level that is appropriate to their cognitive abilities.

the	When pronounced as 'thee', e.g. before words starting with a vowel or used for emphasis, it is easy to decode as 'th' 'ee'. Otherwise this is often pronounced as 'thuh'. The 'uh' sound is a schwa (which is covered extensively in Book 3). The easiest way to describe this is an 'untidy' or lazy' sound.
one	Originally pronounced using an 'u' sound, like in the phrase 'a good 'un'. The 'wun' pronunciation appeared in the south-west of England in the 14th century and spread rapidly.
once	Its history mirrors that of the word one.

two	From the old English **twa** which contained pronounced consonants and an 'a-e' sound 'tway'. The reason for the shift to the 'too' pronunciation is no longer known.
friend	Decodable but unique – the sound spelling **ie** represents the sound 'e' in this word. This word is investigated when working on the 'e' sound in Book 2.
people	Decodable but unique – the sound spelling **eo** represents the sound 'ee' in this word. This word is investigated when working on the 'ee' sound in Book 2.
minute	Middle English from the Latin **minutus** (meaning small) pronounced with an 'oo' sound. This is another example of a schwa.
hour	From the Latin **hora**. Although the 'h' hasn't been pronounced since Roman times, the **h** has persisted to distinguish it visually from the word **our**.
busy	From the Old English **bisig** originally referring to 'having a care or anxious'. Later it referred to being occupied doing something. Spelling shifted from **i** to **u** in the 15th century for a reason no longer known.
business	Source is the same as above **bisgnes**. The original meaning, referring to busyness as 'the state of being busy', has become obsolete and replaced by today's meaning and spelling.
iron	From the Celtic word **isarnon**, which means holy metal (metal made into swords for the Crusades), the Old English word was **iren**.
Mr	A contraction of the word **M**iste**r** – taking just the first and last letter as a short form of the word.
Mrs	A contraction of the word **M**ist**r**es**s** – taking the first and last letter and the middle letter r as a short from of the word 'missus' (which is in itself a short form of mistress which is an out-dated formal title for a woman).

Planning

At the end of this section there is a lesson planner which can be used to plan teaching sessions and track pupil progression through the programme.

All possible activities are listed on the planner which could be viewed as a menu of activities. Do note that not all activities are appropriate for every stage of the programme, so you may not be able to plan certain activities for all sounds. Tables 4 and 5 are helpful to identify which activities are available for each sound when lesson planning.

To use the lesson planner, simply date the column and strike through the small box corresponding to each activity you plan to do in the session. ◹ You can cross check through once completed. ⊠

This provides a simple visual map of the pupil(s)' progress through the programme.

There is space to write brief notes and a larger space at the bottom of the planner where dynamic teacher assessment notes can be written on individual pupil responses / errors, teacher reflections and next steps for the pupil or group.

Structuring a session

Teaching sessions can be of any length but should always include as wide a range of activities as possible. The activities are grouped according to the focus of the activity and this is made clear on the planning sheet:

- Revising the sounds and discover the sound spellings – a multisensory approach
- Reading words using the syllable by syllable / sound by sound strategy
- Spelling Words using the syllable by syllable / sound by sound strategy
- Working in sentences
- Reading text

Sessions should be planned to ensure that over time there is even coverage of all these aspects and all activities available. As a general rule, all sessions should finish with reading text, a book, either listening to the child read or a shared reading activity in a group.

The tasks

Children with special educational needs are often easily distracted and find it difficult to concentrate for long periods on the same task. For this reason, it is recommended that the activities are time limited rather than task limited.

For example, if a child starts a worksheet with support but after five minutes has only completed two items then stop there, record that the sheet is incomplete and move on to the next activity. The child can always continue work on the incomplete sheet in a subsequent session. It is better to keep the lesson interesting and varied to maintain a high level of engagement rather than finish a worksheet for the sake of it. Depending on the child, individual activities should only last between five and ten minutes.

Progress through the programme

Do not feel that a child or group of children must go through every single activity and worksheet in the programme. If you have introduced a set of sounds and sound spellings and the child is able to reliably and consistently recall the sound(s) when shown a sound spelling and identify the sound spellings when told the sound, then move them on to the next sound. Remember that the child takes all previous sounds and their sound spellings with them into the next section so nothing is ever left behind.

They also work on the key skills at every stage in the programme so if they are still learning and developing their blending, segmenting and phoneme manipulation but are secure in their knowledge of sounds and sound spellings you can safely move them on.

Where to start

Ideally a pupil will have worked through Books 1–6 of this programme before starting Book 7. However, some children may start at this point, having had some other previous experience of phonics but needing to work specifically on managing multisyllable words.

Recognise that although these pupils may have knowledge of sounds and sound spellings they may have poor key skills and may need intensive work on blending, segmenting and phoneme manipulation. It may be necessary for these pupils to do some lending, segmenting and phoneme manipulation activities from Books 3–6.

And finally...

You now have an overview of the programme, its approach to written language, how to teach the key skills and the important techniques required to support a child or group of children.

You have all the tools necessary to expand the child's knowledge of sounds and sound spellings, teaching them to become readers and spellers.

Lesson planner Book 7 Part 1

Name(s):		Date	Notes	Date	Notes	Date	Notes	Date	Notes	Date	Notes	Date	Notes
Book 7 Part 1: 2 syllable focus sound													
Introduction	1 Reading / spelling / schwa												
Sound and sound spellings	2 Thinking about the sound												
	3 Sorting word cards												
Reading words	4 Reading 2 syllable words												
	5 Syllable split												
	6 Join the syllables												
	7 Match to a picture												
	8 Two syllable word tech												
	9 Syllable trap												
	10 Sounds like a syllable												
	11 Two syllable anagrams												
	12 Syllable jigsaw												
	13 Spelling challenge												
	14 Writing challenge												
3 Syllable work	15 Reading / spelling 3 syllable words												
Reading text level	16 Reading book*												
NOTES													

Lesson planner Book 7 Part 2

Name(s):			Date	Notes	Date	Notes	Date	Notes	Date	Notes	Date	Notes	Date	Notes
Book 7 Part 2: 3 and 4 syllable / suffix focus															
Reading words	1	Reading word cards													
	2	Syllable split													
	3	Advanced word tech													
	4	Word strings													
	5	Speeding fine													
	6	Syllable trap													
	7	Nonsense word fun													
Spelling words	8	Syllable jigsaw													
	9	Meaning and spelling													
	10	Spelling challenge													
Reading text level	11	Reading book*													
NOTES															

High frequency word list

The following list is the high frequency words organised according to the sounds in the word and in relation to the programme. Each word is explored at an appropriate point in the programme, as indicated. Of course, children are likely to encounter these words at earlier stages in their reading as they share books and will be guided to decode them, with a 'heads up' to sounds not yet studied.

Book	Structure / sound(s)	Top 100 high frequency words	Top 101–200 high frequency words
1	**Set 1 VC** **CVC**	a at sat	
1	**Set 2 VC** **CVC**	in it did	am an dad man
1	**Set 3 VC** **CVC**		on can cat dog got not top
1	**Set 4 VC** **CVC**		up get mum put* ran red run sun
1	**Set 5 VC** **CVC**		if bad bed big but fun had hat him hot let
1	**Set 6** **CVC**		fox
1	**Set 7** **CVC**		yes
2	**All Sets** **VCC**	and ask* it's	end
2	**All Sets** **CVCC**	help just went	best fast* last* lost lots must next wind
2	**All Sets** **CCVC**	from	gran stop
2	**All Sets** **CCVCC+**		didn't grandad plant*
3	**sh**		fish wish

Book	Structure / sound(s)	Top 100 high frequency words	Top 101–200 high frequency words
3	**th**	that this them then with	bath* path*
3	**ng**		along king long **th**ing
3	**ch**		much children
3	**k**	ba**ck**	du**ck**
3	**f**	o**ff**	
3	**l**	wi**ll**	fe**ll** sti**ll** te**ll**
3	**s**		acro**ss** mi**ss**
4	**o-e**	don't go no old so	cold go**ing** most told boat grow snow wind**o**w
4	**z**	a**s** hi**s** i**s**	clo**the**s ha**s** u**s**
4	**ee**	be he me **sh**e we see very	began he's been feet green keep need **qu**een sleep **th**ree tree each eat sea tea even here **th**ese only rea**ll**y
4	**a-e**	day came made make **th**ey	away may play say way gave take great again* baby
4	**er**	her were	after ever every never over under di**ff**erent first girl word work we're

Book	Structure / sound(s)	Top 100 high frequency words	Top 101–200 high frequency words
4	e	again* said head any many friend	any many friend
4	ow		down how now town about found our out round **sh**out
5	oy		boy
5	oo	do into to you look* too	to**day** food room took* **th**rough
5	u	put* look looks come love some could	book good look**ing** took some**th**ing couldn't would com**ing** ano**ther** mo**ther** o**ther**
5	i-e	by my I I'm like time	fly find I'll inside liked night right
5	aw	for a**ll** ca**ll** saw your	morn**ing** or sma**ll** wa**ter** **th**ought before more door
5	air	**th**ere **th**eir	**th**ere's bear air **ch**air

Book	Structure / sound(s)	Top 100 high frequency words	Top 101–200 high frequency words			
5		are				
	ar		after*	can't	fast*	father
			last*			
			car	dark	garden	hard
			park			
6	**s**		horse	house	mouse	
			pla**c**e			
6	**l**		animals			
			p**eo**ple			
6	**b**		ra**bb**it			
6	**d**	**loo**ked ca**ll**ed	jumped	pulled	cried	
			su**dd**enly			
6	**o**	w**a**s	want	wanted		
			gone			
6	**i**		live	lived		
6	**u-e**		use			
Advanced consonants						
6	**f**		**lau**gh			
6	**g**		e**gg**s	ghost		
6	**h**		who	wh**ose**		
6	**j**		giant	magic		
6	**k**		sch**oo**l			
6	**m**		climb			
6	**n**		kn**ow**			
6	**p**		floppy	stopp**ed**		
6	**r**		na**rr**at**or**			
6	**t**		be**tt**er	li**tt**le		
6	**v**		I've			
6	**w**		what	when	wh**ere**	whi**ch**
			wh**ite**	why		
6	**z**		be**cau**se	pl**ea**se		

*These words may be explored at different points in the programme depending on variations in regional pronunciation.

Sounds and their sound spellings 1

ar	star
a	father
al	calm
ear	heart

o	got
a	want
au	fault

i	sit
y	myth

u	music
u-e	cube
ew	few
ue	cue

i-e	kite
i	mind
y	by
igh	night
ie	pie

or	for
au	haunt
aw	saw
ore	more
ar	war
al	walk
our	your
a	also
oar	roar
ough	bought
augh	taught

air	hair
ere	there
are	care
ear	bear

ou	loud
ow	down
ough	plough

oi	soil
oy	boy

oo	moon
u	truth
u-e	rule
ew	grew
o	do
ui	suit
ou	soup
ue	blue

u	put
o	month
oo	book
ou	touch
o-e	come
oul	could

a-e	made
a	angel
ai	train
ay	play
ea	steak
ey	they
eigh	eight

er	her
ur	burn
ir	bird
ear	learn
or	word
our	colour
ar	collar
re	centre
ere	were

e	red
ea	head
a	many
ai	said
ie	friend

a	cat

o	go
o-e	home
oa	boat
ow	grow
oe	toe
ough	though

ea	dream
ee	seen
y	happy
e	be
ie	field
e-e	eve
i	ski

Sounds and their sound spellings 2

x	fox
xc	except
cc	accept

y	yes

z	zip
s	his
zz	buzz
ze	freeze
se	noise

sh	ship
s	sugar
ch	machine

th	think

ng	ring

ch	chip
tch	match

qu	quit

f	fun
ph	phone
ff	stuff
gh	cough

h	hat
wh	whose

l	lamp
ll	bell
le	little
el	travel
il	pupil
al	metal
ol	symbol

j	jam
g	giant
ge	large
dge	bridge

v	van
ve	have

w	wig
wh	which

d	dog
dd	ladder
ed	wagged

g	get
gg	wiggle
gu	guard
gue	plague
gh	ghost

c	can
k	kid
ck	duck
ch	chemist
que	plaque

r	rat
wr	wrong
rr	hurry
rh	rhythm

b	bat
bb	robber
bu	build

s	sat
c	city
sc	scent
ss	less
st	listen
ce	dance
se	house

t	top
tt	better
bt	doubt

p	pet
pp	happy

m	man
mm	summer
mn	hymn
mb	lamb

n	not
kn	knot
nn	sunny
gn	gnat

Suffixes

tion	ac**tion**
cian	op**tician**
ssion	mi**ssion**
sion	ten**sion**
shion	fa**shion**
cion	suspi**cion**

sion	vi**sion**

ture	cap**ture**

sure	mea**sure**
zure	sei**zure**

cious	pre**cious**
scious	con**scious**
tious	cau**tious**

cial	so**cial**
tial	par**tial**

PART 1

Words with an 'o-e' sound – word list of 2 syllable words

o	o	o-e	ow	oa	oe	ough	ou
ago	moment	poem	alone	blowing	approach	oboe	although	boulder
bonus	mostly	poet	awoke	flowing	boasting		doughnut	shoulder
colder	motor	polar	erode	glowing	floating			
clothing	noble	poster	explode	growing	groaning			
colon	notice	process	lonely	knowing	loading			
control	nowhere	progress	remote	owning	moaning			
focus	older	pronoun		owner	poacher			
global	oldest	protein		showing	roasted			
going	only	proton		slowing	roasting			
golden	open	robot		slowly	soaking			
hotel	ova	roman		snowing	toasted			
kosher	ovum	solar		throwing	toasting			
locate	over	total						
molar	photo	vocal						
molten								

This activity introduces the child to the dynamic blending syllable by syllable strategy for reading longer words.

Support the child to read each word.

In the first group, the words have been split into two chunks of sounds or syllables, as indicated by the asterisk * and red and blue colour coding.

Direct the child to dynamically blend the sounds within the first syllable and say the syllable chunk (say what they hear forming), then blend the sounds within the second syllable and say the syllable chunk.

Finally push both syllable chunks together to hear the word forming.

e.g.

	sees:	f i n	i sh		
finish					
	says:	'f'>'i'>'n' = 'fin'	'i'>'sh' = 'ish'	'fin>ish'	'finish'

In the second group, there are no prompts to indicate the syllables. Encourage the child to blend the sounds until they hear that they have made a 'comfortable' chunk of sounds which could be a syllable, then blend the next sounds until they have made a 'comfortable' chunk of sounds and so on. The child can then blend the chunks or syllables together to hear the word form. Refer to the 'Working through the programme' section of this book for a detailed explanation of this.

Activity 1a Introducing the reading strategy   o-e

finish	f i n * i sh	hectic	h e c * t i c
rapid	r a * p i d	contest	c o n * t e s t
rabbit	r a * bb i t	cabin	c a * b i n
traffic	t r a * ff i c	combat	c o m * b a t

solid	panic
comic	contact
magic	upset

This activity introduces the child to the sequential segmenting syllable by syllable strategy for spelling longer words.

Support the child to read the word on the left.

Then look at how the word has been split into two chunks of sounds, or syllables, as indicated by the asterisk * and the red and blue colour coding.

Focus on the grey word and think about the first syllable. Have the child write over each grey sound spelling and say the corresponding sound at the same time.

At the end of the syllable the child then says the syllable chunk. Repeat this for the second syllable and then blend the two syllables together and listen to the word forming. The child then says the whole word.

Ask the child to highlight any sound spellings that they think are tricky, to help them recall them when spelling. Remind the child to take care with split sound spellings.

Cover the words and ask the child to write the word, syllable by syllable and sound by sound, on the two lines underneath, saying the sounds as they write the corresponding sound spelling. The child can then check and correct the answer if necessary.

Finally, the child can write the whole word on the single line but once again work syllable by syllable and sound by sound, saying the sounds as they write the corresponding sound spellings.

Refer to the 'Working through the programme' section of this book for a detailed explanation of this.

Activity 1b Introducing the spelling strategy

			o-e
finish	fin*ish	fin*ish	_____ * _____
rabbit	ra*bbit	ra*bbit	_____ * _____
contest	con*test	con*test	_____ * _____
traffic	tra*ffic	tra*ffic	_____ * _____

This activity results in the child rediscovering all the sound spellings for this sound in the context of 2 syllable words.

Support the child to read the words one by one. Ask the child to say the word again in their head or with their 'thinking voice' and notice how they split up each word into two chunks of sounds, or syllables, as they say it.

For each word, support the child to work out the sound spelling corresponding to the sound 'o-e'.

Words are sorted into lists according to their 'o-e' sound spelling.

There are six sound spellings to find: **o, ow, o-e, oa, ough** and **ou**. The child met the first five in Book 4 but the **ou** sound spelling is new – it only occurs in multisyllable words.

Encourage the child to say each sound as they write each sound spelling in sequence, *syllable by syllable*, in this way:

e.g.

	sees:	b l ow		i ng		
blowing						
	says:	**'b'>'l'>'o-e' = 'blo-e'**	**'i'>'ng' = 'ing'**		**'blo-e>ing'**	**'blowing'**

Break this task into a number of shorter tasks over a number of lessons if necessary.

Activity 2 Thinking about the sound   o-e

blowing	loading	although
oboe	explode	snowing
doughnut	control	toasted
shoulder	remote	awoke
progress	floating	bonus

This set of cards is made up of 2 syllable words containing the sound 'o-e'. Copy onto card and cut out. Practise the dynamic blending – syllable by syllable reading strategy, as described in the 'Working through the programme' section, to read the words on these cards. Model this process for the child if necessary.

Activity 3 Sorting word cards   o-e

ago	progress
control	hotel
throwing	knowing
slowly	toasted
approach	floating
alone	erode
although	shoulder

Support the child to read each word. To help, the words have been split into two chunks of sounds, or syllables, as indicated by the asterisk *.

Direct the child to blend the sounds within the first syllable and say the syllable chunk, then blend the sounds within the second syllable and say the syllable chunk.

Finally push both syllable chunks together to hear the word forming.

e.g.

	sees:	r o	b o t		
robot					
	says:	'r'>'o-e' = 'ro-e'	'b'>'o'>'t' = 'bot'	'ro-e>bot'	**'robot'**

Activity 4 Reading 2 syllable words   o-e

robot	r o * b o t
ago	a * g o
focus	f o * c u s
soaking	s oa * k i ng
alone	a * l o n e
doughnut	d ough * n u t
approach	a * pp r oa ch
knowing	kn ow * i ng
awoke	a * w o k e

Support the child to read the words one by one. Ask the child to say the word again in their head or with their 'thinking voice' and notice how they split up each word into two chunks of sounds, or syllables, as they say it. For each word, support the child to draw a line through the word to show where in the word they split it into two syllables.

It is useful to discuss how they made their choice.

The first group of words has some sound spellings highlighted to help, and the first one is split as an example.

Activity 5 Syllable split   o-e

bo/nus   aw**o**k**e**

sl**ow**i**ng**   moment

ago   coldest

t**oa**sted   s**oa**ki**ng**

d**ough**nut   **sh ou** l d **er**

al**o**ne   open

fl**oa**ti**ng**   total

Careful, the next ones do not have any sound spellings highlighted:

chosen

poem

global

erode

molten

spoken

photo

Support the child to read the clue on the left and work out what the answer word is.

Ask the child to say the word again in their head or with their 'thinking voice' and notice how they split up each word into two chunks of sounds, or syllables, as they say it.

Ask the child to draw a line from the clue to the first syllable of the word and then go on to draw a line to the second syllable of the word.

Finally ask the child to write the whole word on the line at the end indicated by the arrow and read the word out loud.

Activity 6 Join the syllables   o-e

Clue	1st	2nd	→	Word
All of it	ph o	p l o d e	→	
Brave and good	t o	b **le**	→	
Camera's picture	n o	t o	→	
Far away	e x	t **al**	→	*total*
Blow up	r e	m **o** t e	→	
Melted metal	r **oa**	t e n	→	
Oven baked	m o l	s t e d	→	
Place to stay	a	t e l	→	
Have information	h o	i **ng**	→	
Creep up to	**kn ow**	pp r **oa** ch	→	

Ask the child to choose a picture and discuss what the matching word might be.

Then ask the child to think about how that word might be split into two syllables.

The child then finds the first syllable and then the second, drawing a line from picture to syllable to syllable.

The child then writes the complete word on one of the lines in the box at the bottom of the page.

Encourage the child to write the word using the sequential segmenting – syllable by syllable spelling strategy.

Activity 7 Match to a picture   o-e

floa

ing

snow

ting

ex

pho

plode

bot   to

dough   ro

nut

Support the child to read the words one by one. Ask the child to say the word again in their head or with their 'thinking voice' and notice how they split up the word into two chunks of sounds, or syllables, as they say it. Then ask the child to show where they split the word up into two syllables by drawing a line through it. Next ask the child to put a ring round each of the sound spellings.

Activity 8 Two syllable word tech   o-e

total

approach

toasting

ago

knowing

floating

noble

robot

alone

hotel

throwing

Support the child to read the words one by one. Ask the child to say the word again in their head or with their 'thinking voice' and notice how they split up each word into two chunks of sounds, or syllables, as they say it. For each word, ask the child to work out where they split it into two syllables and then draw a line through the word.

Then ask the child to work out how many sounds there are in each syllable. They could write the number next to each syllable.

Support the child to look at the grid underneath and choose the row that contains the right number of lines in the first box (to match the number of sounds in the first syllable) and the right number of lines in the second box (to match the number of sounds in the second syllable). Ask the child to write the word in the grid on the chosen row, writing a sound spelling on each line.

An example is done to help you.

Activity 9 Syllable trap   o-e

3 sounds   grow/ing   2 sounds

ago   control

doughnut   approach

going   clothing

——	—— ——
—— ——	—— —— —— —— ——
—— —— ——	—— —— ——
—— —— ——	—— —— ——
g r ow	i ng
—— —— —— ——	—— —— —— ——
—— —— —— ——	—— —— —— ——

Support the child to read the clue on the left and work out what the word is.

Ask the child to say the word in their head or with their 'thinking voice' and notice how they split up each word into two chunks of sounds, or syllables, as they say it.

Support the child to write the first syllable, sound by sound, in the first boxes, and the second syllable, sound by sound, in the second boxes, noticing that there is a box for each sound within the syllables.

Remind them to be careful with split sound spellings!

Then, covering the boxes, ask the child to write out the word from memory in the box at the end, thinking about the syllables and the sounds in them.

The first two are done for you as examples.

Activity 10 Sounds like a syllable   o-e

Clue	1st syllable			2nd syllable			Word
An extra	b	o		n	u	s	bonus
Wear down rocks	e			r	o-e	d	erode
Getting bigger							
Mechanical person							
Most aged							
Round cake with hole							
On my own							
Melted metal is ...							
On top of the water							

Support the child to read the clue on the left and work out what the answer word is.
The word has been split into two syllables and the sound spellings in each syllable have been mixed up.
Encourage the child to write the first syllable, sound by sound, then the second syllable, sound by sound, on the line on the right.
Ask the child to say the word.
Careful with split sound spellings!

Activity 11 Two syllable anagrams   o-e

Clue	1st syllable	2nd syllable	Word
Melted metal	m l o	t n e	_____
On top of water	l **oa** f	i **ng** t	_____
Having information	**ow kn**	**ng** i	_____
Camera's picture	o **ph**	o t	_____
Blow up	x e	l p d **o-e**	_____
Things you wear	l o c	**ng** i **th**	_____
Place far away	e r	**o-e** m t	_____
A little extra	o b	u s n	_____
Brave and fair	o n	**le** b	_____
Wear away e.g. rocks	e	**o-e** d r	_____
Moving liquid	l **ow** f	**ng** i	_____
Cake with a hole in	**ough** d	t n u	_____
On my own	a	**o-e** n l	_____
Musical instrument	o	**oe** b	_____
Frozen rain	n **ow** s	**ng** i	_____

Support the child to read the clue on the left and work out what the word is.
Ask the child to say the answer word again in their head or with their 'thinking voice' and notice how they split up each word into two chunks of sounds, or syllables, as they say it.
The words have been split into two 'syllable boxes' but are not complete.
Ask the child to finish the word by writing in either the first or second syllable as required in the grey box.
Then ask the child to write out the word in full on the line at the end.
The first one is done for you as an example.

Activity 12 Syllable jigsaw   o-e

Clue	1st syllable	2nd syllable	Word
A long time	a	go	*ago*
Come close to		pproach	
Not with anyone		lone	
Blow up!	ex		
Cake ring		nut	
Place to stay	ho		
Things you wear		thing	
Camera's picture	pho		
Advance, go forward	pro		

o-e

Activity 13 Spelling challenge

throwing th r ow/i ng   *

snowing s n ow/i ng   *

approach a/pp r oa ch   *

floating f l oa/t i ng   *

alone a/l o n e   *

explode e x/p l o d e   *

ago a/g o   *

progress p r o/g r ess   *

Support the child to read each sentence one by one.
Ask the child to re-read the sentence, several times if necessary, and try to remember it.
Then cover the sentence and ask the child to recall the sentence verbally.
Once they can do this confidently, ask the child to write out the sentence from memory.
The child might find it helpful to think about the individual syllables in the words and say the sounds within each as they write. When the sentence is complete, the child reads out their sentence and then compares it to the original.

Alternatively, using text to speech software, the child could type the sentence, with the computer reading back each word and then the completed sentence.

Activity 14 Writing challenge   o-e

Long ago I went to the oldest hotel in Oldtown.

I awoke and was alone on a remote slope.

I had to approach the groaning goat.

I know that the wind is blowing.

Answers

o-e

| Page 5 | Page 10 | Page 11 |

Page 5

Activity 2 Thinking about the sound 'o-e'

ow
blowing snowing
oa
loading toasted floating
ough
although doughnut
oe
oboe
o-e
explode remote awoke
o
control progress bonus
ou
shoulder

Page 10

Activity 5 Syllable split

bo / nus	a / woke
slow / ing	mo / ment
a / go	col / dest
toa / sted	soa / king
d ough / n u t	sh ou l / d er
a / lone	o / pen
floa / ting	to / tal
cho / sen	
po / em	
glo /bal	
e / rode	
mol / ten	
spo / ken	
pho / to	

Page 11

Activity 6 Join the syllables

explode
noble
photo
total
remote
molten
roasted
hotel
knowing
approach

Page 12

Activity 7 Match to a picture

floating
snowing
explode
photo
robot
doughnut

Page 13

Activity 8 Two syllable word tech

a / pp r oa ch
t oa / s t i ng
a / g o
kn ow / i ng
f l oa / t i ng
n o / b le
r o / b o t
a / l o n e
h o / t e l
th r ow / i ng

Page 14

Activity 9 Syllable trap

a	g o
a	pp r oa ch
g o	i ng
d ough	n u t
g r ow	i ng
c l o	th i ng
c on	t r o l

Page 15	Page 16	Page 17
Activity 10 Sounds like a syllable	**Activity 11 Two syllable anagrams**	**Activity 12 Syllable jigsaw**

Page 15

Activity 10 Sounds like a syllable

bo   n u s

e   r o-e d   erode

g r ow   i ng

r o   b o t

o l   d e s t

d ough   n u t

a   l o-e n   alone

m o l   t e n

f l oa   t i ng

Page 16

Activity 11 Two syllable anagrams

molten
floating
knowing
photo
explode
clothing
remote
bonus
noble
erode
flowing
doughnut
alone
oboe
snowing

Page 17

Activity 12 Syllable jigsaw

ago
approach
alone
explode
doughnut
hotel
clothing
photo
progress

Words with an 'ee' sound – word list of 2 syllable words

ea	ee	y	y	y	e	e	ie	others	others
appeal	agree	angry	furry	mummy	being	meter	achieve	kilo	machine
appear	asleep	baby	fussy	nappy	beneath	metre	belief	kiosk	marine
beacon	beetle	badly	gladly	oily	between	methane	believe	kiwi	police
beaker	between	belly	glory	party	decent	neon	chiefly	litre	ravine
beneath	career	berry	grumpy	pastry	decrease	prefect	relief	trio	
conceal	degree	bony	happy	pony	defeat	preview	relieve		honey
creature	eerie	bury	hilly	runny	defect	react		ceiling	money
decrease	exceed	carry	holy	sadly	deflate	receipt		conceit	donkey
defeat	feeble	cherry	itchy	scruffy	defrost	recent		conceive	monkey
disease	freedom	creamy	jelly	silly	degree	relief		deceit	
displease	indeed	crusty	jolly	sleepy	delete	relieve		deceive	faeces
eager	needle	daddy	kitty	steamy	equal	reveal		either	
eagle	proceed	deeply	lady	stony	even	secret		neither	people
easy	steeple	dreamy	lastly	study	evil	Venus		perceive	
feature	succeed	dozy	lately	stuffy	female			receipt	
increase	veneer	dusty	lonely	sunny	fever			receive	
peanut		empty	lucky	tasty	frequent				
reveal		floppy	madly	truly	here				
treacle		fluffy	many	tummy	hero				
treason		friendly	marry	worry	legal				
weaver		funny	moody	ugly	lever				

This activity teaches the child about the schwa and how it impacts on reading multisyllable words.
Refer to the 'Working through the Programme' section of this book for a detailed explanation of this.
Support the child to read each word.
To help, the words have been split into two chunks of sounds, or syllables, as indicated by the asterisk *.
The first group of words are straightforward but the second have a **schwa** and so are a little more 'tricky'
to read.
When supporting the child to read the words in the second group, talk about where in the word the schwa is
and support them to highlight it.
Knowing about schwas can help with reading.

Activity 1a Reading 2 syllable words	Introducing the schwa

ban*dit   sep*tic

gob*lin   man*tis

kid*nap   hum*bug

con*test   splen*did

Watch out for the schwa.

bu***tt**o   ha***pp**en

mag*net   bas*ket

le***ss**on   le*mon

ca***rr**ot   trum*pet

This activity teaches the child about the schwa and how it impacts on spelling multisyllable words.
Refer to the 'Working through the programme' section of this book for a detailed explanation of this.
Support the child to read the word on the left.

Then look at how the word has been split into two chunks of sounds, or syllables, as indicated by the asterisk * and the red and blue colour coding. Ask the child to think about the word and identify whether there is a schwa sound in it, highlighting the corresponding sound spelling.

Focus on the grey word and think about the first syllable. Have the child write over each grey sound spelling and say the corresponding sound at the same time. If there is a schwa in this syllable, then encourage the child to think of and say the 'perfect' sound in place of the schwa. At the end of the syllable the child then says the syllable chunk. Repeat this for the second syllable and then blend the two syllables together and listen to the word forming. The child then says the whole word.

Cover the words and ask the child to write the word, syllable by syllable and sound by sound, on the two lines underneath, saying the sounds as they write the corresponding sound spellings. When the child writes the sound spelling associated with the schwa, encourage them to think about and say the 'perfect' sound. The child can then check and correct the answer if necessary.

Finally, the child can write the whole word on the single line, but once again work syllable by syllable and sound by sound, saying the sounds as they write the corresponding sound spellings.

The child could also highlight any sound spellings that they think are tricky, to help them recall it when spelling. Remind the child to take care with split sound spellings.

Activity 1b Spelling 2 syllable words	**Introducing the schwa**

button   b u * tt o n   b u * tt o n

_____ * _____   _____

chicken   ch i * ck e n   ch i * ck e n

_____ * _____   _____

sudden   s u * dd e n   s u * dd e n

_____ * _____   _____

address   a * dd r e ss   a * dd r e ss

_____ * _____   _____

This activity results in the child rediscovering all the sound spellings for this sound in the context of 2 syllable words.

Support the child to read the words one by one. Ask the child to say the word again in their head or with their 'thinking voice' and notice how they split up each word into two chunks of sounds, or syllables, as they say it.

For each word support the child to work out the sound spelling corresponding to the sound 'ee'.

Words are sorted into lists according to their 'ee' sound spelling.

There are nine sound spellings to find: **ee**, **ea**, **y**, **e**, **ie**, **i**, **i-e**, **e-e** and **ei**. The child met the first eight in Book 4 but the **ei** sound spelling is new – it only occurs in multisyllable words.

Encourage the child to say each sound as they write each sound spelling in sequence, *syllable by syllable*, in this way:

e.g.

	sees:	a n	g r y		
angry					
	says:	'a'>'n' = 'an'	'g'>'r'>'ee' = 'gree'	'an>gree'	'angry'

Break this task into a number of shorter tasks over a number of lessons if necessary.

Activity 2 Thinking about the sound   ee

angry	agree	being
peanut	delete	belief
kilo	police	ceiling
indeed	metre	money
secret	study	eager

This set of cards is made up of 2 syllable words containing the sound 'ee'. Copy onto card and cut out. Practise the dynamic blending – syllable by syllable reading strategy reading strategy, as described in the 'Working through the programme' section, to read the words on these cards. Model this process for the child if necessary.

Activity 3 Sorting word cards   ee

peanut	conceal
indeed	asleep
angry	funny
prefect	secret
believe	achieve
ceiling	receive
police	money

Support the child to read each word. To help, the words have been split into two chunks of sounds, or syllables, as indicated by the asterisk *.

Direct the child to blend the sounds within the first syllable and say the syllable chunk, then blend the sounds within the second syllable and say the syllable chunk. Remind the child to watch out for schwas!

Finally push both syllable chunks together to hear the word forming.

e.g.

	sees:	d e	f ea t		
defeat					
	says:	'd'>'ee' = 'dee'	'f'>'ee'>'t' = 'feet'	'dee>feet'	**'defeat'**

Activity 4 Reading 2 syllable words   ee

defeat	d e * f ea t
ceiling	c ei * l i ng
police	p o * l i c e
being	b e * i ng
kiwi	k i * w i
conceal	c o n * c ea l
indeed	i n * d ee d
tummy	t u * mm y
believe	b e * l ie ve

Support the child to read the words one by one. Ask the child to say the word again in their head or with their 'thinking voice' and notice how they split up each word into two chunks of sounds, or syllables, as they say it. For each word support the child to draw a line through the word to show where in the word they split it into two syllables.

It is useful to discuss how they made their choice.

The first group of words has some sound spellings highlighted to help, and the first one is split as an example.

Activity 5 Syllable split   ee

de/cr **ea** se	c **ei** l i **ng**
i n d **ee** d	d e f r o s t
f l u **ff** y	r a v i n e
k i l o.	g r u m p y
r e c **ei** ve	a **ch** i e ve
p o l i c e	r e v **ea** l
h o n **ey**	s l **ee** p y

Careful, the next ones do not have any sound spellings highlighted:

d e c e i v e

c h e r r y

a g r e e

r e l i e f

d e l e t e

b e n e a t h

s c r e a m i n g

Support the child to read the clue on the left and work out what the answer word is.

Ask the child to say the word again in their head or with their 'thinking voice' and notice how they split up each word into two chunks of sounds, or syllables, as they say it.

Ask the child to draw a line from the clue to the first syllable of the word and then go on to draw a line to the second syllable of the word.

Finally ask the child to write the whole word on the line at the end indicated by the arrow and read the word out loud.

Activity 6 Join the syllables   ee

Clue	1st	2nd		Word
Beat in battle	ea	s y	→	
Phew! What a ...	d e	l ie f	→	
Bird of prey	t u	g le	→	
Stomach	ea	f ea t	→	*defeat*
Not difficult	r e	mm y	→	
Reach a target	p o	ch ie ve	→	
Cops	a	l i c e	→	
A green fruit	s u	w i	→	
Do again	k i	p ea t	→	
Bright weather	r e	nn y	→	

Ask the child to choose a picture and discuss what the matching word might be.

Then ask the child to think about how that word might be split into two syllables.

The child then finds the first syllable and then the second, drawing a line from picture to syllable to syllable.

The child then writes the complete word on one of the lines in the box at the bottom of the page.

Encourage the child to write the word using the sequential segmenting – syllable by syllable spelling strategy.

Activity 7 Match to a picture   ee

a

sleep

ea

gry

lice

nny

po

an   su

gle   ling

cei

_____ _____ _____

_____ _____ _____

32

Support the child to read the words one by one. Ask the child to say the word again in their head or with their 'thinking voice' and notice how they split up the word into two chunks of sounds, or syllables, as they say it.
Then ask the child to show where they split the word up into two syllables by drawing a line through it.
Next ask the child to put a ring round each of the sound spellings.
Finally ask the child to highlight any schwas in the word.

Activity 8 Two syllable word tech   ee

cherry

defeat

receipt

steeple

easy

between

increase

ravine

reveal

ceiling

achieve

Support the child to read the words one by one. Ask the child to say the word again in their head or with their 'thinking voice' and notice how they split up each word into two chunks of sounds, or syllables, as they say it. For each word, ask the child to work out where they split it into two syllables and then draw a line through the word.

Then ask the child to work out how many sounds there are in each syllable. They could write the number next to each syllable.

Support the child to look at the grid underneath and choose the row that contains the right number of lines in the first box (to match the number of sounds in the first syllable) and the right number of lines in the second box (to match the number of sounds in the second syllable). Ask the child to write the word in the grid on the chosen row, writing a sound spelling on each line.

An example is done to help you.

Activity 9 Syllable trap   ee

3 sounds   trea/cle   2 sounds

easy	grumpy
achieve	lucky
prefect	beneath

___	___ ___
___	___ ___ ___
___ ___	___ ___
___ ___	___ ___ ___
t̲ r̲ e̲a	c̲ l̲e
___ ___ ___	___ ___ ___ ___
___ ___ ___	___ ___

Support the child to read the clue on the left and work out what the word is.

Ask the child to say the word in their head or with their 'thinking voice' and notice how they split up each word into two chunks of sounds, or syllables, as they say it.

Support the child to write the first syllable, sound by sound, in the first boxes and the second syllable, sound by sound, in the second boxes, noticing that there is a box for each sound within the syllables.

Remind them to be careful with split sound spellings!

Then, covering the boxes, ask the child to write out the word from memory in the box at the end, thinking about the syllables and the sounds in them.

The first one is done for you as an example.

Activity 10 Sounds like a syllable   ee

Clue	1st syllable			2nd syllable			Word
Fool someone	d	e		c	ei	ve	deceive
Have the same idea							
Not sensible							
Tired							
Group of three							
Not difficult							
Red fruit							
Cute name for a cat							
Sew with this							

Support the child to read the clue on the left and work out what the answer word is.
The word has been split into two syllables and the sound spellings in each syllable have been mixed up.
Encourage the child to write the first syllable, sound by sound, then the second syllable, sound by sound, on the line on the right.
Ask the child to say the word.
Careful with split sound spellings!

Activity 11 Two syllable anagrams   ee

Clue	1ˢᵗ syllable	2ⁿᵈ syllable	Word
Cross	n a	r y g	_____
Bright day	s u	y **nn**	_____
Not hard	**ea**	y s	_____
Under	e b	**ea** n **th**	_____
Do your school work	t u s	y d	_____
Green fruit	i k	w i	_____
Proof of purchase	e r	**ei** pt	_____
Bad tempered	r g u m	y p	_____
Rub out on the computer	e d	**e-e** t l	_____
Reach a target	a	**ie ch** ve	_____
Beat in battle	e d	**ea** t f	_____
Church spire	**ee** t s	**le** p	_____
Group of three	r i t	o	_____
Pet name for a cat	i k	**tt** y	_____
Dark gooey sugar	**ea** r t	**le** c	_____

Support the child to read the clue on the left and work out what the word is.
Ask the child to say the answer word again in their head or with their 'thinking voice' and notice how they split up each word into two chunks of sounds, or syllables, as they say it.
The words have been split into two 'syllable boxes' but are not complete.
Ask the child to finish the word by writing in either the first or second syllable as required in the grey box.
Then ask the child to write out the word in full on the line at the end.
The first one is done for you as an example.

Activity 12 Syllable jigsaw ee

Clue	1st syllable	2nd syllable	Word
Yum yum	ta	sty	tasty
Have faith		lieve	
Bright weather	su		
Rub out on screen	de		
Father	da		
Not difficult	ea		
Bird of prey		gle	
A green fruit	ki		
Show dramatically	re		

ee

Activity 13 Spelling challenge

indeed   i n/d ee d

agree   a/g r ee

funny   f u/nn y

empty   e m p/t y

between   b e/t w ee n

believe   b e/l ie ve

defeat   d e/f ea t

reveal   r e/v ea l

Support the child to read each sentence one by one.
Ask the child to re-read the sentence, several times if necessary, and try to remember it.
Then cover the sentence and ask the child to recall the sentence verbally.
Once they can do this confidently, ask the child to write out the sentence from memory.
The child might find it helpful to think about the individual syllables in the words and say the sounds within each as they write. When the sentence is complete, the child reads out their sentence and then compares it to the original.

Alternatively, using text to speech software, the child could type the sentence, with the computer reading back each word and then the completed sentence.

Activity 14 Writing challenge   ee

Please teach the eagle to eat peanuts.

I keep beetles in the beech tree.

Daddy's jelly is runny and floppy.

I believe the chief left his shield in the field.

The hero defeated the evil beings.

Mimi b**ough**t a li**tre** of kiwis from the kiosk.

We recei**ve**d a recei**pt** from the **build**ers **wh**en we **p**ai**d** f**or** the **r**e**pair** w**or**k on the ceili**ng**.

Monkeys and donkeys like lots of honey.

The police f**ou**nd the ma**ch**ine stu**ck** in the ravine.

Answers

Page 23
Activity 1a Introducing the schwa

button	happen
magnet	basket
lesson	lemon
carrot	trumpet

Page 25
Activity 2 Thinking about the sound 'ee'

y
angry   study
ey
money
ee
agree   indeed
e
being   delete   belief   metre   secret
ea
peanut   eager

e-e	**ie**
delete	belief
i	**i-e**
kilo	police

ei
ceiling

Page 30
Activity 5 Syllable split

de / crease	cei / ling
in / deed	de / frost
flu / ffy	ra / vine
ki / lo	grum/py
re / ceive	a / chieve
po / lice	re / veal
ho / ney	slee / py
de / ceive	
che / rry	
a / gree	
re / lief	
de / lete	
be / neath	
screa / ming	

Page 31
Activity 6 Join the syllables

easy
relief
eagle
defeat
tummy
achieve
police
kiwi
repeat
sunny

Page 32
Activity 7 Match to a picture

asleep
police
sunny
eagle
ceiling
angry

Page 33
Activity 8 Two syllable word tech

d e / f e a t
r e / c ei pt
s t ee / p le
ea / s y
b e / t w ee n
in / c r ea se
r a / v i n e
r e / v ea l
c ei / l i ng
a / ch ie ve

Page 34
Activity 9 Syllable trap

ea	s y
a	chi e ve
l u	ck y
b e	n ea th
t r ea	c le
p r e	f e c t
g r u m	p y

Page 35	Page 36	Page 37
Activity 10 Sounds like a syllable	**Activity 11 Two syllable anagrams**	**Activity 12 syllable jigsaw**

Page 35

Activity 10 Sounds like a syllable

d e	c ei ve
a	g r ee
s i	ll y
s l ee	p y
t r i	o
ea	s y
ch e	rr y
k i	tt y
n ee	d le

Page 36

Activity 11 Two syllable anagrams

angry
sunny
easy
beneath
study
kiwi
receipt
grumpy
delete
achieve
defeat
steeple
trio
kitty
treacle

Page 37

Activity 12 syllable jigsaw

tasty
believe
sunny
delete
daddy
easy
eagle
kiwi
reveal

Words with an 'a-e' sound – word list of 2 syllable words

a-e	ai	a	ay	eigh	others
amaze	afraid	ancient	away	eighteen	convey
ashamed	again	arrange	betray	eighty	survey
awake	against	bacon	crayon	neighbour	
became	attain	basic	decay		
behave	await	chamber	delay		
decade	complain	cradle	dismay		greater
dictate	contain	crater	display		greatest
embrace	detain	crazy	repay		
engage	domain	data	today		
erase	exclaim	exchange			
escape	explain	famous			reindeer
estate	failure	fatal			
exhale	obtain	favour			
inflame	retain	flavour			
inflate	retrain	label			
inhale	trailer	labour			
insane	trainer	ladies			
invade		laser			
lately		lazy			
parade		matrix			
relate		navy			
replace		radar			
		razor			
		saline			
		saving			
		shady			
		stable			
		stamen			
		staple			
		table			
		taken			
		vacant			
		wafer			

This activity builds on previous work about the schwa and requires the child to identify schwas in words.
Support the child to read each word.
To help, the words have been split into two chunks of sounds, or syllables, as indicated by the asterisk *.
The first group of words are straightforward but the second have a **schwa** and so are a little more 'tricky'
to read.
When supporting the child to read the words in the second group, talk about where in the word the schwa is
and support them to highlight it.
Remind them that knowing about schwas can help with reading and spelling.

Activity 1a Reading 2 syllable words   Spot the schwa

Words without a schwa

a d * m i t   f r a n * t i c

i n * s u l t   c a t * n i p

Highlight the schwa

p a * **ck** e t   s u * **dd** e n

f o * r e s t   b u * **ck** e t

t a n * **d e m**   b l o * **ss** o m

w i t * n e **ss**   a * **dd** r e **ss**

ch i * **ck** e n   k i * **tch** e n

c o * **tt** o n   h e l p * l e **ss**

This activity results in the child rediscovering all the sound spellings for this sound in the context of 2 syllable words.

Support the child to read the words one by one. Ask the child to say the word again in their head or with their 'thinking voice' and notice how they split up each word into two chunks of sounds, or syllables, as they say it.

For each word support the child to work out the sound spelling corresponding to the sound 'a-e'.

Words are sorted into lists according to their 'a-e' sound spelling.

There are eight sound spellings to find: **a-e**, **ai**, **a**, **ay**, **eigh**, **ey**, **ea** and **ei**.

Encourage the child to say each sound as they write each sound spelling in sequence, *syllable by syllable*, in this way:

e.g.

contain

sees:　　c　o　n　　　　　t　ai　n

says:　　'c'>'o'>'n' = 'con'　　't'>'a-e'>'n' = 'ta-en'　　**'con>ta-en'**　　**'contain'**

Remind the child to watch out for schwas! There is a schwa in the first syllable of 'contain'.

Break this task into a number of shorter tasks over a number of lessons if necessary.

Activity 2 Thinking about the sound   a-e

contain	amaze	display
eighteen	convey	awake
table	away	explain
greatest	reindeer	basic
complain	delay	ashamed

This set of cards is made up of 2 syllable words containing the sound 'a-e'. Copy onto card and cut out. Practise the dynamic blending – syllable by syllable reading strategy, as described in the 'Working through the programme' section, to read the words on these cards. Model this process for the child if necessary.

Activity 3 Sorting word cards a-e

escape	inflate
afraid	contain
explain	obtain
basic	crazy
lazy	reindeer
today	away
greatest	eighty

Support the child to read each word. To help, the words have been split into two chunks of sounds, or syllables, as indicated by the asterisk *.

Direct the child to blend the sounds within the first syllable and say the syllable chunk, then blend the sounds within the second syllable and say the syllable chunk. Remind the child to watch out for schwas!

Finally push both syllable chunks together to hear the word forming.

e.g.

	sees:	c o m	p l a i n		
complain					
	says:	'c'>'o'>'m' = 'com'	'p'>'l'>'a-e'> 'n' = 'pla-en'	'com>pla-en'	**'complain'**

Activity 4 Reading 2 syllable words   a-e

complain	c o m * p l a i n
display	d i s * p l ay
invade	i n * v a d e
convey	c o n * v ey
reindeer	r ei n * d ee r
explain	e x * p l a i n
delay	d e * l ay
lazy	l a * z y
eighty	eigh * t y
greatest	g r ea * t e s t

Support the child to read the words one by one. Ask the child to say the word again in their head or with their 'thinking voice' and notice how they split up each word into two chunks of sounds, or syllables, as they say it.
For each word support the child to draw a line through the word to show where in the word they split it into two syllables.
It is useful to discuss how they made their choice. Remind the child to watch out for schwas.
The first group of words has some sound spellings highlighted to help, and the first one is split as an example.

Activity 5 Syllable split   a-e

in/va de   dec **ay**

r **ei** n d **ee** r   r **ai** l w **ay**

o b t **ai** n   d i s p l **ay**

d a t a   g r **ea** t e s t

a **rr** a n g e   c o n t **ai** n

c o n v **ey**   b e h a v e

t a b **le**   **eigh** t **ee** n

Careful, the next do not have any sound spellings highlighted:

r e m a i n

l a b e l

e s c a p e

l a t e s t

a w a y

t o d a y

e x p l a i n

Support the child to read the clue on the left and work out what the answer word is.

Ask the child to say the word again in their head or with their 'thinking voice' and notice how they split up each word into two chunks of sounds, or syllables, as they say it.

Ask the child to draw a line from the clue to the first syllable of the word and then go on to draw a line to the second syllable of the word.

Finally ask the child to write the whole word on the line at the end indicated by the arrow and read the word out loud.

Activity 6 Join the syllables   a-e

Clue	1st	2nd	→	Word
Scared	g r **ea**	f r **ai** d	→	
This day	a	t e s t	→	
The best	c o m	d **ay**	→	
18	t o	d **ee** r	→	*reindeer*
Grumble	**eigh**	p l **ai** n	→	
Horse's home	s t a	t **ee** n	→	
Pulls Santa's sleigh	b e	b **le**	→	
Rub out	r **ei** n	r a s e	→	
Be good!	e	d **ie** s	→	
Women	l a	h a v e	→	

Ask the child to choose a picture and discuss what the matching word might be.

Then ask the child to think about how that word might be split into two syllables.

The child then finds the first syllable and then the second, drawing a line from picture to syllable to syllable.

The child then writes the complete word on one of the lines in the box at the bottom of the page.

Encourage the child to write the word using the sequential segmenting – syllable by syllable spelling strategy.

Activity 7 Match to a picture   a-e

sta

80

bel

la

ble

eigh

ty

deer

rade   on

rein   cray

pa

Support the child to read the words one by one. Ask the child to say the word again in their head or with their 'thinking voice' and notice how they split up the word into two chunks of sounds, or syllables, as they say it.
Then ask the child to show where they split the word up into two syllables by drawing a line through it.
Next ask the child to put a ring round each of the sound spellings.
Finally ask the child to highlight any schwas in the word.

Activity 8 Two syllable word tech   a-e

greatest

invade

explain

eighteen

replay

became

latest

afraid

painting

display

Support the child to read the words one by one. Ask the child to say the word again in their head or with their 'thinking voice' and notice how they split up each word into two chunks of sounds, or syllables, as they say it. For each word, ask the child to work out where they split it into two syllables and then draw a line through the word.

Then ask the child to work out how many sounds there are in each syllable. They could write the number next to each syllable.

Support the child to look at the grid underneath and choose the row that contains the right number of lines in the first box (to match the number of sounds in the first syllable) and the right number of lines in the second box (to match the number of sounds in the second syllable). Ask the child to write the word in the grid on the chosen row, writing a sound spelling on each line.

An example is done to help you.

Activity 9 Syllable trap   a-e

3 sounds   railway   2 sounds

data	display
straighten	afraid
greatest	obtain

—	— — — — —
— —	— — —
— — —	— — — —
r ai l	w ay
— — — —	— — —
— — —	— — —
— — — — —	— — — —

Support the child to read the clue on the left and work out what the word is.

Ask the child to say the word in their head or with their 'thinking voice' and notice how they split up each word into two chunks of sounds, or syllables, as they say it.

Support the child to write the first syllable, sound by sound, in the first boxes and the second syllable, sound by sound, in the second boxes, noticing that there is a box for each sound within the syllables.

Remind them to be careful with split sound spellings!

Then, covering the boxes, ask the child to write out the word from memory in the box at the end, thinking about the syllables and the sounds in them.

The first two are done for you as an example.

Activity 10 Sounds like a syllable   a-e

Clue	1st syllable	2nd syllable	Word
10 years	d | e	c | a-e | d	decade
Santa's transport	r | ei | n	d | ee | r	reindeer
70 + 10			
Can't be bothered			
Astound			
Frightened			
.... agents sell houses			
This very day			
18 in a word			

Support the child to read the clue on the left and work out what the answer word is.
The word has been split into two syllables and the sound spellings in each syllable have been mixed up.
Encourage the child to write the first syllable, sound by sound, then the second syllable, sound by sound, on the line on the right.
Ask the child to say the word.
Careful with split sound spellings!

Activity 11 Two syllable anagrams   a-e

Clue	1st syllable	2nd syllable	Word
Zero gravity	**eigh** w t	**ss** l e	_____
Scared	a	**ai** f d r	_____
To get something	b o	**ai** n t	_____
10 years	e d	c d **a-e**	_____
Pull Santa's sleigh	**ei** n r	**ee** d r	_____
Make late	e d	**ay** l	_____
Run away from	e s	**a-e** p c	_____
Biggest and best	g **ea** r	t t s e	_____
Swap	x e	n **a-e** ch g	_____
Deadly	a f	t **al**	_____
Put back	e r	**a-e** l c p	_____
Grumble	c m o	l p **ai**	_____
A baby's bed	r a c	**le** d	_____
Not in use	a v	n c t a	_____
Stay behind	e r	**ai** n m	_____

Support the child to read the clue on the left and work out what the word is.

Ask the child to say the answer word again in their head or with their 'thinking voice' and notice how they split up each word into two chunks of sounds, or syllables, as they say it.

The words have been split into two 'syllable boxes' but are not complete.

Ask the child to finish the word by writing in either the first or second syllable as required in the grey box.

Then ask the child to write out the word in full on the line at the end.

The first one is done for you as an example.

Activity 12 Syllable jigsaw   a-e

Clue	1st syllable	2nd syllable	Word
Horse's home	sta	ble	_stable_
80		ty	_____
Work surface		ble	_____
This day	to		_____
Give money owed	re		_____
Run away	es		_____
Pull Santa's sleigh		deer	_____
Grumble	com		_____
Women		dies	_____

Activity 13 Spelling challenge

a/f r ai d	* _ _ _ _	*	afraid
e x/p l ai n	* _ _ _ _	*	explain
d i s/p l ay	* _ _ _ _	* _ _ _ _	display
d e/l ay	* _ _ _ _	*	delay
b a/b y	* _ _ _ _	*	baby
t a/b le	* _ _ _ _	*	table
a/m a z e	* _ _ _ _	*	amaze
i n/v a d e	* _ _ _ _	*	invade

Support the child to read each sentence one by one.
Ask the child to re-read the sentence, several times if necessary, and try to remember it.
Then cover the sentence and ask the child to recall the sentence verbally.
Once they can do this confidently, ask the child to write out the sentence from memory.
The child might find it helpful to think about the individual syllables in the words and say the sounds within each as they write. When the sentence is complete, the child reads out their sentence and then compares it to the original.

Alternatively, using text to speech software, the child could type the sentence, with the computer reading back each word and then the completed sentence.

Activity 14 Writing challenge   a-e

He is a**sh**am**e**d **th**at **sh**e beh**a**v**e**s **th**at w**ay**.

I am afr**ai**d I cannot explai**n th**at again.

I m**ay** p**ay** to **see** the displ**ay** tod**ay**.

The cr**a**zy **a**lien went to a v**a**cant t**a**b**le**.

My **eigh**t**een** n**eigh**b**ours** are the gr**ea**t**e**st.

Support the child to read each word.

To help, the words have been split into three chunks of sounds, or syllables, as indicated by the asterisk * and red, blue and green colour coding.

Direct the child to blend the sounds within the first syllable and say the syllable chunk, then blend the sounds within the second syllable and say the syllable chunk, then blend the sounds within the third syllable and say the syllable chunk. Finally push all three syllable chunks together to hear the word forming.

e.g.

fantastic

sees: f a n   t a   s t i c

says: 'f'>'a'>'n' = 'fan' 't'>'a' = 'ra' 's'>'t'>'i'>'c' = 'stic' 'fan>ta>stic' **'fantastic'**

Remind the child to watch out for schwas highlighted.

Activity 15 Introducing 3 syllable words   a-e

fantastic   f a n * t a * s t ic

historic   h i s * t o * r i c

inhabit   i n * h a * b i t

caravan   c a * r a * v a n

gorilla   g o * r i * ll a

recommend   r e * c o * mm e n d

Africa   A * f r i * c a

vitamin   v i * t a * m i n

Answers a-e

Page 44

Activity 1a Reading 2 syllable words Spot the schwa

packet	sudden
forest	bucket
tandem	blossom
witness	address
chicken	kitchen
cotton	helpless

Page 45

Activity 2 Thinking about the sound 'a-e'

ai
contain explain complain
a-e
amaze awake ashamed
ay
display delay
eigh
eighteen
ey   **a**
convey   table basic
ay   **ea**
away   greatest
ei
reindeer

Page 49

Activity 5 Syllable split

in / vade	de / cay
rein / deer	rail / way
ob / tain	dis / play
da / ta	grea / test
a / rrange	con / tain
con / vey	be / have
ta / ble	eigh / teen
re / main	
la / bel	
es / cape	
la / test	
a / way	
to / day	
ex / plain	

Page 50

Activity 6 Join the syllables

afraid
greatest
today
reindeer
complain
eighteen
stable
erase
ladies
behave

Page 51

Activity 7 Match to a picture

label
stable
eighty
reindeer
parade
crayon

Page 52

Activity 8 Two syllable word tech

grea / test
in / vade
ex / plain
eigh / teen
re / play
be / came
la / test
a / fraid
pain / ting
dis / play

Page 53

Activity 9 Syllable trap

a	fraid
da	ta
ob	tain
rail	way
dis	play
grea	test
straigh	ten

Page 54	Page 55	Page 56
Activity 10 Sounds like a syllable	**Activity 11 Two syllable anagrams**	**Activity 12 Syllable jigsaw**

Page 54

Activity 10 Sounds like a syllable

d e	c a-e d	decade
r ei n	d ee r	
eigh	t y	
l a	z y	
a	m a-e z	amaze
a	f r ai d	
e	s t a-e t	estate
t o	d ay	
eigh	t ee n	

Page 55

Activity 11 Two syllable anagrams

weightless
afraid
obtain
decade
reindeer
delay
escape
greatest
exchange
fatal
replace
complain
cradle
vacant
remain

Page 56

Activity 12 Syllable jigsaw

eigh ty
sta ble
to day
re pay
es cape
rein deer
com plain
la dies

Words with an 'er' sound – word list of 2 syllable words

er	ur	ir	ear	our	or
alert	burger	birthday	early	colour	worker
assert	burner	circle	earning	favour	working
adverb	curtain	circuit	earthquake	flavour	worthy
burger	disturb	circus	earthworm	harbour	
burner	further	confirm	learning	journal	
center (USA)	gurgle	infirm	research	journey	
certain	hurdle	thirteen			
concern	murder	thirty			**ar**
conserve	murmur				burglar
convert	occur				collar
desert	purchase				dollar
dessert	purple				
deter	purpose				
divert	return				**re**
emerge	surface				centre
further	surname				litre
gerbil	survey				metre
hermit	Thursday				
immerse	turkey				
inert	urban				**urr**
insert	urgent				furry
invert					purring
meter					
merchant					
mercy					**yr**
murder					zephyr
nervous					myrtle
observe					
perfect					
permit					**irr**
person					stirring
prefer				·	whirring
preserve					
reserve					
reverse					
servant					
service					
thermal					
verbal					
worker					

This activity results in the child rediscovering all the sound spellings for this sound in the context of 2 syllable words.

Support the child to read the words one by one. Ask the child to say the word again in their head or with their 'thinking voice' and notice how they split up each word into two chunks of sounds, or syllables, as they say it.

For each word support the child to work out the sound spelling corresponding to the sound 'er'.

Words are sorted into lists according to their 'er' sound spelling.

There are eight sound spellings to find: **er**, **ur**, **ir**, **ear**, **our**, **or**, **ar** and **re**.

Encourage the child to say each sound as they write each sound spelling in sequence, *syllable by syllable*, in this way:

e.g.

	sees:	p er		s o n
person				
	says:	'p'>'er' = 'per'	's'>'o'>'n' = 'son'	'per>son'	**'person'**

Remind the child to watch out for schwas! There is a schwa in the second syllable of person.

Break this task into a number of shorter tasks over a number of lessons if necessary.

Activity 2 Thinking about the sound   er

person	disturb	thirteen
early	metre	prefer
confirm	working	purple
perfect	flavour	searching
collar	burger	litre

_____	_____
_____	_____
_____	_____
_____	_____
_____	_____

This set of cards is made up of 2 syllable words containing the sound 'er'. Copy onto card and cut out.
Practise the dynamic blending – syllable by syllable reading strategy, as described in the 'Working through the programme' section, to read the words on these cards. Model this process for the child if necessary.

Activity 3 Sorting word cards	er

advert	prefer
return	disturb
purple	birthday
thirteen	early
learning	colour
journey	working
collar	metre

Support the child to read each word. To help, the words have been split into two chunks of sounds, or syllables, as indicated by the asterisk *.
Direct the child to blend the sounds within the first syllable and say the syllable chunk, then blend the sounds within the second syllable and say the syllable chunk. Remind the child to watch out for schwas!
Finally push both syllable chunks together to hear the word forming.
e.g.

	sees:	th ir	t ee n		
thirteen	says:	'th'>'er' = 'ther'	't'>'ee'> 'n' = 'teen'	'ther>teen'	**'thirteen'**

Activity 4 Reading 2 syllable words   er

thirteen	th ir * t ee n
murder	m ur * d er
journey	j our * n ey
working	w or * k i ng
centre	c e n * t re
occur	o * cc ur
circle	c ir * c le
favour	f a * v our
burglar	b ur * g l ar

Support the child to read the words one by one. Ask the child to say the word again in their head or with their 'thinking voice' and notice how they split up each word into two chunks of sounds, or syllables, as they say it. For each word support the child to draw a line through the word to show where in the word they split it into two syllables.

It is useful to discuss how they made their choice. Remind the child to watch out for schwas!

The first group of words has some sound spellings highlighted to help, and the first one is split as an example.

Activity 5 Syllable split   er

f l a/v **our**   c e n t **re**

d i v **er** t   p **er** s o n

th i **r** t y   d i s p l **ay**

j **our** n **ey**   b **ur** g l **ar**

m e t **re**   c **ir** c le

m **ur** d **er**   c **ur** t **ai** n

g **er** b **il**   l **ear** n i **ng**

Careful, the next do not have any sound spellings highlighted:

c i r c u s

l i t r e

w o r k e r

b u r g e r

r e t u r n

c o n v e r t

d o l l a r

Support the child to read the clue on the left and work out what the answer word is.

Ask the child to say the word again in their head or with their 'thinking voice' and notice how they split up each word into two chunks of sounds, or syllables, as they say it.

Ask the child to draw a line from the clue to the first syllable of the word and then go on to draw a line to the second syllable of the word.

Finally ask the child to write the whole word on the line at the end indicated by the arrow and read the word out loud.

Activity 6 Join the syllables   er

Clue	1st	2nd	→	Word
Nice in a bun	c e n	g **er**	→	*burger*
Wide awake	b **ur**	t **re**	→	
Middle	a	b **il**	→	
Rodent pet	**Th ur s**	l **er** t	→	
Wiggly minibeast	g **er**	ll **ar**	→	
After Wednesday	**ear th**	d **ay**	→	
USA money, $	r e	w **or** m	→	
Taste	d o	t **ur** n	→	
Go back	f l a	c **er** n	→	
A worry	c o n	v **our**	→	

Ask the child to choose a picture and discuss what the matching word might be.
Then ask the child to think about how that word might be split into two syllables.
The child then finds the first syllable and then the second, drawing a line from picture to syllable to syllable.
The child then writes the complete word on one of the lines in the box at the bottom of the page.
Encourage the child to write the word using the sequential segmenting – syllable by syllable spelling strategy.

Activity 7 Match to a picture   er

quake

li

earth

tre   per

de

son

ger   sert

bur   tre

me

_____   _____   _____

_____   _____   _____

Support the child to read the words one by one. Ask the child to say the word again in their head or with their 'thinking voice' and notice how they split up the word into two chunks of sounds, or syllables, as they say it.

Then ask the child to show where they split the word up into two syllables by drawing a line through it.

Next ask the child to put a ring round each of the sound spellings.

Finally ask the child to highlight any schwas in the word.

Activity 8 Two syllable word tech   er

burglar

disturb

centre

worker

journey

purple

perfect

return

early

flavour

litre

Support the child to read the words one by one. Ask the child to say the word again in their head or with their 'thinking voice' and notice how they split up each word into two chunks of sounds, or syllables, as they say it. For each word, ask the child to work out where they split it into two syllables and then draw a line through the word.

Then ask the child to work out how many sounds there are in each syllable. They could write the number next to each syllable.

Support the child to look at the grid underneath and choose the row that contains the right number of lines in the first box (to match the number of sounds in the first syllable) and the right number of lines in the second box (to match the number of sounds in the second syllable). Ask the child to write the word in the grid on the chosen row, writing a sound spelling on each line.

An example is done to help you.

Activity 9 Syllable trap   er

| 3 sounds | 2 sounds |

fla\vour   circle

perfect   urgent

early   return

confirm   alert

——	—— ——
——	—— —— ——
——	—— —— —— ——
—— ——	—— ——
—— ——	—— —— ——
—— ——	—— —— —— ——
<u>f l a</u>	<u>v our</u>
—— —— ——	—— —— —— ——

Support the child to read the clue on the left and work out what the word is.

Ask the child to say the word in their head or with their 'thinking voice' and notice how they split up each word into two chunks of sounds, or syllables, as they say it.

Support the child to write the first syllable, sound by sound, in the first boxes and the second syllable, sound by sound, in the second boxes, noticing that there is a box for each sound within the syllables.

Remind them to be careful with split sound spellings!

Then, covering the boxes, ask the child to write out the word from memory in the box at the end, thinking about the syllables and the sounds in them.

The first one is done for you as an example.

Activity 10 Sounds like a syllable   er

Clue	1st syllable			2nd syllable			Word
Last name	s	ur		n	a-e	m	surname
Come back							
The middle							
Day you were born							
100 cm							
Red and blue make							
Dry, sandy place							
Arrive before the agreed time							
Round shape							

Support the child to read the clue on the left and work out what the answer word is.
The word has been split into two syllables and the sound spellings in each syllable have been mixed up.
Encourage the child to write the first syllable, sound by sound, then the second syllable, sound by sound, on the line on the right.
Ask the child to say the word.
Careful with split sound spellings!

Activity 11 Two syllable anagrams   er

Clue	1ˢᵗ syllable	2ⁿᵈ syllable	Word
Wiggly animal	th ear	m w or	*earthworm*
30	ir th	y t	_____
Last name	ur s	a-e m n	_____
100 cm	e m	re t	_____
Has no faults	er p	c f t e	_____
Window cover	c ur	ai n t	_____
Shade or tint	o c	our l	_____
House robber	ur b	ar l g	_____
USA money, $	o d	ar ll	_____
Taste	l a f	our v	_____
Go backwards	e r	er v se	_____
Buy	ur p	a-e s ch	_____
Round shape	ir c	le c	_____
Allow	er p	m t i	_____
Like better	e p r	er f	_____

Support the child to read the clue on the left and work out what the word is.

Ask the child to say the answer word again in their head or with their 'thinking voice' and notice how they split up each word into two chunks of sounds, or syllables, as they say it.

The words have been split into two 'syllable boxes' but are not complete.

Ask the child to finish the word by writing in either the first or second syllable as required in the grey box.

Then ask the child to write out the word in full on the line at the end.

The first one is done for you as an example.

Activity 12 Syllable jigsaw   er

Clue	1st syllable	2nd syllable	Word
Come back	re	turn	return
1000 ml	li		_____
Family name		name	_____
Allow		mit	_____
Go backwards	re		_____
Sandy land	de		_____
Round shape		cle	_____
Shade or tint	co		_____
Meat in a bun		ger	_____

Activity 13 Spelling challenge

er

perfect	p er|f e c t	* _ | _ _ _	*
person	p er|s o n	* | _ _	*
return	r e|t ur n	* | _ _ _	*
birthday	b ir th|d ay	* | _ _	*
early	ear|l y	* _ | _	*
centre	c e n|t re	* | _ _	*
journey	j our|n ey	* | _ _	*
burger	b ur|g er	* _ | _ _	*

Support the child to read each sentence one by one.

Ask the child to re-read the sentence, several times if necessary, and try to remember it.

Then cover the sentence and ask the child to recall the sentence verbally.

Once they can do this confidently, ask the child to write out the sentence from memory.

The child might find it helpful to think about the individual syllables in the words and say the sounds within each as they write. When the sentence is complete, the child reads out their sentence and then compares it to the original.

Alternatively, using text to speech software, the child could type the sentence, with the computer reading back each word and then the completed sentence.

Activity 14 Writing challenge   er

That person has a German dog.

Let's return to the Turkish church.

The world has lots of worms.

I am ten metres from the town centre.

We went to the circus for my thirteenth birthday.

We are learning about earthquakes and have to do some research.

Support the child to read each word.

To help, the words have been split into three chunks of sounds, or syllables, as indicated by the asterisk * and red, blue and green colour coding.

Direct the child to blend the sounds within the first syllable and say the syllable chunk, then blend the sounds within the second syllable and say the syllable chunk, then blend the sounds within the third syllable and say the syllable chunk. Finally push all three syllable chunks together to hear the word forming.

e.g.

deserted

sees: d e   s er   t e d

says: 'd'>'ee' = 'dee'   'z'>'er' = 'zer'   't'>'e'>'d' = 'ted'   'dee>zer>ted'   'deserted'

Remind the child to watch out for schwas highlighted.

Activity 15 Reading 3 syllable words   er

deserted	d e * s er * t e d
colouring	c o * l our * i ng
perfectly	p er * f e c t * l y
returning	r e * t ur * n i ng
researcher	r e * s ear * ch er
murderer	m ur * d er * er
observant	o b * s er * v a n t
earlier	ear * l i * er

Answers er

Page 63

Activity 2 Thinking about the sound 'er'

er
person prefer perfect burger
ur
disturb purple burger
ir
thirteen confirm
ear
early searching

re	**or**
metre litre	working
our	**ar**
flavour	collar

Page 67

Activity 5 Syllable split

fla / vour	cen / tre
di / vert	per / son
thir / ty	dis / play
jour / ney	bur / glar
me / tre	cir / cle
mur / der	cur / tain
ger / bil	lear / ning
cir / cus	
li / tre	
wor / ker	
bur / ger	
re / turn	
con / vert	
do / llar	

Page 68

Activity 6 Join the syllables

burger
centre
gerbil
alert
dollar
Thursday
earthworm
return
concern
flavour

Page 69

Activity 7 Match to a picture

earthquake
litre
person
desert
burger
metre

Page 70

Activity 8 Two syllable word tech

d i s / t u r b
c e n / t r e
w or / k er
j our / n ey
p ur / p le
p er / f e c t
r e / t u r n
ear / l y
f l a / v our
l i / t re

Page 71

Activity 9 Syllable trap

ear	l y
a	l er t
ur	g e n t
c ir	c le
r e	t u r n
p er	f e c t
f l a	v our
c o n	f ir m

Page 72	Page 73	Page 74
Activity 10 Sounds like a syllable	**Activity 11 Two syllable anagrams**	**Activity 12 Syllable jigsaw**

Page 72

Activity 10 Sounds like a syllable

s ur   n a-e m   surname
r e   t ur n
c e n   t re
b ir th d ay
m e   t re
p ur   p le
d e   s er t
ear   l y
c ir   c le

Page 73

Activity 11 Two syllable anagrams

earthworm
thirty
surname
metre
perfect
curtain
colour
burglar
dollar
flavour
reverse
purchase
circle
permit
prefer

Page 74

Activity 12 Syllable jigsaw

re   turn
li   tre
sur   name
per   mit
re   verse
de   sert
cir   cle
co   lour
bur   ger

Words with an 'e' sound – word list of 2 syllable words

e	e	e	e	e	e	e	e	e	ea	ea	a	ie	ai
address	correct	eject	fellow	level	perfect	restful	suspend	very	ahead	threaded	any	friendless	against
affect	credit	elbow	gentle	medal	perish	revenge	suspense	vessel	behead	threaten	anything	friendly	captain
ascend	debit	eldest	gently	mellow	petal	second	telling	vetting	breakfast	wealthy	anyone	unfriend	fountain
assess	decade	elect	getting	melting	plenty	segment	temper	wedding	breathless	weapon	many		mountain
attempt	defect	empty	hello	member	possess	seldom	tempest	welfare	cleansing	weather			
attend	defence	ending	helper	membrane	presence	select	temple	western	deaden	weathered			
begging	defend	endless	helpful	merit	present	selfish	tender	wetter	dreaded				
belly	deflect	envy	himself	method	pretend	senses	tendon	whether	dreadful				
berry	denim	epic	impress	metric	prevent	sensor	tennis	yelling	deadly				
better	dentist	error	infect	misled	progress	sentence	tepid	yellow	feather				
blessing	depend	essay	inject	neglect	project	seven	testing	zebra	headed				
centre	descend	event	inspect	nettle	protect	shelter	texting		healthy				
checking	desert	ever	intend	network	protest	slender	themselves		heaven				
chemist	detect	excess	invent	never	reflect	spectrum	treble		heavy				
clever	detest	exhale	invest	object	refresh	spending	tremble		instead				
commence	devil	exit	itself	obsess	regret	splendid	trendy		leather				
confess	direct	expect	jelly	offend	reject	stepping	twenty		meadow				
connect	distress	expense	kestrel	pedal	relish	stretching	unless		peasant				
consent	dressing	expert	kettle	pelvis	rental	subject	vector		ready				
contempt	echo	extend	legend	pencil	repent	success	velvet		spreading				
content	edit	extra	lemon	penny	resent	suggest	vendor		steady				
contest	effect	extract	letter	pepper	respect	suspect	venom		sweater				

This activity results in the child rediscovering all the sound spellings for this sound in the context of 2 syllable words.

Support the child to read the words one by one. Ask the child to say the word again in their head or with their 'thinking voice' and notice how they split up each word into two chunks of sounds, or syllables, as they say it. For each word, support the child to work out the sound spelling corresponding to the sound 'e'.

Words are sorted into lists according to their 'e' sound spelling.

There are five sound spellings to find: **e**, **ea**, **ai**, **a** and **ie**. By far the most common is the sound spelling **e**. Encourage the child to say each sound as they write each sound spelling in sequence, *syllable by syllable*, in this way:

e.g.

address

       sees: a   **dd** r e **ss**

       says: 'a' = 'a'   'd'>'r'>'e'>'s' = 'dres'   'a>dres'   **'address'**

Remind the child to watch out for schwas! There is a schwa in the first syllable of 'address'.
Break this task into a number of shorter tasks over a number of lessons if necessary.

Activity 2 Thinking about the sound   e

address	heavy	many
instead	friendly	mountain
any	captain	extra
friendless	steady	inspect
fountain	helpful	ready

This set of cards is made up of 2 syllable words containing the sound 'e'. Copy onto card and cut out. Practise the dynamic blending – syllable by syllable reading strategy, as described in the 'Working through the programme' section, to read the words on these cards. Model this process for the child if necessary.

Activity 3 Sorting word cards   e

address	attend
expect	impress
present	subject
instead	ready
healthy	mountain
captain	friendly
any	many

Support the child to read each word. To help, the words have been split into two chunks of sounds, or syllables, as indicated by the asterisk *.
Direct the child to blend the sounds within the first syllable and say the syllable chunk, then blend the sounds within the second syllable and say the syllable chunk. Remind the child to watch out for schwas!
Finally push both syllable chunks together to hear the word forming.
e.g.

sees: u n   l e ss

unless

says: 'u'>'n' = 'un'   'l'>'e'>'s' = 'les'   'un>les'   **'unless'**

Activity 4 Reading 2 syllable words   e

unless   u n * l e ss

sending   s e n * d i ng

ahead   a * h ea d

captain   c a p * t ai n

itself   i t * s e l f

dressing   d r e * ss i ng

instead   i n * s t ea d

many   m a * n y

friendly   f r ie n d * l y

Support the child to read the words one by one. Ask the child to say the word again in their head or with their 'thinking voice' and notice how they split up each word into two chunks of sounds, or syllables, as they say it. For each word support the child to draw a line through the word to show where in the word they split it into two syllables.

It is useful to discuss how they made their choice. Remind the child to watch out for schwas!

The first group of words has some sound spellings highlighted to help, and the first one is split as an example.

Activity 5 Syllable split   e

o b/j e c t   h ea l th y

s e n t e n ce   z e b r a

m a n y   d r ea d f u l

e x p er t   g e n t le

h e l p er   w ea th er

th r ea t e n   a g ai n s t

f r ie n d l e ss   p er f e c t

Careful, the next ones do not have any sound spellings highlighted:

a n y

s w e a t e r

h e a v y

e n d l e s s

c e n t r e

b r e a k f a s t

n e t w o r k

Support the child to read the clue on the left and work out what the answer word is.

Ask the child to say the word again in their head or with their 'thinking voice' and notice how they split up each word into two chunks of sounds, or syllables, as they say it.

Ask the child to draw a line from the clue to the first syllable of the word and then go on to draw a line to the second syllable of the word.

Finally ask the child to write the whole word on the line at the end indicated by the arrow and read the word out loud.

Activity 6 Join the syllables   e

Clue	1st	2nd	→	Word
Large hill	f **ea**	v y	→	
On birds' wings	m **ou** n	**th** er	→	*feather*
Weighty	f r **ie** n d	t **ai** n	→	
Stripy animal	h **ea**	s t **ea** d	→	
Wants to play	z e	l y	→	
In place of	t r e m	**th** y	→	
Feel fit and well	i n	b r a	→	
Boil water for tea	h **ea** l	b **le**	→	
Shake with fear	p e	**tt le**	→	
'Hot' vegetable	k e	**pp** er	→	

Ask the child to choose a picture and discuss what the matching word might be.

Then ask the child to think about how that word might be split into two syllables.

The child then finds the first syllable and then the second, drawing a line from picture to syllable to syllable.

The child then writes the complete word on one of the lines in the box at the bottom of the page.

Encourage the child to write the word using the sequential segmenting – syllable by syllable spelling strategy.

Activity 7 Match to a picture   e

ze

fea

ther

bra

pe

pper

break

moun   tain

fast

nnis

te

_____   _____   _____

_____   _____   _____

Support the child to read the words one by one. Ask the child to say the word again in their head or with their 'thinking voice' and notice how they split up the word into two chunks of sounds, or syllables, as they say it.
Then ask the child to show where they split the word up into two syllables by drawing a line through it.
Next ask the child to put a ring round each of the sound spellings.
Finally ask the child to highlight any schwas in the word.

Activity 8 Two syllable word tech   e

heaven

descend

unless

spreading

friendly

against

event

wealthy

detect

lemon

many

Support the child to read the words one by one. Ask the child to say the word again in their head or with their 'thinking voice' and notice how they split up each word into two chunks of sounds, or syllables, as they say it. For each word, ask the child to work out where they split it into two syllables and then draw a line through the word.

Then ask the child to work out how many sounds there are in each syllable. They could write the number next to each syllable.

Support the child to look at the grid underneath and choose the row that contains the right number of lines in the first box (to match the number of sounds in the first syllable) and the right number of lines in the second box (to match the number of sounds in the second syllable). Ask the child to write the word in the grid on the chosen row, writing a sound spelling on each line.

Activity 9 Syllable trap   e

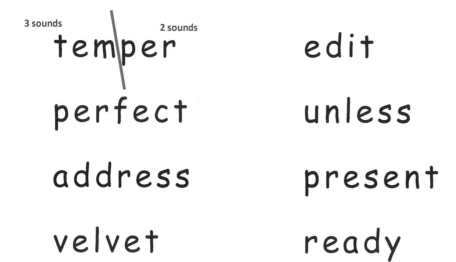

3 sounds   2 sounds

tem|per   edit

perfect   unless

address   present

velvet   ready

Support the child to read the clue on the left and work out what the word is.

Ask the child to say the word in their head or with their 'thinking voice' and notice how they split up each word into two chunks of sounds, or syllables, as they say it.

Support the child to write the first syllable, sound by sound, in the first boxes and the second syllable, sound by sound, in the second boxes, noticing that there is a box for each sound within the syllables.

Remind them to be careful with split sound spellings!

Then, covering the boxes, ask the child to write out the word from memory in the box at the end, thinking about the syllables and the sounds in them.

The first one is done for you as an example.

Activity 10 Sounds like a syllable   e

Clue	1st syllable	2nd syllable	Word
In front	a	h | ea | d	ahead
Not ever			
Very well			
Boss on a ship			
Lots			
Not light			
Rain, sun, wind…			
Burger sauce			
Jeans material			

Copyright material from Ann Sullivan (2019), *Phonics for Pupils with Special Educational Needs*, Routledge

Support the child to read the clue on the left and work out what the answer word is.
The word has been split into two syllables and the sound spellings in each syllable have been mixed up.
Encourage the child to write the first syllable, sound by sound, then the second syllable, sound by sound, on the line on the right.
Ask the child to say the word.

Activity 11 Two syllable anagrams   e

Clue	1st syllable	2nd syllable	Word
Tooth doctor	d n e	t t s i	_____
Has lots of money	l w **ea**	y **th**	_____
Leads on a ship	p c a	**ai** n t	_____
Happy	n o c	n t e t	_____
Lots and lots	a m	y n	_____
Ground bird	**ea ph**	s t n a	_____
Hang	u s s	n p d e	_____
First meal	k b **ea** r	s f t a	_____
Choose a leader	e	e l t c	_____
All set	**ea** r	d y	_____
A human	**er** p	n s o	_____
Wobbly dessert	e j	y ll	_____
Jumper	w s **ea**	**er** t	_____
Gift	r p e	n t s e	_____
20	w t n e	y t	_____

Support the child to read the clue on the left and work out what the word is.

Ask the child to say the answer word again in their head or with their 'thinking voice' and notice how they split up each word into two chunks of sounds, or syllables, as they say it.

The words have been split into two 'syllable boxes' but are not complete.

Ask the child to finish the word by writing in either the first or second syllable as required in the grey box.

Then ask the child to write out the word in full on the line at the end.

The first one is done for you as an example.

Activity 12 Syllable jigsaw   e

Clue	1st syllable	2nd syllable	Word
Sun, rain, fog e.g.	wea	ther	weather
Shake with fear		ble	_____
Yellow fruit		mon	_____
Water display	foun		_____
Has lots of money		thy	_____
Lots of people		ny	_____
Occasion	e		_____
Tooth doctor		tist	_____
First meal of the day		fast	_____

e

Activity 13 Spelling challenge

Word	Syllable breakdown		
ahead	a/h ea d	* –––	* –––
instead	i n/s t ea d	* –––	* –––
weather	w ea/th er	* –––	* –––
address	a/dd r e ss	* –––	* –––
contest	c o n/t e s t	* –––	* –––
never	n e/v er	* –––	* –––
many	m a/n y	* –––	* –––
mountain	m ou n/t ai n	* –––	* –––

Support the child to read each sentence one by one.
Ask the child to re-read the sentence, several times if necessary, and try to remember it.
Then cover the sentence and ask the child to recall the sentence verbally.
Once they can do this confidently, ask the child to write out the sentence from memory.
The child might find it helpful to think about the individual syllables in the words and say the sounds within each as they write. When the sentence is complete, the child reads out their sentence and then compares it to the original.

Alternatively, using text to speech software, the child could type the sentence, with the computer reading back each word and then the completed sentence.

Activity 14 Writing challenge   e

I intend to collect the berries.

She had a dreadful breakfast in the meadow.

Anyone can have many friends.

The fountain is on the mountain.

Support the child to read each word.

To help, the words have been split into three chunks of sounds, or syllables, as indicated by the asterisk * and red, blue and green colour coding.

Direct the child to blend the sounds within the first syllable and say the syllable chunk, then blend the sounds within the second syllable and say the syllable chunk, then blend the sounds within the third syllable and say the syllable chunk. Finally push all three syllable chunks together to hear the word forming.

e.g.

disinfect

sees: d i s   i n   f e c t

says: 'd'>'i'>'s' = 'dis'   'i'>'n' = 'in'   'f'>'e'>'c'>'t' = 'fect'   'dis>in>fect'   **'disinfect'**

Remind the child to watch out for schwas highlighted.

Activity 15 Reading 3 syllable words   e

disinfect	d i s * i n * f e c t
anything	a * n y * th i ng
lemonade	l e * m o n * a d e
heavenly	h ea * v e n * l y
incorrect	i n * c o * rr e c t
expensive	e x * p e n * s i ve
threatening	th r ea * t e * n i ng
perfectly	p er * f e c t * l y

Answers

Page 81
Activity 2 Thinking about the sound 'e'

e
address extra inspect
helpful
ea
heavy instead steady ready
a
many any
ie
friendly friendless
ai
mountain captain fountain

Page 86
Activity 5 Syllable split

ob / ject	heal / thy
sen / tence	zeb / ra
ma / ny	dread / ful
ex / pert	gen / tle
hel / per	wea / ther
threa / ten	a / gainst
friend / less	per / fect
a / ny	
swea / ter	
hea / vy	
end / less	
cen / tre	
break / fast	
net / work	

Page 87
Activity 6 Join the syllables

heavy
feather
mountain
instead
friendly
healthy
zebra
tremble
kettle
pepper

Page 88
Activity 7 Match to a picture

feather
zebra
pepper
breakfast
tennis
mountain

Page 89
Activity 8 Two syllable word tech

d e / s c e n d
u n / l e s s
s p r e a / d i n g
f r i e n d / l y
a / g a i n s t
e / v e n t
w e a l / t h y
d e / t e c t
l e / m o n
m a / n y

Page 90
Activity 9 Syllable trap

e	d i t
a	d d r e s s
r e a	d y
u n	l e s s
p e r	f e c t
t e m	p e r
v e l	v e t
p r e	s e n t

Page 91	Page 92	Page 93
Activity 10 Sounds like a syllable	**Activity 11 Two syllable anagrams**	**Activity 12 Syllable jigsaw**

Page 91
Activity 10 Sounds like a syllable

a   h ea d
n e   v er
h ea l   th y
c a p   t ai n
m a   n y
h ea   v y
w ea   th er
r e   l i sh
d e n   i m

Page 92
Activity 11 Two syllable anagrams

dentist
wealthy
captain
content
many
pheasant
suspend
breakfast
elect
ready
person
jelly
sweater
present
twenty

Page 93
Activity 12 Syllable jigsaw

wea   ther
trem   ble
le   mon
foun   tain
weal   thy
ma   ny
e   vent
den   tist
break   fast

Words with an 'ow' sound – word list of 2 syllable words

ow	ou	ough
allow	about	ploughing
allowed	aloud	ploughman
bowel	amount	
dowel	around	
flower	clouded	
powder	cloudy	
power	council	
shower	counter	
towel	discount	
tower	flour	
trowel	grounded	
vowel	surround	
	thousand	
	trousers	

This activity results in the child rediscovering all the sound spellings for this sound in the context of 2 syllable words.

Support the child to read the words one by one. Ask the child to say the word again in their head or with their 'thinking voice' and notice how they split up each word into two chunks of sounds, or syllables, as they say it.

For each word support the child to work out the sound spelling corresponding to the sound 'ow'.

Words are sorted into lists according to their 'ow' sound spelling.

There are three sound spellings to find: **ow, ou** and **ough**.

Encourage the child to say each sound as they write each sound spelling in sequence, *syllable by syllable*, in this way:

e.g.

	sees: s u	rr ou n d

surround

| | says: 's'>'u' = 'su' | 'r'>'ow'>'n'>'d' = 'rownd' | **'su>rownd'** | **'surround'** |

Remind the child to watch out for schwas!

Break this task into a number of shorter tasks over a number of lessons if necessary.

Activity 2 Thinking about the sound   ow

surround	vowel	ploughman
tower	thousand	powder
ploughing	flower	amount
aloud	trousers	allow
shower	council	around

This set of cards is made up of 2 syllable words containing the sound 'ow'. Copy onto card and cut out. Practise the dynamic blending – syllable by syllable reading strategy, as described in the 'Working through the programme' section, to read the words on these cards. Model this process for the child if necessary.

Activity 3 Sorting word cards	ow
allow	flower
power	shower
towel	vowel
about	amount
around	clouded
counter	discount
surround	ploughing

Support the child to read each word. To help, the words have been split into two chunks of sounds, or syllables, as indicated by the asterisk *.
Direct the child to blend the sounds within the first syllable and say the syllable chunk, then blend the sounds within the second syllable and say the syllable chunk. Remind the child to watch out for schwas!
Finally push both syllable chunks together to hear the word forming.
e.g.

clouded

sees: c l ou   d e d

says: 'c'>'l'>'ow' = 'clow'   'd'>'e'>'d' = 'ded'   'clow>ded'   **'clouded'**

Activity 4 Reading 2 syllable words   ow

clouded	c l ou * d e d
amount	a * m ou n t
towel	t ow * el
flower	f l ow * er
ploughing	p l ough * i ng
counter	c ou n * t er
allow	a * ll ow
discount	d i s * c ou n t
shower	sh ow * er

Support the child to read the words one by one. Ask the child to say the word again in their head or with their 'thinking voice' and notice how they split up each word into two chunks of sounds, or syllables, as they say it. For each word support the child to draw a line through the word to show where in the word they split it into two syllables.

It is useful to discuss how they made their choice. Remind the child to watch out for schwas!

The first group of words has some sound spellings highlighted to help, and the first one is split as an example.

Activity 5 Syllable split   ow

a/ll **ow**   g r **ou** n d e d

c **ou** n c **il**   t r **ou** s **er** s

t **ow er**   s u rr **ou** n d

p l **ough** m a n   t r **ow** e l

a r **ou** n d   sh **ow er**

v **ow** e l   p **ow** d **er**

c l **ou** d e d   b **ow** e l

Careful, the next ones do not have any sound spellings highlighted:

a b o u t

p l o u g h i n g

p o w e r

c o u n t e r

t h o u s a n d

d i s c o u n t

f l o w e r

Support the child to read the clue on the left and work out what the answer word is.

Ask the child to say the word again in their head or with their 'thinking voice' and notice how they split up each word into two chunks of sounds, or syllables, as they say it.

Ask the child to draw a line from the clue to the first syllable of the word and then go on to draw a line to the second syllable of the word.

Finally ask the child to write the whole word on the line at the end indicated by the arrow and read the word out loud.

Activity 6 Join the syllables   ow

Clue	1st	2nd	→	Word
Fine grains	c **ou** n	rr **ou** n d	→	
Local leaders	p **ow**	c **il**	→	
Dry with this	s u	d **er**	→	*powder*
All around	t **ow**	d y	→	
Misty skies	**th ou**	**el**	→	
1000	c l **ou**	s a n d	→	
Money off	f l **ou**	r	→	
Use to make cake	d i s	**er**	→	
Wear on legs	t **ow**	c **ou** n t	→	
Eiffel, Blackpool, e.g.	t r **ou**	s **er** s	→	

Ask the child to choose a picture and discuss what the matching word might be.

Then ask the child to think about how that word might be split into two syllables.

The child then finds the first syllable and then the second, drawing a line from picture to syllable to syllable.

The child then writes the complete word on one of the lines in the box at the bottom of the page.

Encourage the child to write the word using the sequential segmenting – syllable by syllable spelling strategy.

Activity 7 Match to a picture   ow

el   plough

show   tow

er

flow

ing

er

dy

clou   1000

thou

sand

Support the child to read the words one by one. Ask the child to say the word again in their head or with their 'thinking voice' and notice how they split up the word into two chunks of sounds, or syllables, as they say it.
Then ask the child to show where they split the word up into two syllables by drawing a line through it.
Next ask the child to put a ring round each of the sound spellings.
Finally ask the child to highlight any schwas in the word.

Activity 8 Two syllable word tech ow

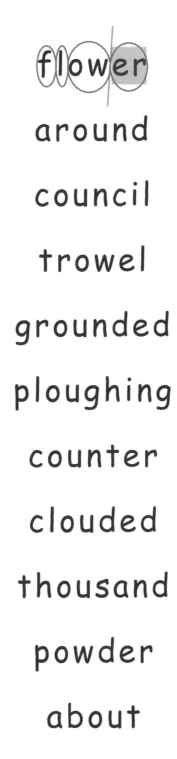

around

council

trowel

grounded

ploughing

counter

clouded

thousand

powder

about

Support the child to read the words one by one. Ask the child to say the word again in their head or with their 'thinking voice' and notice how they split up each word into two chunks of sounds, or syllables, as they say it. For each word, ask the child to work out where they split it into two syllables and then draw a line through the word.

Then ask the child to work out how many sounds there are in each syllable. They could write the number next to each syllable.

Support the child to look at the grid underneath and choose the row that contains the right number of lines in the first box (to match the number of sounds in the first syllable) and the right number of lines in the second box (to match the number of sounds in the second syllable). Ask the child to write the word in the grid on the chosen row, writing a sound spelling on each line.

An example is done to help you.

Activity 9 Syllable trap   ow

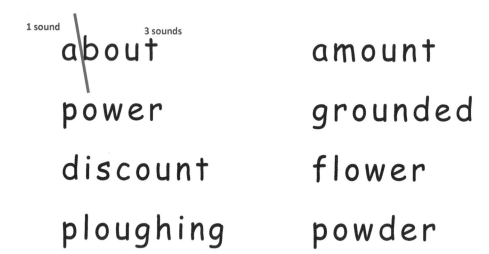

1 sound   a|bout   3 sounds

amount

power   grounded

discount   flower

ploughing powder

a	b ou t
___	___ ___ ___ ___
___ ___	___
___ ___	___ ___
___ ___ ___	___
___ ___ ___	___ ___ ___
___ ___ ___	___ ___ ___ ___
___ ___ ___ ___	___ ___ ___

Support the child to read the clue on the left and work out what the word is.
Ask the child to say the word in their head or with their 'thinking voice' and notice how they split up each word into two chunks of sounds, or syllables, as they say it.
Support the child to write the first syllable, sound by sound, in the first boxes and the second syllable, sound by sound, in the second boxes, noticing that there is a box for each sound within the syllables.
Remind them to be careful with split sound spellings!
Then, covering the boxes, ask the child to write out the word from memory in the box at the end, thinking about the syllables and the sounds in them.
The first one is done for you as an example.

Activity 10 Sounds like a syllable   ow

Clue	1st syllable			2nd syllable		Word
Small loose particles	p	ow		d	er	powder
Let						
Use this to dry body						
Use to make cakes						
Making a track in soil						
Clothes for the legs						
Has petals						
Tall building						
Water drops to clean						

Support the child to read the clue on the left and work out what the answer word is.
The word has been split into two syllables and the sound spellings in each syllable have been mixed up.
Encourage the child to write the first syllable, sound by sound, then the second syllable, sound by sound, on the line on the right.
Ask the child to say the word.

Activity 11 Two syllable anagrams   ow

Clue	1st syllable	2nd syllable	Word
Let, permit	a	**ow** ll	_____
Fine grains	**ow** p	**er** d	_____
Making a track in soil	**ough** l p	**ng** i	_____
Local government	**ou** c n	**il** c	_____
Cleansing water spray	**ow** sh	**er**	_____
Wear on legs	r **ou** t	s s **er**	_____
Use to make bread	**ou** f l	r	_____
Has petals and a stem	**ow** f l	**er**	_____
Be all around	u s	**ou** n d **rr**	_____
Money off	i d s	c t **ou** n	_____
Misty sky	**ou** l c	y d	_____
1000	**ou** th	a n s d	_____
Not allowed out	g **ou** r n	d d e	_____

Support the child to read the clue on the left and work out what the word is.
Ask the child to say the answer word again in their head or with their 'thinking voice' and notice how they split up each word into two chunks of sounds, or syllables, as they say it.
The words have been split into two 'syllable boxes' but are not complete.
Ask the child to finish the word by writing in either the first or second syllable as required in the grey box.
Then ask the child to write out the word in full on the line at the end.
The first one is done for you as an example.

Activity 12 Syllable jigsaw ow

Clue	1st syllable	2nd syllable	Word
Local government	coun	cil	council
Misty skies		dy	
Tall building		er	
A quantity	a		
1000		sand	
Making track in soil		ing	
All around	su		
Fine grains		der	
Use to dig soil		el	

Activity 13 Spelling challenge

ow

allow	a/ll ow	* | | |	*
flower	f l ow/er	* | | |	*
shower	**sh** ow/er	* | |	*
about	a/b ou t	* | |	*
around	a/r ou n d	* | |	*
surround	s u/rr ou n d	* | | |	*
thousand	**th** ou/s a n d	* | | |	*
council	c ou n/c il	* | | |	*

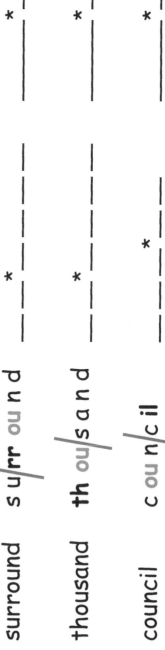

Support the child to read each sentence one by one.

Ask the child to re-read the sentence, several times if necessary, and try to remember it.

Then cover the sentence and ask the child to recall the sentence verbally.

Once they can do this confidently, ask the child to write out the sentence from memory.

The child might find it helpful to think about the individual syllables in the words and say the sounds within each as they write. When the sentence is complete, the child reads out their sentence and then compares it to the original.

Alternatively, using text to speech software, the child could type the sentence, with the computer reading back each word and then the completed sentence.

Activity 14 Writing challenge   **ow**

I get a **tho**usand p**o**unds disc**o**unt from the **sh**op.

The c**o**uncil was surr**o**unded by **sh**outing Sc**o**uts.

I lost a br**ow**n t**ow**el in the **sh**owers.

He will not all**ow** the cr**ow**d into the t**ow**er.

Support the child to read each word.

To help, the words have been split into three chunks of sounds, or syllables, as indicated by the asterisk * and red, blue and green colour coding.

Direct the child to blend the sounds within the first syllable and say the syllable chunk, then blend the sounds within the second syllable and say the syllable chunk, then blend the sounds within the third syllable and say the syllable chunk. Finally push all three syllable chunks together to hear the word forming.

e.g.

	sees:	p ow	er	f u l
powerful				
	says:	'p'>'ow' = 'pow'	'er' = 'er'	'f'>'u'>'l' = 'ful'	'pow>er>ful'	**'powerful'**

Remind the child to watch out for schwas highlighted.

Activity 15 Reading 3 syllable words   ow

powerful	p ow * er * f u l
surrounded	s u * rr ou n * d e d
roundabout	r ou n * d a * b ou t
powdery	p ow * d er * y
cloudier	c l ou * d i * er
discounted	d i s * c ou n * t e d
showering	sh ow * er * i ng
allowance	a * ll ow * a n ce

Answers ow

Page 100 **Activity 2 Thinking about the sound 'ow'**	**Page 104** **Activity 5 Syllable split**	**Page 105** **Activity 6 Join the syllables**

Page 100
Activity 2 Thinking about the sound 'ow'

ou
surround thousand amount aloud
trousers council around
ow
vowel tower powder flower allow shower
ough
ploughman ploughing

Page 104
Activity 5 Syllable split

a / llow	groun / ded
coun / cil	trou / sers
tow / er	su / rround
plough / man	trow /el
a / round	show / er
vow / el	pow / der
clou / ded	bow / el
a / bout	
plough / ing	
pow / er	
coun / ter	
thou / sand	
dis / count	
flow / er	

Page 105
Activity 6 Join the syllables

surround
council
powder
cloudy
towel
thousand
flour
tower
discount
trousers

Page 106
Activity 7 Match to a picture

shower
towel
ploughing
flower
thousand
cloudy

Page 107
Activity 8 Two syllable word tech

a / r ou n d
c ou n / c il
t r ow / el
g r ou n /d ed
p l ough / i ng
c ou n /t er
c l ou /d ed
th ou /s a nd
p ow / d er
a / b ou t

Page 108
Activity 9 Syllable trap

a	b ou t
a	m ou n t
p ow	er
p ow	d er
f l ow	er
p l ough	i ng
d is	c ou n t
g r ou n	d ed

Page 109	Page 110	Page 111
Activity 10 Sounds like a syllable	**Activity 11 Two syllable anagrams**	**Activity 12 Syllable jigsaw**

Page 109

Activity 10 Sounds like a syllable

p ow   d er
a   ll ow
t ow   el
f l ou   r
p l ough   i ng
t r ou   s er s
f l ow   er
t ow   er
sh ow   er

Page 110

Activity 11 Two syllable anagrams

allow
powder
ploughing
council
shower
trousers
flour
flower
surround
discount
cloudy
thousand
grounded

Page 111

Activity 12 Syllable jigsaw

coun   cil
clou   dy
tow   er
a   mount
thou   sand
plough   ing
su   rround
pow   der
trow   el

Words with an 'oy' sound – word list of 2 syllable words

oi	oy
anoint	annoy
appoint	buoyant
avoid	cowboy
boiled	destroy
boiler	disloyal
boiling	employ
choices	joyful
coiling	joyous
exploit	loyal
joined	oyster
joiner	royal
joining	soya
noises	voyage
noisy	
oily	
ointment	
pointed	
pointer	
pointed	
poison	
recoil	
rejoin	
toilet	
voices	

This activity results in the child rediscovering all the sound spellings for this sound in the context of 2 syllable words.

Support the child to read the words one by one. Ask the child to say the word again in their head or with their 'thinking voice' and notice how they split up each word into two chunks of sounds, or syllables, as they say it.

For each word support the child to work out the sound spelling corresponding to the sound 'oy'.

Words are sorted into lists according to their 'oy' sound spelling.

There are two sound spellings to find: **oi** and **oy**.

Encourage the child to say each sound as they write each sound spelling in sequence, *syllable by syllable*, in this way:

e.g.

sees: a   v oi d

avoid

says: 'a' = 'a'   'v'>'oy'>'d' = 'voyd'   'a>voyd'   **'avoid'**

Remind the child to watch out for schwas! There is a schwa in the first syllable of 'avoid'.

Break this task into a number of shorter tasks over a number of lessons if necessary.

Activity 2 Thinking about the sound 'oy'

avoid	annoy	boiling
employ	toilet	destroy
royal	poison	choices
noisy	cowboy	joyful

This set of cards is made up of 2 syllable words containing the sound 'oy'. Copy onto card and cut out. Practise the dynamic blending – syllable by syllable reading strategy, as described in the 'Working through the programme' section, to read the words on these cards. Model this process for the child if necessary.

Activity 3 Sorting word cards	oy

avoid	boiling
poison	noisy
jointed	toilet
choices	appoint
annoy	cowboy
destroy	employ
joyful	loyal

Support the child to read each word. To help, the words have been split into two chunks of sounds, or syllables, as indicated by the asterisk *.
Direct the child to blend the sounds within the first syllable and say the syllable chunk, then blend the sounds within the second syllable and say the syllable chunk. Remind the child to watch out for schwas!
Finally push both syllable chunks together to hear the word forming.
e.g.

employ

sees: e m　　　　p l　oy

says: 'e'>'m' = 'em'　　'p'>'l'>'oy' = 'ploy'　　'em>ploy'　　**'employ'**

Activity 4 Reading 2 syllable words　　　　　　　oy

employ	e m * p l oy
noisy	n oi * s y
toilet	t oi * l e t
cowboy	c ow * b oy
avoid	a * v oi d
voices	v oi * c e s
annoy	a * nn oy
royal	r oy * al
poison	p oi * s o n

Support the child to read the words one by one. Ask the child to say the word again in their head or with their 'thinking voice' and notice how they split up each word into two chunks of sounds, or syllables, as they say it. For each word support the child to draw a line through the word to show where in the word they split it into two syllables.

It is useful to discuss how they made their choice. Remind the child to watch out for schwas!

The first group of words has some sound spellings highlighted to help, and the first one is split as an example.

Activity 5 Syllable split   oy

a/v **oi** d   r **oy** al

c **ow** b **oy**   n **oi** s y

t **oi** l e t   e m p l **oy**

d e s t r **oy**   j **oi** n i **ng**

a **nn oy**   **oi** n t m e n t

Careful, the next ones do not have any sound spellings highlighted:

voices

joyful

poison

pointer

appoint

soya

oyster

boiling

Support the child to read the clue on the left and work out what the answer word is.

Ask the child to say the word again in their head or with their 'thinking voice' and notice how they split up each word into two chunks of sounds, or syllables, as they say it.

Ask the child to draw a line from the clue to the first syllable of the word and then go on to draw a line to the second syllable of the word.

Finally ask the child to write the whole word on the line at the end indicated by the arrow and read the word out loud.

Activity 6 Join the syllables   oy

Clue	1st	2nd	→	Word
Healing cream	oy	a g e	→	
Shelled animal	oi n t	s t er	→	
Journey by sea	b oi	m e n t	→	*ointment*
To do with kings	v oy	l er	→	
Controls heating	a	al	→	
In the bathroom	r oy	v oi d	→	
Keep away from	p oi	l e t	→	
Herds cattle	t oi	s o n	→	
Lethal drink	a	b oy	→	
Irritate	c ow	nn oy	→	

Ask the child to choose a picture and discuss what the matching word might be.

Then ask the child to think about how that word might be split into two syllables.

The child then finds the first syllable and then the second, drawing a line from picture to syllable to syllable.

The child then writes the complete word on one of the lines in the box at the bottom of the page.

Encourage the child to write the word using the sequential segmenting – syllable by syllable spelling strategy.

Activity 7 Match to a picture   oy

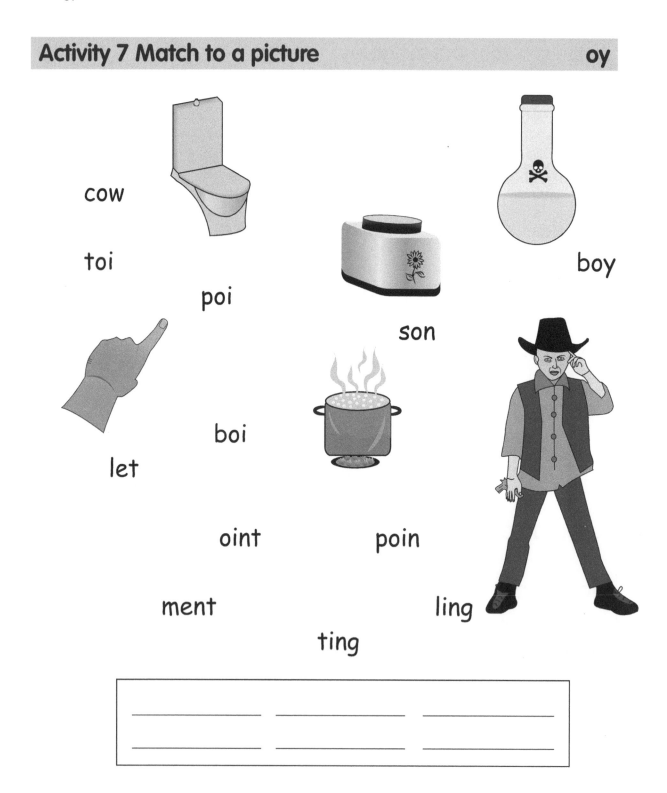

Support the child to read the words one by one. Ask the child to say the word again in their head or with their 'thinking voice' and notice how they split up the word into two chunks of sounds, or syllables, as they say it.

Then ask the child to show where they split the word up into two syllables by drawing a line through it.

Next ask the child to put a ring round each of the sound spellings.

Finally ask the child to highlight any schwas in the word.

Activity 8 Two syllable word tech   oy

avoid

appoint

cowboy

employ

choices

royal

poison

oyster

joyful

annoy

boiling

Support the child to read the words one by one. Ask the child to say the word again in their head or with their 'thinking voice' and notice how they split up each word into two chunks of sounds, or syllables, as they say it. For each word, ask the child to work out where they split it into two syllables and then draw a line through the word.

Then ask the child to work out how many sounds there are in each syllable. They could write the number next to each syllable.

Support the child to look at the grid underneath and choose the row that contains the right number of lines in the first box (to match the number of sounds in the first syllable) and the right number of lines in the second box (to match the number of sounds in the second syllable). Ask the child to write the word in the grid on the chosen row, writing a sound spelling on each line.

An example is done to help you.

Activity 9 Syllable trap   oy

1 sound   2 sounds

oi|ly   toilet

destroy   disloyal

boiler   avoid

soya   appoint

oi	⊥ y
——	—— —— ——
——	—— —— —— ——
—— ——	——
—— ——	—— ——
—— ——	—— —— ——
—— —— ——	—— —— —— ——
—— —— —— ——	—— —— —— ——

Support the child to read the clue on the left and work out what the word is.
Ask the child to say the word in their head or with their 'thinking voice' and notice how they split up each word into two chunks of sounds, or syllables, as they say it.
Support the child to write the first syllable, sound by sound, in the first boxes and the second syllable, sound by sound, in the second boxes, noticing that there is a box for each sound within the syllables.
Remind them to be careful with split sound spellings!
Then, covering the boxes, ask the child to write out the word from memory in the box at the end, thinking about the syllables and the sounds in them.
The first one is done for you as an example.

Activity 10 Sounds like a syllable   oy

Clue	1st syllable			2nd syllable			Word
Keep away from	a			v	oi	d	avoid
Full of happiness							
Irritate							
Sharp and spiky							
Shelled sea animal							
Wrapping around							
Cattle herder							
In the bathroom							
Controls the heating							

Support the child to read the clue on the left and work out what the answer word is.
The word has been split into two syllables and the sound spellings in each syllable have been mixed up.
Encourage the child to write the first syllable, sound by sound, then the second syllable, sound by sound, on the line on the right.
Ask the child to say the word.

Activity 11 Two syllable anagrams   oy

Clue	1st syllable	2nd syllable	Word
Very loud	**oi** n	s y	_____
Choose for a job	a	**pp oi** t n	_____
To do with kings etc.	**oy** r	al	_____
Shelled sea animal	**oy**	**er** t s	_____
Controls the heating	**oi** b	**er** l	_____
In the bathroom	**oi** t	e t l	_____
Meat substitute	**oy** s	a	_____
Healing cream	n t **oi**	n t e m	_____
Lethal drink	**oi** p	o n s	_____
Keep away from	a	**oi** d v	_____
Ruin completely	e d	**oy** r t	_____
Give a job	m e	l **oy** p	_____
Very happy	**oy** j	l f u	_____
Greasy	**oi**	y l	_____
People speaking	**oi** v	e c s	_____

Support the child to read the clue on the left and work out what the word is.
Ask the child to say the answer word again in their head or with their 'thinking voice' and notice how they split up each word into two chunks of sounds, or syllables, as they say it.
The words have been split into two 'syllable boxes' but are not complete.
Ask the child to finish the word by writing in either the first or second syllable as required in the grey box.
Then ask the child to write out the word in full on the line at the end.
The first one is done for you as an example.

Activity 12 Syllable jigsaw   oy

Clue	1st syllable	2nd syllable	Word
Indicated	poin	ted	pointed
Very loud		sy	
Lethal drink		son	
Ruin completely	de		
Builds with wood		ner	
Travel by sea		age	
Give a job	em		
People speaking		ces	
Wrapping around		ling	

Activity 13 Spelling challenge

oy

avoid	a/v oi d	* ⫶	⫶
noisy	n oi/s y	* ⫶	* ⫶
toilet	t oi/l e t	* ⫶	* ⫶
joining	j oi/n i ng	* ⫶	* ⫶
boiler	b oi/l er	* ⫶	* ⫶
annoy	a/nn oy	* ⫶	* ⫶
employ	e m/p l oy	* ⫶	* ⫶
royal	r oy/al	* ⫶	* ⫶

Support the child to read each sentence one by one.
Ask the child to re-read the sentence, several times if necessary, and try to remember it.
Then cover the sentence and ask the child to recall the sentence verbally.
Once they can do this confidently, ask the child to write out the sentence from memory.
The child might find it helpful to think about the individual syllables in the words and say the sounds within each as they write. When the sentence is complete, the child reads out their sentence and then compares it to the original.

Alternatively, using text to speech software, the child could type the sentence, with the computer reading back each word and then the completed sentence.

Activity 14 Writing challenge   oy

My v**oice** a**dds** to the n**oise** of the cr**ow**d.

The wi**tch** p**o**inted to the p**o**ison.

I am empl**oy**ed to get **oys**ters.

That b**oy** destr**oy**ed his t**oy**s.

Support the child to read each word.

To help, the words have been split into three chunks of sounds, or syllables, as indicated by the asterisk * and red, blue and green colour coding.

Direct the child to blend the sounds within the first syllable and say the syllable chunk, then blend the sounds within the second syllable and say the syllable chunk, then blend the sounds within the third syllable and say the syllable chunk. Finally push all three syllable chunks together to hear the word forming.

e.g.

employment

sees: e m   p l oy   m e n t

says: 'e'>'m' = 'em' 'p'>'l'>'oy' = 'ploy' 'm'>'e'>'n'>'t' = 'ment' 'em>ploy>ment'

'employment'

Remind the child to watch out for schwas highlighted!

Activity 15 Reading 3 syllable words   oy

employment	e m * p l oy * m e n t
noisier	n oi * s i * er
avoidance	a * v oi * d a n ce
annoying	a * nn oy * i ng
rejoicing	r e * j oi * c i ng
employee	e m * p l oy * ee
overjoyed	o * v er * j oy ed
appointment	a * pp oi n t * m e n t

Answers oy

Page 118
Activity 2 Thinking about the sound 'oy'

oi
avoid boiling toilet poison
choices noisy
oy
annoy employ destroy royal
cowboy joyful

Page 122
Activity 5 Syllable split

a / v oi d	r oy / al
c ow / b oy	n oi / s y
t oi / l et	em / p l oy
de / s t r oy	j oi / n i ng
a / nn oy	oi n t / m e n t
v oi / c e s	
j oy / f u l	
p oi / s o n	
p oi n / t er	
a / pp oi n t	
s oy / a	
oy / s t er	
b oi / l i ng	

Page 123
Activity 6 Join the syllables

voyage
oyster
ointment
boiler
royal
avoid
toilet
poison
cowboy
annoy

Page 124
Activity 7 Match to a picture
cowboy
poison
toilet
ointment
boiling
pointing

Page 125
Activity 8 Two syllable word tech

a / pp oi n t
c ow / b oy
em / p l oy
ch oi / c e s
r oy / al
p oi / s o n
oy / s t er
j oy / f u l
a / nn oy
b oi / l i ng

Page 126
Activity 9 Syllable trap

oi	l y
a	v oi d
a	pp oi n t
s oy	a
b oi	l er
t oi	l et
de	s t r oy
d i s	l oy al

Page 127	Page 128	Page 129
Activity 10 Sounds like a syllable	**Activity 11 Two syllable anagrams**	**Activity 12 Syllable jigsaw**

Page 127

Activity 10 Sounds like a syllable

a   v oi d
j oy   f u l
a   nn oy
p oi n t e d
oy   s t er
c oi   l i ng
c ow b oy
t oi   l e t
b oi   l er

Page 128

Activity 11 Two syllable anagrams

noisy
appoint
royal
oyster
boiler
toilet
soya
ointment
poison
avoid
destroy
employ
joyful
oily
voices

Page 129

Activity 12 Syllable jigsaw

poin   ted
noi   sy
poi   son
de   stroy
joi   ner
voy   age
em   ploy
voi   ces
coi   ling

Words with an 'oo' sound – word list of 2 syllable words

oo	u	ew	u-e	o	ui	others
aloof	brutal	cashew	conclude	doing	cruiser	**ou**
balloon	crucial	chewing	elude	loser	fruitful	grouping
choosing	cruel	jewel	exclude	losing	fruity	recoup
cooler	crusade	newly	extrude	movie	juicy	regroup
doodle	fluent	renew	pollute	moving	nuisance	routine
foolish	fluid	sewage	protrude	today	recruit	toucan
gloomy	glucose	sewer	salute	tonight	suitcase	wounded
lagoon	judo		seclude	towards		youthful
loosen	July					
maroon	lucid					**o-e**
moonlight	lunar					approve
platoon	Pluto					disprove
poodle	prudence					movement
racoon	rhubarb					remove
rooftop	ruby					
rooster	ruin					**ue**
saloon	rumour					bluebell
scooter	scuba					gruesome
shooting	super					
smoothly	superb					**eu**
snooker	supreme					neutral
sooner	truly					neutron
tattoo	truthful					
toothbrush						**oe**
toothpaste						canoe
						ough
						throughout

This activity results in the child rediscovering all the sound spellings for this sound in the context of 2 syllable words.

Support the child to read the words one by one. Ask the child to say the word again in their head or with their 'thinking voice' and notice how they split up each word into two chunks of sounds, or syllables, as they say it.

For each word support the child to work out the sound spelling corresponding to the sound 'oo'.

Words are sorted into lists according to their 'oo' sound spelling.

There are many sound spellings to find; some are less common than others: **oo, u, ew, u-e, o, ui, ou, o-e, ue** and **oe**. One sound spelling is new to the child - **eu** - it only occurs in multisyllable words.

Encourage the child to say each sound as they write each sound spelling in sequence, *syllable by syllable*, in this way:

e.g.

> sees: b a   ll oo n

balloon

> says: 'b''a' = 'ba'   'l'>'oo'>'n' = 'loon'   'ba>loon'   'balloon'

Remind the child to watch out for schwas! There is a schwa in the first syllable of 'balloon'.

Break this task into a number of shorter tasks over a number of lessons if necessary.

Activity 2 Thinking about the sound   oo

balloon	July	cashew
conclude	doing	movement
Pluto	choosing	judo
fruity	jewel	pollute
gruesome	routine	losing
salute	bluebell	foolish
remove	ruin	juicy
renew	today	neutral
youthful	approve	throughout
canoe	maroon	chewing

This set of cards is made up of 2 syllable words containing the sound 'oo'. Copy onto card and cut out. Practise the dynamic blending – syllable by syllable reading strategy, as described in the 'Working through the programme' section, to read the words on these cards. Model this process for the child if necessary.

Activity 3 Sorting word cards	oo

balloon	sooner
ruin	super
jewel	fewer
pollute	conclude
today	doing
suitcase	juicy
routine	approve

Support the child to read each word. To help, the words have been split into two chunks of sounds, or syllables, as indicated by the asterisk *.

Direct the child to blend the sounds within the first syllable and say the syllable chunk, then blend the sounds within the second syllable and say the syllable chunk. Remind the child to watch out for schwas!

Finally push both syllable chunks together to hear the word forming.

e.g.

	sees: f oo	l i sh		
foolish	says: 'f'>'oo' = 'foo'	'l'>'i'>'sh' = 'lish'	'foo>lish'	**'foolish'**

Activity 4 Reading Two syllable words   oo

foolish	f oo * l i sh
exclude	e x * c l u d e
juicy	j ui * c y
scooter	s c oo * t er
ruby	r u * b y
routine	r ou * t i n e
bluebell	b l ue * b e ll
movie	m o * v ie
remove	r e * m o v e

Support the child to read the words one by one. Ask the child to say the word again in their head or with their 'thinking voice' and notice how they split up each word into two chunks of sounds, or syllables, as they say it. For each word support the child to draw a line through the word to show where in the word they split it into two syllables.

It is useful to discuss how they made their choice. Remind the child to watch out for schwas!

The first group of words has some sound spellings highlighted to help and the first one is split as an example.

Activity 5 Syllable split   oo

d **oo**/d le   ch **ew** i ng

n **ui** s a n ce   s a l u t e

t o w **ar** d s   a **pp** r o v e

c a n **oe**   r **ui** n

s **oo** n er   th r **ough** ou t

Careful, the next ones do not have any sound spellings highlighted:

maroon

movie

exclude

bluebell

youthful

routine

truthful

Support the child to read the clue on the left and work out what the answer word is.

Ask the child to say the word again in their head or with their 'thinking voice' and notice how they split up each word into two chunks of sounds, or syllables, as they say it.

Ask the child to draw a line from the clue to the first syllable of the word and then go on to draw a line to the second syllable of the word.

Finally ask the child to write the whole word on the line at the end indicated by the arrow and read the word out loud.

Activity 6 Join the syllables   oo

Clue	1ˢᵗ	2ⁿᵈ	→	Word
Rub out	t r u **th**	g **oo** n	→	
Honest	r e	f u l	→	
Like a lake	t **oo th**	m o v e	→	*remove*
On a toothbrush	l a	**sh ew**	→	
Kind of nut	r **oo**	v **ie**	→	
Male chicken	m o	p a s t e	→	
Make dirty	c a	s t **er**	→	
Film	p o	**pp** r o v e	→	
Like something	a	l y	→	
After June	J u	**ll** u t e	→	

Ask the child to choose a picture and discuss what the matching word might be.
Then ask the child to think about how that word might be split into two syllables.
The child then finds the first syllable and then the second, drawing a line from picture to syllable to syllable.
The child then writes the complete word on one of the lines in the box at the bottom of the page.
Encourage the child to write the word using the sequential segmenting – syllable by syllable spelling strategy.

Activity 7 Match to a picture   oo

can

bell

tou

lu

blue

ter

nar

scoo

suit

case

noe

ca

```
_____    _____    _____

_____    _____    _____
```

Support the child to read the words one by one. Ask the child to say the word again in their head or with their 'thinking voice' and notice how they split up the word into two chunks of sounds, or syllables, as they say it.

Then ask the child to show where they split the word up into two syllables by drawing a line through it.

Next ask the child to put a ring round each of the sound spellings.

Finally ask the child to highlight any schwas in the word.

Activity 8 Two syllable word tech   oo

foolish

bluebell

jewel

poodle

remove

salute

routine

July

movie

ruby

Support the child to read the words one by one. Ask the child to say the word again in their head or with their 'thinking voice' and notice how they split up each word into two chunks of sounds, or syllables, as they say it. For each word, ask the child to work out where they split it into two syllables and then draw a line through the word.

Then ask the child to work out how many sounds there are in each syllable. They could write the number next to each syllable.

Support the child to look at the grid underneath and choose the row that contains the right number of lines in the first box (to match the number of sounds in the first syllable) and the right number of lines in the second box (to match the number of sounds in the second syllable). Ask the child to write the word in the grid on the chosen row, writing a sound spelling on each line.

An example is done to help you.

Activity 9 Syllable trap   oo

2 sounds   mo|vie   2 sounds

tonight

throughout   approve

movement   recruit

wounded   sewer

___	___ ___ ___ ___
___ ___	___
_m_ _o_	_v_ _i_ _e_
___ ___	___ ___
___ ___	___ ___ ___
___ ___ ___	___ ___ ___
___ ___ ___	___ ___ ___
___ ___ ___	___ ___ ___

Support the child to read the clue on the left and work out what the word is.

Ask the child to say the word in their head or with their 'thinking voice' and notice how they split up each word into two chunks of sounds, or syllables, as they say it.

Support the child to write the first syllable, sound by sound, in the first boxes and the second syllable, sound by sound, in the second boxes, noticing that there is a box for each sound within the syllables.

Remind them to be careful with split sound spellings!

Then, covering the boxes, ask the child to write out the word from memory in the box at the end, thinking about the syllables and the sounds in them.

The first one is done for you as an example.

Activity 10 Sounds like a syllable   oo

Clue	1st syllable	2nd syllable	Word
After June	J | u	l | y	July
Film			
This evening			
Take away			
Honestly			
Long thin boat			
A complete wreck			
Spring flower			
Random drawing			

Support the child to read the clue on the left and work out what the answer word is.
The word has been split into two syllables and the sound spellings in each syllable have been mixed up.
Encourage the child to write the first syllable, sound by sound, then the second syllable, sound by sound, on the line on the right.
Ask the child to say the word.

Activity 11 Two syllable anagrams   oo

Clue	1ˢᵗ syllable	2ⁿᵈ syllable	Word
Leave out	x e	l u-e d c	_____
This evening	o t	igh t n	_____
Exotic bird	ou t	n c a	_____
Sweet with crumble	u rh	ar b b	_____
Fantastic	u s	er p	_____
Spring flower	ue l b	ll b e	_____
Film	o m	ie v	_____
Rub out	e r	v o-e m	_____
Thin boat	a c	oe n	_____
Like a lake	a l	oo n g	_____
Destroy	u r	n i	_____
Gossip	u r	our m	_____
Unkind	r c u	el	_____
Silly	oo f	i sh l	_____
Gem	ew j	el	_____

Support the child to read the clue on the left and work out what the word is.

Ask the child to say the answer word again in their head or with their 'thinking voice' and notice how they split up each word into two chunks of sounds, or syllables, as they say it.

The words have been split into two 'syllable boxes' but are not complete.

Ask the child to finish the word by writing in either the first or second syllable as required in the grey box.

Then ask the child to write out the word in full on the line at the end.

The first one is done for you as an example.

Activity 12 Syllable jigsaw   oo

Clue	1st syllable	2nd syllable	Word
In everything	through	out	_throughout_
Gem		el	_____
Kind of crumble		barb	_____
Take away	re		_____
To do with the moon		nar	_____
Spring flower		bell	_____
Kind of nut	ca		_____
Gossip		mour	_____
Great		per	_____

Activity 13 Spelling challenge

oo

balloon	b a/ll oo n	*	*
foolish	f oo/l i sh	*	*
sooner	s oo/n er	*	*
remove	r e/m o v e	*	*
approve	a/pp r o v e	*	*
tonight	t o/n igh t	*	*
today	t o/d ay	*	*
doing	d o/i ng	*	*

Support the child to read each sentence one by one.

Ask the child to re-read the sentence, several times if necessary, and try to remember it.

Then cover the sentence and ask the child to recall the sentence verbally.

Once they can do this confidently, ask the child to write out the sentence from memory.

The child might find it helpful to think about the individual syllables in the words and say the sounds within each as they write. When the sentence is complete, the child reads out their sentence and then compares it to the original.

Alternatively, using text to speech software, the child could type the sentence, with the computer reading back each word and then the completed sentence.

Activity 14 Writing challenge   oo

By the lagoon we **saw** a **shoo**ting star in the moonlight.

I made a **super rhu**barb crumble in July.

I conclude **th**at it is not good to pollute.

Tonight I will go to **see that** new movie.

Support the child to read each word.
To help, the words have been split into three chunks of sounds, or syllables, as indicated by the asterisk * and red, blue and green colour coding.
Direct the child to blend the sounds within the first syllable and say the syllable chunk, then blend the sounds within the second syllable and say the syllable chunk, then blend the sounds within the third syllable and say the syllable chunk. Finally push all three syllable chunks together to hear the word forming.
e.g.

polluted

sees:	p o	ll u	t e d		
says:	'p'>'o' = 'po'	'l'>'oo' = 'loo'	't'>'e'>'d' = 'ted'	'po>llu>ted'	**'polluted'**

Remind the child to watch out for schwas highlighted.

Activity 15 Reading 3 syllable words   oo

polluted   p o * ll u * t e d

beautiful   b ea u * t i * f u l

included   i n * c l u * d e d

suitable   s ui * t a * b le

juiciest   j ui * c i * e s t

removing   r e * m o * v i ng

luminous   l u * m i n * ou s

fluently   f l u * e n t * l y

Answers

oo

Page 136

Activity 2 Thinking about the sound 'oo'

oo
balloon choosing foolish
maroon
u
July Pluto judo ruin
ew
cashew jewel renew chewing
u-e
conclude pollute salute
o
doing losing today
o-e
movement remove approve
ui   **ou**
fruity juicy routine youthful
ue   **eu**
gruesome bluebell neutral
ough   **oe**
throughout   canoe

Page 141

Activity 5 Syllable split

doo / dle   chew / ing
nui / sance   sa / lute
to /wards   a / pprove
ca / noe   ru / in
soo / ner   through / out
ma / roon
mo / vie
ex / clude
blue / bell
youth / ful
rou / tine
truth / ful

Page 142

Activity 6 Join the syllables

lagoon
truthful
remove
cashew
movie
toothpaste
rooster
approve
July
pollute

Page 143
Activity 7 Match to a picture

toucan
bluebell
lunar
canoe
suitcase
scooter

Page 144
Activity 8 Two syllable word tech

f oo / l i sh
b l ue / b e ll
j ew / el
p oo / d le
re / m o v e
s a / l u t e
r ou / t i n e
Ju / ly
m o / v ie
r u / b y

Page 145
Activity 9 Syllable trap

a	pp r o-e v
s ew	er
m o	v ie
t o	n igh t
r e	c r u i t
th r ough	ou t
w ou n	d e d
m o-e v	m e n t

Page 146
Activity 10 Sounds like a syllable

J u	l y	
m o	v ie	
t o	n igh t	
r e	m o-e v	remove
t r u	l y	
c a	n oe	
r u	i n	
b l ue	b e ll	
d oo	d le	

Page 147
Activity 11 Two syllable anagrams

exclude
tonight
toucan
rhubarb
super
bluebell
movie
remove
canoe
lagoon
ruin
rumour
cruel
foolish
jewel

Page 148
Activity 12 Syllable jigsaw

through	out
jew	el
rhu	barb
re	move
lu	nar
blue	bell
ca	shew
ru	mour
su	per

Words with a 'u' sound – word list of 2 syllable words

u	u	oo	ou	o	o-e
abrupt	jungle	bloody	couple	among	above
adult	lucky	booking*	cousin	brother	become
ambush	muddle	cooker*	double	dozen	lovely
bubble	muddy	cooking*	enough	money	outdone
buckle	mumble	cookie	nougat*	monkey	
buddy	muscle	crooked*	rougher	monthly	
bullet	public	flooded	roughest	mother	
bumble	pulling	floodlit	touches	nothing	
bumpy	pumpkin	footie	touching	other	
bundle	puppet	footstep	toughen	oven	**oul**
buzzer	pushing	goodbye	trouble	shovel	couldn't
careful	putting	goodness	younger	stomach	shouldn't
discuss	struggle	handbook	youngest	woman	wouldn't
fuller	subject	hooded	youngster		
funfair	tunnel	looking*			
funnel	ugly	wooded	*any 2*		
grumpy	uncle	woodland	*syllable*		
hungry		woody	*words ending*		
hurried		woollen	*in ous*		
husband		woolly			
jumper					

*any 2 syllable
un- words & up- words*

This activity results in the child rediscovering all the sound spellings for this sound in the context of 2 syllable words.

Support the child to read the words one by one. Ask the child to say the word again in their head or with their 'thinking voice' and notice how they split up each word into two chunks of sounds, or syllables, as they say it.

For each word support the child to work out the sound spelling corresponding to the sound 'u'.

Words are sorted into lists according to their 'u' sound spelling.

There are many sound spellings to find; some are less common than others: **u, oo, ou, o, o-e** and **oul**.

Encourage the child to say each sound as they write each sound spelling in sequence, *syllable by syllable*, in this way:

e.g.

	sees: w o	m a n		
woman				
	says: 'w"u' = 'wu'	'm'>'a'>'n' = 'man'	'wu>man'	'woman'

Remind the child to watch out for schwas!

Break this task into a number of shorter tasks over a number of lessons if necessary.

Activity 2 Thinking about the sound 'u'

grumpy	woman	floodlit
cookie	above	couldn't
double	public	mother
among	woolly	youngest
lovely	cousin	ambush
hungry	wouldn't	become
goodness	money	shouldn't

This set of cards is made up of 2 syllable words containing the sound 'u'. Copy onto card and cut out. Practise the dynamic blending – syllable by syllable reading strategy, as described in the 'Working through the programme' section, to read the words on these cards. Model this process for the child if necessary.

Activity 3 Sorting word cards   U

grumpy	public
adult	footstep
woolly	cookie
enough	trouble
cousin	money
brother	above
lovely	couldn't

Support the child to read each word. To help, the words have been split into two chunks of sounds, or syllables, as indicated by the asterisk *.

Direct the child to blend the sounds within the first syllable and say the syllable chunk, then blend the sounds within the second syllable and say the syllable chunk. Remind the child to watch out for schwas!

Finally push both syllable chunks together to hear the word forming.

e.g.

double

sees: d ou   b le

says: 'd'>'u' = 'du'   'b'>'l' = 'bl'   'du>bl'   **'double'**

Activity 4 Reading 2 syllable words   U

double   d ou * b le

enough   e * n ou gh

among   a * m o ng

woman   w o * m a n

above   a * b o v e

become   b e * c o m e

couldn't   c oul d * n't

goodness   g oo d * n e ss

adult   a * d u l t

Support the child to read the words one by one. Ask the child to say the word again in their head or with their 'thinking voice' and notice how they split up each word into two chunks of sounds, or syllables, as they say it. For each word support the child to draw a line through the word to show where in the word they split it into two syllables.

It is useful to discuss how they made their choice. Remind the child to watch out for schwas!

The first group of words has some sound spellings highlighted to help, and the first one is split as an example.

Activity 5 Syllable split   U

w o / m a n   t r **ou** b **le**

m o n **th** l y   d i s c u **ss**

h u s b a n d   l o v e l y

e n **ou** **gh**   w **oo** **ll** y

l u **ck** y   t u **nn** e l

Careful, the next ones do not have any sound spellings highlighted:

footstep

flooded

stomach

couple

grumpy

struggle

youngster

Support the child to read the clue on the left and work out what the answer word is.
Ask the child to say the word again in their head or with their 'thinking voice' and notice how they split up each word into two chunks of sounds, or syllables, as they say it.
Ask the child to draw a line from the clue to the first syllable of the word and then go on to draw a line to the second syllable of the word.
Finally ask the child to write the whole word on the line at the end indicated by the arrow and read the word out loud.

Activity 6 Join the syllables   U

Clue	1st	2nd	→	Word
Rushed along	h u n	c **le**	→	
Need food	h u	g r y	→	
Dad's brother	s t o	**rr ie** d	→	*hurried*
Tummy	o	**th er**	→	
Something else	u n	g **le**	→	
Little one	w o	m a **ch**	→	
Lady	j u n	s t **er**	→	
Directs liquid	y **ou ng**	m a n	→	
Rainforest	p u	**nn el**	→	
Talking toy	f u	**pp** e t	→	

Copyright material from Ann Sullivan (2019), *Phonics for Pupils with Special Educational Needs*, Routledge

161

Ask the child to choose a picture and discuss what the matching word might be.

Then ask the child to think about how that word might be split into two syllables.

The child then finds the first syllable and then the second, drawing a line from picture to syllable to syllable.

The child then writes the complete word on one of the lines in the box at the bottom of the page.

Encourage the child to write the word using the sequential segmenting – syllable by syllable spelling strategy.

Activity 7 Match to a picture   u

jum

mo

coo

kin

ther

per

fu

mon

nnel

pump

kie

key

Support the child to read the words one by one. Ask the child to say the word again in their head or with their 'thinking voice' and notice how they split up the word into two chunks of sounds, or syllables, as they say it.
Then ask the child to show where they split the word up into two syllables by drawing a line through it.
Next ask the child to put a ring round each of the sound spellings.
Finally ask the child to highlight any schwas in the word.

Activity 8 Two syllable word tech   U

lovely

stomach

couldn't

discuss

trouble

jungle

subject

cookie

enough

become

puppet

Support the child to read the words one by one. Ask the child to say the word again in their head or with their 'thinking voice' and notice how they split up each word into two chunks of sounds, or syllables, as they say it. For each word, ask the child to work out where they split it into two syllables and then draw a line through the word.

Then ask the child to work out how many sounds there are in each syllable. They could write the number next to each syllable.

Support the child to look at the grid underneath and choose the row that contains the right number of lines in the first box (to match the number of sounds in the first syllable) and the right number of lines in the second box (to match the number of sounds in the second syllable). Ask the child to write the word in the grid on the chosen row, writing a sound spelling on each line.

An example is done to help you.

Activity 9 Syllable trap   U

2 sounds   2 sounds

dou|ble   footstep

enough   jumper

discuss   nothing

adult   pumpkin

—	— — —
—	— — — —
d̲ o̲u̲	b̲ l̲e̲
— —	— — —
— — —	— —
— — —	— —
— — —	— — —
— — — —	— — —

Support the child to read the clue on the left and work out what the word is.

Ask the child to say the word in their head or with their 'thinking voice' and notice how they split up each word into two chunks of sounds, or syllables, as they say it.

Support the child to write the first syllable, sound by sound, in the first boxes and the second syllable, sound by sound, in the second boxes, noticing that there is a box for each sound within the syllables.

Remind them to be careful with split sound spellings!

Then, covering the boxes, ask the child to write out the word from memory in the box at the end, thinking about the syllables and the sounds in them.

The first one is done for you as an example.

Activity 10 Sounds like a syllable u

Clue	1st syllable			2nd syllable			Word
Mummy	m	o		th	er		mother
Made of wool							
Auntie's child							
Nought, zero...							
Uh oh! Problems!							
Lady							
Cash							
Born last							
Ought not to							

Support the child to read the clue on the left and work out what the answer word is.
The word has been split into two syllables and the sound spellings in each syllable have been mixed up.
Encourage the child to write the first syllable, sound by sound, then the second syllable, sound by sound, on the line on the right.
Ask the child to say the word.

Activity 11 Two syllable anagrams   U

Clue	1st syllable	2nd syllable	Word
Ought not to	d **sh** **oul**	n' t	_____
Bad tempered	r u g m	y p	_____
Less aged than	**ou** y **ng**	er	_____
Tummy	o t s	**ch** a m	_____
Delightful	**o-e** v l	y l	_____
12	o d	n z e	_____
Talking toy	u p	**pp** t e	_____
Wrestle	r t u s	le **gg**	_____
Mummy	o m	er **th**	_____
Talk about	s d i	**ss** c u	_____
Covered in wet dirt	u m	y **dd**	_____
Biscuit	**oo** c	**ie** k	_____
Sufficient	e	**gh** **ou** n	_____
Upwards	a	v b **o-e**	_____
Covered in trees	**oo** w	y d	_____

Support the child to read the clue on the left and work out what the word is.
Ask the child to say the answer word again in their head or with their 'thinking voice' and notice how they split up each word into two chunks of sounds, or syllables, as they say it.
The words have been split into two 'syllable boxes' but are not complete.
Ask the child to finish the word by writing in either the first or second syllable as required in the grey box.
Then ask the child to write out the word in full on the line at the end.
The first one is done for you as an example.

Activity 12 Syllable jigsaw   U

Clue	1st syllable	2nd syllable	Word
Dig with this	shov	el	_shovel_
Sweater		per	_____
Rushed to do it		rried	_____
Sufficient	e		_____
Use these to move		scles	_____
Times two		ble	_____
Upwards, on top	a		_____
Dad's brother		cle	_____
Need food		gry	_____

Activity 13 Spelling challenge

u

d ou/b le	* ————	* ————————
t r ou/b le	* ————	* ————————
e/n ou gh	* ————	* ————————
w o/m a n	* ————	* ————————
m o/n ey	* ————	* ————————
c ou l/d n' t	* ————	* ————————
b e/c o m e	* ————	* ————————
d i s/c u ss	* ————	* ————————

double

trouble

enough

woman

money

couldn't

become

discuss

Support the child to read each sentence one by one.

Ask the child to re-read the sentence, several times if necessary, and try to remember it.

Then cover the sentence and ask the child to recall the sentence verbally.

Once they can do this confidently, ask the child to write out the sentence from memory.

The child might find it helpful to think about the individual syllables in the words and say the sounds within each as they write. When the sentence is complete, the child reads out their sentence and then compares it to the original.

Alternatively, using text to speech software, the child could type the sentence, with the computer reading back each word and then the completed sentence.

Activity 14 Writing challenge   u

Up above were some lovely doves.

I couldn't sing, but should I?

The thunder made me jump suddenly.

The monkey gave money to his brother.

My cousin is younger than me; I am double his age.

Support the child to read each word.

To help, the words have been split into three chunks of sounds, or syllables, as indicated by the asterisk * and red, blue and green colour coding.

Direct the child to blend the sounds within the first syllable and say the syllable chunk, then blend the sounds within the second syllable and say the syllable chunk, then blend the sounds within the third syllable and say the syllable chunk. Finally push all three syllable chunks together to hear the word forming.

e.g.

sees: u n   d er   s t a n d

understand

says: 'u'>'n' = 'un'   'd'>'er' = 'der'   's'>'t'>'a'>'n'>'d' = 'stand'   'un>der>stand'

                                                              '**understand**'

Remind the child to watch out for schwas highlighted.

Activity 15 Reading 3 syllable words   U

understand   u n * d er * s t a n d

unlucky   u n * l u * ck y

multiply   m u l * t i * p l y

butterfly   b u * tt er * f l y

umbrella   u m * b r e * ll a

unhappy   u n * h a * pp y

another   a * n o * th er

government   g o * v er n * m e n t

Answers

Page 155
Activity 2 Thinking about the sound 'u'

u
grumpy public ambush hungry
o
woman mother among money
oo
floodlit cookie woolly goodness
o-e
above lovely become
oul
couldn't wouldn't shouldn't
ou
double youngest cousin

Page 160
Activity 5 Syllable split

wo/man   trou/ble
month/ly   dis/cuss
hus/band   love/ly
e/nough   woo/lly
lu/cky   tu/nnel
foot/step
floo/ded
sto/mach
cou/ple
grum/py
stru/ggle
young/ster

Page 161
Activity 6 Join the syllables

uncle
hungry
hurried
other
jungle
stomach
youngster
woman
funnel
puppet

Page 162
Activity 7 Match to a picture

mother
jumper
cookie
monkey
pumpkin
funnel

Page 163
Activity 8 Two syllable word tech

sto/mach
could/n't
dis/cuss
trou/ble
jun/gle
sub/ject
coo/kie
e/nough
be/come
pu/ppet

Page 164
Activity 9 Syllable trap

e   nough
a   dult
dou   ble
no   thing
jum   per
dis   cuss
foot   step
pump   kin

Page 165	Page 166	Page 167
Activity 10 Sounds like a syllable	**Activity 11 Two syllable anagrams**	**Activity 12 Syllable jigsaw**

Page 165

Activity 10 Sounds like a syllable

m o	th er
w oo	ll y
c ou	s i n
n o	th i ng
t r ou	b le
w o	m e n
m o	n ey
y ou ng	e s t
sh ou l d	n ' t

Page 166

Activity 11 Two syllable anagrams

shouldn't
grumpy
younger
stomach
lovely
dozen
puppet
struggle
mother
discuss
muddy
cookie
enough
above
woody

Page 167

Activity 12 Syllable jigsaw

shov	el
jum	per
hu	rried
e	nough
mu	scles
dou	ble
a	bove
un	cle
hun	gry

Words with an 'i-e' sound – word list of 2 syllable words

i	i	i-e	y	igh	eigh	Misc
behind	silence	admire	crying	brightly	heighten	island
binding	silo	advice	deny	delight	heightened	
blinded	signage	advise	dryer	frighten		
design	signer	alike	drying	higher		iron
digest	spider	arrive	flyer	highest		
dilute	tiger	beside	flying	mighty		
diner	tiler	climber	fryer	nightly		
direct	tiny	climbing	frying	rightly		
divert	virus	collide	imply	sighing		
final		confine	lying	tighten		
finer		define	myself	tighter		
finest		divide	rely	tightly		
fibre		driver	reply			
giant		excite	supply			
kinder		inside	trying			
liar		invite				
liner		likely				
lion		nineteen				
minder		ninety				
mining		outside				
miner		provide				
minor		require				
minus		reside				
nitric		revise				
pilot		survive				
quiet		timer				
resign		timely				
science		widen				
silent		wider				

This activity results in the child rediscovering all the sound spellings for this sound in the context of 2 syllable words.

Support the child to read the words one by one. Ask the child to say the word again in their head or with their 'thinking voice' and notice how they split up each word into two chunks of sounds, or syllables, as they say it.

For each word support the child to work out the sound spelling corresponding to the sound 'i-e'.

Words are sorted into lists according to their 'i-e' sound spelling.

There are many sound spellings to find; some are less common than others: **i, i-e, y, igh** and **eigh**.

Encourage the child to say each sound as they write each sound spelling in sequence, *syllable by syllable*, in this way:

e.g.

admire

sees: a d   m i r e

says: 'a"d' = 'ad'   'm'>'i-e'>'r' = 'mi-er'   'ad>mi-er'   **'admire'**

Remind the child to watch out for schwas!

Break this task into a number of shorter tasks over a number of lessons if necessary.

Activity 2 Thinking about the sound 'i-e'

admire	flying	mighty
minus	arrive	imply
myself	direct	inside
brightly	heighten	pilot
lion	collide	higher
reply	sighing	provide

This set of cards is made up of 2 syllable words containing the sound 'i-e'. Copy onto card and cut out. Practise the dynamic blending – syllable by syllable reading strategy, as described in the 'Working through the programme' section, to read the words on these cards. Model this process for the child if necessary.

Activity 3 Sorting word cards i-e

behind	design
direct	quiet
silence	excite
invite	inside
myself	flying
reply	delight
frighten	heighten

Support the child to read each word. To help, the words have been split into two chunks of sounds, or syllables, as indicated by the asterisk *.

Direct the child to blend the sounds within the first syllable and say the syllable chunk, then blend the sounds within the second syllable and say the syllable chunk. Remind the child to watch out for schwas!

Finally push both syllable chunks together to hear the word forming.

e.g.

silent

sees: s i   l e n t

says: 's'>'i-e' = 'si-e'   'l'>'e'>'n'>'t' = 'lent'   'si-e>lent'   **'silent'**

Activity 4 Reading 2 syllable words   i-e

silent	s i * l e n t
quiet	qu i * e t
spider	s p i * d er
inside	i n * s i d e
divide	d i * v i d e
myself	m y * s e l f
reply	r e * p l y
delight	d e * l igh t
higher	h igh * er

Support the child to read the words one by one. Ask the child to say the word again in their head or with their 'thinking voice' and notice how they split up each word into two chunks of sounds, or syllables, as they say it. For each word support the child to draw a line through the word to show where in the word they split it into two syllables.

It is useful to discuss how they made their choice. Remind the child to watch out for schwas!

The first group of words has some sound spellings highlighted to help, and the first one is split as an example.

Activity 5 Syllable split	**i-e**

de/sign   collide

provide   mighty

myself   heighten

science   advice

reply   digest

Careful, the next ones do not have any sound spellings highlighted:

highest

invite

giant

supply

spider

divide

frighten

Support the child to read the clue on the left and work out what the answer word is.

Ask the child to say the word again in their head or with their 'thinking voice' and notice how they split up each word into two chunks of sounds, or syllables, as they say it.

Ask the child to draw a line from the clue to the first syllable of the word and then go on to draw a line to the second syllable of the word.

Finally ask the child to write the whole word on the line at the end indicated by the arrow and read the word out loud.

Activity 6 Join the syllables   i-e

Clue	1st	2nd	→	Word
Flies a plane	l i	d **er**	→	
Steers a car	p i	v **er**	→	
Big cat	s p i	l o t	→	*pilot*
Me, all on my own	d r i	o n	→	
Need	m y	t e n	→	
Beast with eight legs	f r **igh**	qu i r e	→	
Strong	r e	s e l f	→	
Scare	a	t y	→	
Get here	c o	rr i v e	→	
Crash	m **igh**	ll i d e	→	

Ask the child to choose a picture and discuss what the matching word might be.

Then ask the child to think about how that word might be split into two syllables.

The child then finds the first syllable and then the second, drawing a line from picture to syllable to syllable.

The child then writes the complete word on one of the lines in the box at the bottom of the page.

Encourage the child to write the word using the sequential segmenting – syllable by syllable spelling strategy.

Activity 7 Match to a picture   i-e

sci

li   nine

ger

on

ence

pi   teen

ti

lot   mber

cli

Support the child to read the words one by one. Ask the child to say the word again in their head or their 'thinking voice' and notice how they split up the word into two chunks of sounds, or syllables, as they say it.
Then ask the child to show where they split the word up into two syllables by drawing a line through it.
Next ask the child to put a ring round each of the sound spellings.
Finally ask the child to highlight any schwas in the word.

Activity 8 Two syllable word tech   i-e

design

collide

direct

giant

miner

science

survive

beside

provide

delight

supply

Support the child to read the words one by one. Ask the child to say the word again in their head or with their 'thinking voice' and notice how they split up each word into two chunks of sounds, or syllables, as they say it. For each word, ask the child to work out where they split it into two syllables and then draw a line through the word.

Then ask the child to work out how many sounds there are in each syllable. They could write the number next to each syllable.

Support the child to look at the grid underneath and choose the row that contains the right number of lines in the first box (to match the number of sounds in the first syllable) and the right number of lines in the second box (to match the number of sounds in the second syllable). Ask the child to write the word in the grid on the chosen row, writing a sound spelling on each line.

An example is done to help you.

Activity 9 Syllable trap   i-e

2 sounds   3 sounds

gi|ant   tiger

brightly   myself

frighten   dryer

alike   flying

___	___ ___ ___
___ ___ ___	___ ___
<u>g</u> <u>i</u>	<u>a</u> <u>n</u> <u>t</u>
___ ___ ___	___ ___ ___ ___ ___
___ ___ ___ ___	___
___ ___ ___	___ ___
___ ___ ___	___ ___ ___
___ ___ ___ ___ ___	___ ___ ___

Support the child to read the clue on the left and work out what the word is.
Ask the child to say the word in their head or with their 'thinking voice' and notice how they split up each word into two chunks of sounds, or syllables, as they say it.
Support the child to write the first syllable, sound by sound, in the first boxes and the second syllable, sound by sound, in the second boxes, noticing that there is a box for each sound within the syllables.
Remind them to be careful with split sound spellings!
Then, covering the boxes, ask the child to write out the word from memory in the box at the end, thinking about the syllables and the sounds in them.
The first one is done for you as an example.

Activity 10 Sounds like a syllable   i-e

Clue	1st syllable		2nd syllable			Word
Split up	d	i	v	i-e	d	divide
Very, very small						
Pattern						
19						
Big cat						
Joy and happiness						
Indoors						
Tall person						
Scare						

Support the child to read the clue on the left and work out what the answer word is.
The word has been split into two syllables and the sound spellings in each syllable have been mixed up.
Encourage the child to write the first syllable, sound by sound, then the second syllable, sound by sound, on the line on the right.
Ask the child to say the word.

Activity 11 Two syllable anagrams   i-e

Clue	1st syllable	2nd syllable	Word
Big cat	i l	n o	_____
Study for a test	e r	i-e v s	_____
90	i-e n n	y t	_____
Tall person	i g	t n a	_____
Last football match	i f	al n	_____
Next to	e b	d s i-e	_____
Mini-beast with 8 legs	i s p	er d	_____
Scare	igh r f	e n t	_____
Tallest	igh h	t s e	_____
Answer	e r	l y p	_____
Take away	i m	u s n	_____
Pattern	e d	gn i s	_____
Crash into	o c	i-e d ll	_____
Flies a plane	i p	o t l	_____
Not in front	e b	n i h d	_____

Support the child to read the clue on the left and work out what the word is.
Ask the child to say the answer word again in their head or with their 'thinking voice' and notice how they split up each word into two chunks of sounds, or syllables, as they say it.
The words have been split into two 'syllable boxes' but are not complete.
Ask the child to finish the word by writing in either the first or second syllable as required in the grey box.
Then ask the child to write out the word in full on the line at the end.
The first one is done for you as an example.

Activity 12 Syllable jigsaw   i-e

Clue	1st syllable	2nd syllable	Word
Mountaineer	*cli*	mber	_climber_
Not noisy		et	
Very last		nal	
Crash into	co		
Take away		nus	
All on my own, by		self	
Similar	a		
Scare		ten	
Gives us flu		rus	

Activity 13 Spelling challenge

i-e

behind	be/hind	*	*	
giant	gi/ant	*	*	
arrive	a/rr/ive	*	*	
divide	di/vide	*	*	
invite	in/vite	*	*	
reply	re/ply	*	*	
highest	high/est	*	*	
frighten	frigh/ten	*	*	

Support the child to read each sentence one by one.
Ask the child to re-read the sentence, several times if necessary, and try to remember it.
Then cover the sentence and ask the child to recall the sentence verbally.
Once they can do this confidently, ask the child to write out the sentence from memory.
The child might find it helpful to think about the individual syllables in the words and say the sounds within each as they write. When the sentence is complete, the child reads out their sentence and then compares it to the original.

Alternatively, using text to speech software, the child could type the sentence, with the computer reading back each word and then the completed sentence.

Activity 14 Writing challenge   i-e

To **sur**viv**e** exams, revis**e**!

The lion di**g**ests **foo**d silently, the ti**g**er violently.

I was **bu**ying myself a **supp**ly of sw**ee**ts.

He was del**igh**ted by the s**igh**t of l**igh**tning.

Support the child to read each word.

To help, the words have been split into three chunks of sounds, or syllables, as indicated by the asterisk * and red, blue and green colour coding.

Direct the child to blend the sounds within the first syllable and say the syllable chunk, then blend the sounds within the second syllable and say the syllable chunk, then blend the sounds within the third syllable and say the syllable chunk. Finally push all three syllable chunks together to hear the word forming.

e.g.

overnight

sees: o   v er   n igh t

says: 'o-e' = 'o-e'   'v>er' = 'ver'   'n'>'i-e'>'t' = 'ni-et'   'o-e>ver>ni-et'   **'overnight'**

Remind the child to watch out for schwas highlighted.

Activity 15a Reading 3 syllable words   i-e

overnight	o * v er * n igh t
arrival	a * rr i * v al
untidy	u n * t i * d y
realise	r e * a * l i s e
idea	i * d e * a
requirement	r e * qu i r e * m en t
scientist	sc i * e n * t i s t
inquiry	i n * qu i * r y

Support the child to read the word on the left.
Then look at how the word has been split into three chunks of sounds, or syllables, as indicated by the asterisk * and red, blue and green colour coding.
Then ask the child to work through the word syllable by syllable, writing over each grey sound spelling and saying the corresponding sounds. At the end of each syllable the child says the chunk of sounds and at the end of the word the child says the whole word.
Cover the words and ask the child to write the word syllable by syllable and sound by sound on the three lines, saying the sounds as they write the corresponding sound spellings. The child can then check and correct the answer if necessary.
Finally, the child can write the whole word on the single line, but once again work syllable by syllable and sound by sound, saying the sounds as they write the corresponding sound spellings.
Remind the child to watch out for schwas which are highlighted and to take care with split sound spellings. The child could highlight any sound spellings that they think are tricky, to help them recall them when spelling.

Activity 15b Spelling 3 syllable words

i-e

organise or*ga*nise   or*ga*nise   _____ * _____ * _____

underline un*der*line un*der*line _____ * _____ * _____

multiply mul*ti*ply   mul*ti*ply   _____ * _____ * _____

united u*ni*ted   u*ni*ted   _____ * _____ * _____

untidy un*ti*dy   un*ti*dy   _____ * _____ * _____

Answers
i-e

Page 174
Activity 2 Thinking about the sound 'i-e'

i-e
admire arrive inside collide
provide
y
flying imply myself reply
igh
mighty brightly higher
sighing
i
minus direct pilot lion
eigh
heighten

Page 178
Activity 5 Syllable split

de/sign   co/llide
pro/vide   migh/ty
my/self   heigh/ten
sci/ence   ad/vice
re/ply   di/gest
high/est
in/vite
gi/ant
su/pply
spi/der
di/vide
frigh/ten

Page 179
Activity 6 Join the syllables

spider
driver
pilot
lion
frighten
require
myself
mighty
arrive
collide

Page 180
Activity 7 Match to a picture

science
nineteen
lion
climber
pilot
tiger

Page 181
Activity 8 Two syllable word tech

co/llide
di/rect
gi/ant
mi/ner
sci/ence
sur/vive
be/side
pro/vide
de/light
su/pply

Page 182
Activity 9 Syllable trap

a   li-e k   alike
ti   g er
gi   a nt
my   self
dry   er
fly   ing
frigh   ten
bright   ly

Page 183

Activity 10 Sounds like a syllable

d i	v i-e d	divide
t i	n y	
d e	s i gn	
n i-e n	t ee n	nineteen
t i	g er	
d e	l igh t	
i n	s i-e d	inside
g i	a n t	
f r igh	t e n	

Page 184

Activity 11 Two syllable anagrams

lion
revise
ninety
giant
final
beside
spider
frighten
highest
reply
minus
design
collide
pilot
behind

Page 185

Activity 12 Syllable jigsaw

cli	mber
qui	et
fi	nal
co	llide
mi	nus
my	self
a	like
frigh	ten
vi	rus

Words with an 'aw' sound – word list of 2 syllable words

or	or	or	a	au	ore
absorb	forty	orchard	almost	applaud	adore
adorn	forward	ordeal	also	applause	ashore
afford	fourteen	order	although	auburn	before
border	glory	organ	always	August	boredom
chloride	gorgeous	ornate	caller	author	explore
chlorine	hormone	orphan	calling	autumn	ignore
chorus	hornet	perform	falling	caustic	implore
conform	import	porous	recall	laundry	restore
corner	inform	porthole	smaller	nautical	storey
deform	Jordan	portrait	smallest	saucer	
deport	morning	portray	walnut		**ar**
dormant	morsel	record	walrus		award
dorsal	mortal	reform	water		quarter
endorse	mortar	report			quartet
enforce	normal	resort			reward
export	orbit	snorkel			toward
fiord		story			towards
flora		support			warble
formal		thorax			warden
format		torment			wardrobe
former					
fortnight					

al	augh	aw	oar	Misc
chalking	daughter	awful	aboard	indoors
stalker	haughty	awkward	roaring	
stalking	naughty	dawdle	soaring	
talker	slaughter	hawthorn		abroad
talking				
walker				
walking			awesome
				fluorine

This activity results in the child rediscovering all the sound spellings for this sound in the context of 2 syllable words.

Support the child to read the words one by one. Ask the child to say the word again in their head or with their 'thinking voice' and notice how they split up each word into two chunks of sounds, or syllables, as they say it.

For each word support the child to work out the sound spelling corresponding to the sound 'aw'.

Words are sorted into lists according to their 'aw' sound spelling.

There are many sound spellings to find; some are less common than others: **or, a, au, ore, ar, al, augh, aw, oar** and **oor**.

Encourage the child to say each sound as they write each sound spelling in sequence, *syllable by syllable,* in this way:

e.g.

        sees: a l   m o s t

almost

        says: 'aw''l' = 'awl'   'm'>'o-e'>'s'>'t' = 'mo-est'   'awl>mo-est'   **'almost'**

Remind the child to watch out for schwas!

Break this task into a number of shorter tasks over a number of lessons if necessary.

Activity 2 Thinking about the sound 'aw'

almost	August	walker
afford	award	also
before	daughter	story
towards	morning	ignore
talking	although	awful
applaud	explore	reward
naughty	indoors	report
corner	always	autumn

This set of cards is made up of 2 syllable words containing the sound 'aw'. Copy onto card and cut out. Practise the dynamic blending – syllable by syllable reading strategy, as described in the 'Working through the programme' section, to read the words on these cards. Model this process for the child if necessary.

Activity 3 Sorting word cards   aw

afford	also
although	applaud
autumn	before
award	towards
talking	daughter
awful	aboard
indoors	awesome

Support the child to read each word. To help, the words have been split into two chunks of sounds, or syllables, as indicated by the asterisk *.

Direct the child to blend the sounds within the first syllable and say the syllable chunk, then blend the sounds within the second syllable and say the syllable chunk. Remind the child to watch out for schwas!

Finally push both syllable chunks together to hear the word forming.

e.g.

absorb   sees: a b   s or b

    says: 'a'>'b' = 'ab'   'z'>'aw'>'b' = 'zawb'   'ab>zawb'   **'absorb'**

Activity 4 Reading 2 syllable words   aw

absorb	a b * s or b
perform	p er * f or m
forward	f or * w ar d
although	a l * th ough
always	a l * w ay s
autumn	au * t u mn
ignore	i g * n ore
award	a * w ar d
daughter	d augh * t er
naughty	n augh * t y

Support the child to read the words one by one. Ask the child to say the word again in their head or with their 'thinking voice' and notice how they split up each word into two chunks of sounds, or syllables, as they say it. For each word support the child to draw a line through the word to show where in the word they split it into two syllables.

It is useful to discuss how they made their choice. Remind the child to watch out for schwas!

The first group of words has some sound spellings highlighted to help, and the first one is split as an example.

Activity 5 Syllable split   aw

c **or**/**n** **er**   w a t **er**

e x p l **ore**   r e w **ar** d

g **or** g e **ou** s   n **augh** t y

qu **ar** t **er**   **au** t u **mn**

a l **th** **ough**   b **ore** d o m

Careful, the next ones do not have any sound spellings highlighted:

always

report

orbit

walking

August

towards

daughter

Support the child to read the clue on the left and work out what the answer word is.
Ask the child to say the word again in their head or with their 'thinking voice' and notice how they split up each word into two chunks of sounds, or syllables, as they say it.
Ask the child to draw a line from the clue to the first syllable of the word and then go on to draw a line to the second syllable of the word.
Finally ask the child to write the whole word on the line at the end indicated by the arrow and read the word out loud.

Activity 6 Join the syllables   aw

Clue	1st	2nd	→	Word
Goes with a cup	f **our**	r o b e	→	
Clothes cupboard	s **au**	t **ee** n	→	
14	w **ar** d	c **er**	→	*saucer*
Holiday place	**Au**	s o m e	→	
After July	n **augh**	s **or** t	→	
Badly behaved	r e	g u s t	→	
Amazing	**awe**	t y	→	
.... and forever	a l	t r **ai** t	→	
Picture of a person	l **au** n	d r y	→	
Washing	p **or**	w **ay** s	→	

Copyright material from Ann Sullivan (2019), *Phonics for Pupils with Special Educational Needs*, Routledge

Ask the child to choose a picture and discuss what the matching word might be.

Then ask the child to think about how that word might be split into two syllables.

The child then finds the first syllable and then the second, drawing a line from picture to syllable to syllable.

The child then writes the complete word on one of the lines in the box at the bottom of the page.

Encourage the child to write the word using the sequential segmenting – syllable by syllable spelling strategy.

Activity 7 Match to a picture   aw

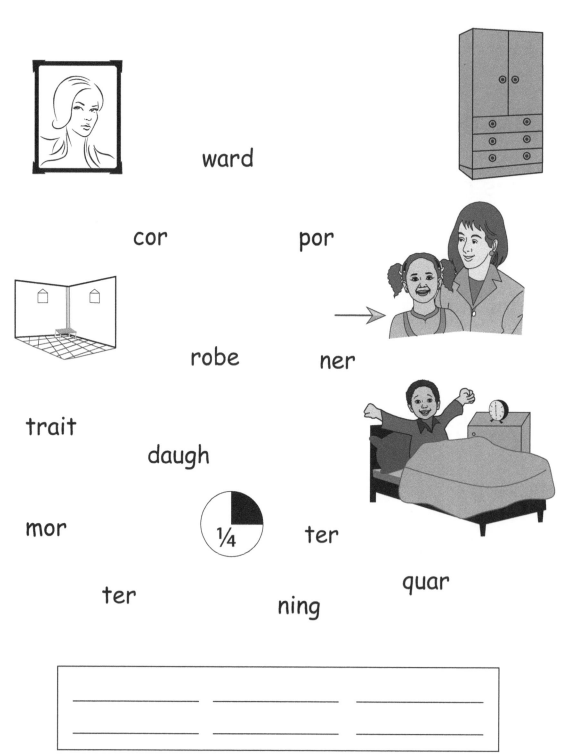

ward

cor   por

robe   ner

trait

daugh

mor   ¼   ter

ter   quar

ning

_____   _____   _____

_____   _____   _____

Support the child to read the words one by one. Ask the child to say the word again in their head or with their 'thinking voice' and notice how they split up the word into two chunks of sounds, or syllables, as they say it.
Then ask the child to show where they split the word up into two syllables by drawing a line through it.
Next ask the child to put a ring round each of the sound spellings.
Finally ask the child to highlight any schwas in the word.

Activity 8 Two syllable word tech   aw

towards

applaud

report

indoors

daughter

wardrobe

boredom

corner

fourteen

although

walnut

Support the child to read the words one by one. Ask the child to say the word again in their head or with their 'thinking voice' and notice how they split up each word into two chunks of sounds, or syllables, as they say it. For each word, ask the child to work out where they split it into two syllables and then draw a line through the word.

Then ask the child to work out how many sounds there are in each syllable. They could write the number next to each syllable.

Support the child to look at the grid underneath and choose the row that contains the right number of lines in the first box (to match the number of sounds in the first syllable) and the right number of lines in the second box (to match the number of sounds in the second syllable). Ask the child to write the word in the grid on the chosen row, writing a sound spelling on each line.

An example is done to help you.

Activity 9 Syllable trap   aw

2 sounds   3 sounds

re/port   portrait

adore   walnut

orbit   applause

also   smaller

——	—— ——
——	—— —— ——
——	—— —— —— ——
—— ——	—— —— ——
r e	p or t
—— —— ——	—— —— ——
—— —— —— ——	—— —— ——
—— —— —— ——	—— —— —— ——

Support the child to read the clue on the left and work out what the word is.
Ask the child to say the word in their head or with their 'thinking voice' and notice how they split up each word into two chunks of sounds, or syllables, as they say it.
Support the child to write the first syllable, sound by sound, in the first boxes and the second syllable, sound by sound, in the second boxes, noticing that there is a box for each sound within the syllables.
Remind them to be careful with split sound spellings!
Then, covering the boxes, ask the child to write out the word from memory in the box at the end, thinking about the syllables and the sounds in them.
The first one is done for you as an example.

Activity 10 Sounds like a syllable aw

Clue	1st syllable		2nd syllable			Word
Not backward	f	or	w	ar	d	forward
Season after summer						
As well						
Beginning of the day						
Female child						
Not outside						
Prize						
Act on stage						
Don't speak to						

Support the child to read the clue on the left and work out what the answer word is.
The word has been split into two syllables and the sound spellings in each syllable have been mixed up.
Encourage the child to write the first syllable, sound by sound, then the second syllable, sound by sound, on the line on the right.
Ask the child to say the word.

Activity 11 Two syllable anagrams   aw

Clue	1st syllable	2nd syllable	Word
Shouting to someone	a c	i **ng** **ll**	_____
Holiday place	e r	**or** t s	_____
Investigate	x e	l **ore** p	_____
Washing	**au** l n	r d y	_____
40	**or** f	y t	_____
Comes out of the tap	a w	**er** t	_____
Goes with a cup	**au** s	**er** c	_____
¼	**ar** qu	**er** t	_____
Sea animal with long tusks	l w a	u s r	_____
Two weeks	t f **or**	t n **igh**	_____
Don't talk to	g i	**ore** n	_____
Clapping	a	**au** se pp l	_____
Despite	l a	**ough** th	_____
Inside	i n	**oor** d s	_____
Act	**er** p	m f **or**	_____

Support the child to read the clue on the left and work out what the word is.

Ask the child to say the answer word again in their head or with their 'thinking voice' and notice how they split up each word into two chunks of sounds, or syllables, as they say it.

The words have been split into two 'syllable boxes' but are not complete.

Ask the child to finish the word by writing in either the first or second syllable as required in the grey box.

Then ask the child to write out the word in full on the line at the end.

The first one is done for you as an example.

Activity 12 Syllable jigsaw　　　　　　　aw

Clue	1st syllable	2nd syllable	Word
Start of the day	mor	ning	*morning*
40		ty	_____
Move round the earth		bit	_____
Love and worship	a		_____
Nearly		most	_____
After July		gust	_____
Clapping	a		_____
Female child		ter	_____
Amazing		some	_____

aw

Activity 13 Spelling challenge

a l/m o s t	*	*	
almost			
a l/w ay s	*	*	
always			
a l/th ough	*	*	
although			
b e/f ore	*	*	
before			
t o/w ar d s	*	*	
towards			
d augh/t er	*	*	
daughter			
t al/k i ng	*	*	
talking			
au/t u mn	*	*	
autumn			

Support the child to read each sentence one by one.
Ask the child to re-read the sentence, several times if necessary, and try to remember it.
Then cover the sentence and ask the child to recall the sentence verbally.
Once they can do this confidently, ask the child to write out the sentence from memory.
The child might find it helpful to think about the individual syllables in the words and say the sounds within each as they write. When the sentence is complete, the child reads out their sentence and then compares it to the original.

Alternatively, using text to speech software, the child could type the sentence, with the computer reading back each word and then the completed sentence.

Activity 14 Writing challenge   aw

In the morning Jordan informed us he was leaving.

I watched the walrus falling in the water.

August in summer, not autumn.

The pirates went ashore to explore.

The quartet won an award.

Her daughter was naughty.

Support the child to read the word on the left.

Then look at how the word has been split into three chunks of sounds, or syllables, as indicated by the asterisk * and red, blue and green colour coding.

Then ask the child to work through the word syllable by syllable, writing over each grey sound spelling and saying the corresponding sounds. At the end of each syllable the child says the chunk of sounds and at the end of the word the child says the whole word.

Cover the words and ask the child to write the word syllable by syllable and sound by sound on the three lines, saying the sounds as they write the corresponding sound spellings. The child can then check and correct the answer if necessary.

Finally, the child can write the whole word on the single line, but once again work syllable by syllable and sound by sound, saying the sounds as they write the corresponding sound spellings.

Remind the child to watch out for schwas which are highlighted and to take care with split sound spellings. The child could highlight any sound spellings that they think are tricky, to help them recall them when spelling.

Activity 15 Spelling 3 syllable words

		aw

important	i m * p o r * t a n t	i m * p o r * t a n t	___ * ___ * ___
performance	p er * f o r * m a n ce	p er * f o r * m a n ce	___ * ___ * ___
supporter	s u * pp or * t er	s u * pp or * t er	___ * ___ * ___
uniform	u * n i * f o r m	u * n i * f o r m	___ * ___ * ___
audience	au * d i * e n ce	au * d i * e n ce	___ * ___ * ___

Answers

Page 193
Activity 2 Thinking about the sound 'aw'

a
almost also although
always
au
August applaud autumn
al
walker talking
or
afford story morning report
corner
ar
award towards reward
ore
before ignore explore
augh
daughter naughty
aw
awful
oors
indoors

Page 198
Activity 5 Syllable split

cor / ner   wa / ter
ex / plore   re / ward
gor / geous   naugh / ty
quar / ter   au / tumn
al / though   bore / dom
al / ways
re / port
or / bit
wal / king
Au / gust
to / wards
daugh / ter

Page 199
Activity 6 Join the syllables

wardrobe
fourteen
saucer
awesome
resort
August
naughty
portrait
laundry
always

Page 200
Activity 7 Match to a picture

portrait
quarter
daughter
morning
corner
wardrobe

Page 201
Activity 8 Two syllable word tech

a / pp l au d
r e / p or t
i n / d oor s
d augh / t er
w ar d / r o b e
b ore / d o m
c or / n er
f our / t ee n
a l / th ough
w a l / n u t

Page 202
Activity 9 Syllable trap

a   d ore
or   b i t
a   pp l au se
a l   s o
r e   p or t
p or   t r ai t
s m a   ll er
w a l   n u t

Page 203	Page 204	Page 205
Activity 10 Sounds like a syllable	**Activity 11 Two syllable anagrams**	**Activity 12 Syllable jigsaw**

Page 203

Activity 10 Sounds like a syllable

f or	w ar d
au	t u mn
a l	s o
m or	n i ng
d augh	t er
i n	d oor s
r e	w ar d
p er	f or m
i g	n ore

Page 204

Activity 11 Two syllable anagrams

calling
resort
explore
laundry
forty
water
saucer
quarter
walrus
fortnight
ignore
applause
although
indoors
perform

Page 205

Activity 12 Syllable jigsaw

mor	ning
for	ty
or	b i t
a	d ore
al	m o st
Au	g u st
a	pp l au se
d augh	t er
awe	s o m e

Words with an 'air' sound – word list of 2 syllable words

air	are	ar	ear	ere
affair	aware	caring	bearer	therefore
aircraft	barely	daring	bearing	werewolf
airfield	beware	parent	forbear	whereas
airline	careful	pharaoh	forswear	whereby
airmail	careless	scarcely	swearing	wherefore
airport	compare	scary	tearing	
airtight	declare	sharing	wearing	
airway	farewell	vary		
chairman	prepare	wary		
dairy	rarely			
despair	scarecrow			
éclair	warehouse			
fairground				
fairly				
fairy				
hairbrush				
haircut				
hairspray				
hairstyle				
hairy				
impair				
prairie				
repair				
staircase				

This activity results in the child rediscovering all the sound spellings for this sound in the context of 2 syllable words.

Support the child to read the words one by one. Ask the child to say the word again in their head or with their 'thinking voice' and notice how they split up each word into two chunks of sounds, or syllables, as they say it.

For each word support the child to work out the sound spelling corresponding to the sound 'air'.

Words are sorted into lists according to their 'air' sound spelling.

There are many sound spellings to find; some are less common than others: **air, are, ar, ear** and **ere**.

Encourage the child to say each sound as they write each sound spelling in sequence, *syllable by syllable*, in this way:

e.g.

	sees:	a		w are		
aware						
	says:	'a' = 'a'		'w'>'air' = 'wair'	'a>wair'	'aware'

Remind the child to watch out for schwas! There is a schwa in the first syllable of 'aware'.

Break this task into a number of shorter tasks over a number of lessons if necessary.

Activity 2 Thinking about the sound 'air'

aware	therefore	parent
hairbrush	scary	airline
caring	staircase	beware
swearing	repair	prepare
werewolf	compare	bearing

This set of cards is made up of 2 syllable words containing the sound 'air'. Copy onto card and cut out. Practise the dynamic blending – syllable by syllable reading strategy, as described in the 'Working through the programme' section, to read the words on these cards. Model this process for the child if necessary.

Activity 3 Sorting word cards	**air**
aware	careful
prepare	farewell
airport	repair
haircut	parent
caring	scary
wearing	tearing
therefore	werewolf

Support the child to read each word. To help, the words have been split into two chunks of sounds, or syllables, as indicated by the asterisk *.

Direct the child to blend the sounds within the first syllable and say the syllable chunk, then blend the sounds within the second syllable and say the syllable chunk. Remind the child to watch out for schwas!

Finally push both syllable chunks together to hear the word forming.

e.g.

	sees:	b e	w are		
beware					
	says:	'b'>'ee' = 'bee'	'w'>'air' = 'wair'	'be>wair'	**'beware'**

Activity 4 Reading 2 syllable words   air

beware	b e * w are
therefore	th ere * f ore
daring	d ar * i ng
compare	c o m * p are
airport	air * p or t
repair	r e * p air
swearing	s w ear * i ng
prepare	p r e * p are
parent	p ar * e n t
scary	s c ar * y

Support the child to read the words one by one. Ask the child to say the word again in their head or with their 'thinking voice' and notice how they split up each word into two chunks of sounds, or syllables, as they say it. For each word support the child to draw a line through the word to show where in the word they split it into two syllables.

It is useful to discuss how they made their choice. Remind the child to watch out for schwas!

The first group of words has some sound spellings highlighted to help, and the first one is split as an example.

Activity 5 Syllable split   air

b e/w **are**   th ere f ore

f **air** g r **ou** n d   sh **ar** i ng

r e p **air**   s w **ear** i ng

p **ar** e n t   c **are** f u l

c o m p **are**   w **are** h **ou** se

Careful, the next ones do not have any sound spellings highlighted:

prepare

haircut

scary

daring

airport

aware

scarecrow

Support the child to read the clue on the left and work out what the answer word is.

Ask the child to say the word again in their head or with their 'thinking voice' and notice how they split up each word into two chunks of sounds, or syllables, as they say it.

Ask the child to draw a line from the clue to the first syllable of the word and then go on to draw a line to the second syllable of the word.

Finally ask the child to write the whole word on the line at the end indicated by the arrow and read the word out loud.

Activity 6 Join the syllables   air

Clue	1st	2nd	→	Word
Own planes	s c ar	i ng	→	
Frightening	air	y	→	
Bad language	th ere	l i n e	→	*airline*
...and so...	s w ear	i ng	→	
Generous	c are	f ore	→	
Watch out, be...	sh ar	f u l	→	
Dressing in...	r e	i ng	→	
Taking risks	w ear	c r ow	→	
Mend	s c are	p air	→	
Frightens birds	d ar	i ng	→	

Ask the child to choose a picture and discuss what the matching word might be.
Then ask the child to think about how that word might be split into two syllables.
The child then finds the first syllable and then the second, drawing a line from picture to syllable to syllable.
The child then writes the complete word on one of the lines in the box at the bottom of the page.
Encourage the child to write the word using the syllable by sequential segmenting – syllable by syllable spelling strategy.

Activity 7 Match to a picture   air

air

scare

hair

craft

crow

brush

par

stair

ing

ents

case

shar

_____ _____ _____

_____ _____ _____

Support the child to read the words one by one. Ask the child to say the word again in their head or with their 'thinking voice' and notice how they split up the word into two chunks of sounds, or syllables, as they say it.

Then ask the child to show where they split the word up into two syllables by drawing a line through it.

Next ask the child to put a ring round each of the sound spellings.

Finally ask the child to highlight any schwas in the word.

Activity 8 Two syllable word tech   air

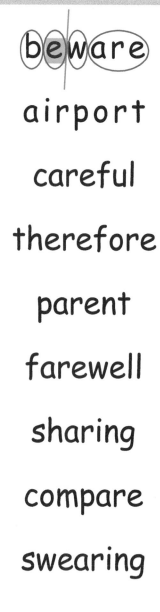

beware

airport

careful

therefore

parent

farewell

sharing

compare

swearing

scary

repair

Support the child to read the words one by one. Ask the child to say the word again in their head or with their 'thinking voice' and notice how they split up each word into two chunks of sounds, or syllables, as they say it. For each word, ask the child to work out where they split it into two syllables and then draw a line through the word.

Then ask the child to work out how many sounds there are in each syllable. They could write the number next to each syllable.

Support the child to look at the grid underneath and choose the row that contains the right number of lines in the first box (to match the number of sounds in the first syllable) and the right number of lines in the second box (to match the number of sounds in the second syllable). Ask the child to write the word in the grid on the chosen row, writing a sound spelling on each line.

An example is done to help you.

Activity 9 Syllable trap   air

2 sounds	2 sounds
be|ware	parent
airport	scarecrow
compare	hairbrush
affair	airfield

——	—— ——
——	—— —— ——
——	—— —— —— ——
b e	w are
—— —— ——	—— —— ——
—— —— ——	—— —— —— ——
—— —— —— ——	—— —— ——
—— —— —— ——	—— —— —— ——

Support the child to read the clue on the left and work out what the word is.

Ask the child to say the word in their head or with their 'thinking voice' and notice how they split up each word into two chunks of sounds, or syllables, as they say it.

Support the child to write the first syllable, sound by sound, in the first boxes and the second syllable, sound by sound, in the second boxes, noticing that there is a box for each sound within the syllables.

Remind them to be careful with split sound spellings!

Then, covering the boxes, ask the child to write out the word from memory in the box at the end, thinking about the syllables and the sounds in them.

The first one is done for you as an example.

Activity 10 Sounds like a syllable   air

Clue	1st syllable		2nd syllable		Word
Considerate	c	ar	i	ng	caring
Get ready					
Bad language					
Old fashioned goodbye					
Watch out					
Not very often					
Frightens birds					
Mum or dad					
Where planes land					

Support the child to read the clue on the left and work out what the answer word is.
The word has been split into two syllables and the sound spellings in each syllable have been mixed up.
Encourage the child to write the first syllable, sound by sound, then the second syllable, sound by sound, on the line on the right.
Ask the child to say the word.

Activity 11 Two syllable anagrams   air

Clue	1st syllable	2nd syllable	Word
Watch out	e b	**are** w	_____
Bad language	w **ear** s	**ng** i	_____
Get ready	r p e	**are** p	_____
Taking risks	**ar** d	**ng** i	_____
Good bye	**are** f	w **ll** e	_____
... and so...	**ere** **th**	**ore** f	_____
Frightens birds	**are** s c	**ow** r c	_____
Mum or dad	**ar** p	n t e	_____
Grooming tool	**air** h	u **sh** r b	_____
Frightening	c **ar** s	y	_____
Mend	e r	**air** p	_____
Place where planes land	**air**	t p **or**	_____
Kind and generous	**ar** **sh**	**ng** i	_____
Stores	**are** w	**se** **ou** h	_____
Not very often	**are** r	y l	_____

Support the child to read the clue on the left and work out what the word is.

Ask the child to say the answer word again in their head or with their 'thinking voice' and notice how they split up each word into two chunks of sounds, or syllables, as they say it.

The words have been split into two 'syllable boxes' but are not complete.

Ask the child to finish the word by writing in either the first or second syllable as required in the grey box.

Then ask the child to write out the word in full on the line at the end.

The first one is done for you as an example.

Activity 12 Syllable jigsaw   air

Clue	1st syllable	2nd syllable	Word
Store	ware	house	warehouse
Bad language		ing	_____
Frightens birds		crow	_____
Mend	re		_____
Place for planes		port	_____
Goodbye		well	_____
Similar or different?	com		_____
Not often		ly	_____
Grooming tool		brush	_____

Activity 13 Spelling challenge

air

repair	r e/p air	*	*
airport	air/p or t	*	*
prepare	p r e/p are	*	*
careful	c are/f u l	*	*
compare	c o m/p are	*	*
parent	p ar/e n t	*	*
caring	c ar/i ng	*	*
wearing	w ear/i ng	*	*

Support the child to read each sentence one by one.

Ask the child to re-read the sentence, several times if necessary, and try to remember it.

Then cover the sentence and ask the child to recall the sentence verbally.

Once they can do this confidently, ask the child to write out the sentence from memory.

The child might find it helpful to think about the individual syllables in the words and say the sounds within each as they write. When the sentence is complete, the child reads out their sentence and then compares it to the original.

Break this task into smaller ones as necessary.

Alternatively, using text to speech software, the child could type the sentence, with the computer reading back each word and then the completed sentence.

Activity 14 Writing challenge   air

They desp**air**ed **th**at the **air**craft was lost.

I rarely **sh**are my **squ**are crisps.

He sw**ears** he do**es**n't w**ear** bear fur.

The scary canary is **now** a parent.

Support the child to read the word on the left.

Then look at how the word has been split into three chunks of sounds, or syllables, as indicated by the asterisk * and red, blue and green colour coding.

Then ask the child to work through the word syllable by syllable, writing over each grey sound spelling and saying the corresponding sounds. At the end of each syllable the child says the chunk of sounds and at the end of the word the child says the whole word.

Cover the words and ask the child to write the word syllable by syllable and sound by sound on the three lines, saying the sounds as they write the corresponding sound spellings.

Finally, the child can write the whole word on the single line, but once again work syllable by syllable and sound by sound, saying the sounds as they write the corresponding sound spellings.

Remind the child to watch out for schwas which are highlighted and to take care with split sound spellings. The child could highlight any sound spellings that they think are tricky, to help them recall them when spelling.

Activity 15 Spelling 3 syllable words

air

repairing   r e * p air * i ng   r e * p air * i ng   __ * __ * __

unfairness   u n * f air * n e ss   u n * f air * n e ss   __ * __ * __

unfairly   u n * f air * l y   s u * pp or * t er   __ * __ * __

airliner   air * l i * n er   air * l i * n er   __ * __ * __

hairdresser h air * d r e ss * er   h air * d r e ss * er   __ * __ * __

Answers

Page 212
Activity 2 Thinking about the sound 'air'

are
aware beware prepare
compare
ere
therefore werewolf
ar
parent scary caring
air
hairbrush airline staircase
repair
ear
swearing bearing

Page 217
Activity 5 Syllable split

be / ware   there / fore
fair / ground   shar / ing
re / pair   swear / ing
par / ent   care / ful
com /pare   ware / house
pre / pare
hair / cut
scar / y
dar / ing
air / port
a / ware
scare / crow

Page 218
Activity 6 Join the syllables

swearing
scary
airline
sharing
therefore
careful
daring
scarecrow
repair
wearing

Page 219
Activity 7 Match to a picture

aircraft
hairbrush
scarecrow
parent
staircase
sharing

Page 220
Activity 8 Two syllable word tech

air / p or t
c are / f u l
th ere / f ore
p ar / e n t
f are / w e ll
sh ar / i ng
c om / p are
s w ear / i ng
s c ar / y
r e / p air

Page 221
Activity 9 Syllable trap

a   ff air
air   p or t
air   f ie l d
b e   w are
p ar   e n t
h air   b r u sh
c o m   p are
s c are   c r ow

Page 222	Page 223	Page 224
Activity 10 Sounds like a syllable	**Activity 11 Two syllable anagrams**	**Activity 12 Syllable jigsaw**

Page 222

Activity 10 Sounds like a syllable

c ar	i ng
p r e	p are
s w ear	i ng
f are	w e ll
b e	w are
r are	l y
s c are	c r ow
p ar	e n t
air	p or t

Page 223

Activity 11 Two syllable anagrams

beware
swearing
prepare
daring
farewell
therefore
scarecrow
parent
hairbrush
scary
repair
airport
sharing
warehouse
rarely

Page 224

Activity 12 Syllable jigsaw

ware	house
swear	ing
scare	crow
re	pair
air	port
fare	well
com	pare
rare	ly
hair	brush

Words with an 'ar' sound – word list of 2 syllable words

ar	ar	ar	a	al	ear
afar	darkness	marvel	amen	almond	heartbeat
ajar	darling	parcel	corral	balmy	heartbreak
alarm	depart	pardon	drama	behalf	heartburn
apart	discard	parking	father	calming	hearty
arcade	discharge	parlour	gala	calmly	
archer	embark	parsley	khaki		
archive	enlarge	parson	lager		
argon	farmer	partly	lather		
argue	garden	partner	lava		
armchair	garlic	party	llama		
armful	garment	sardine	massage		
armpit	guitar	scarlet	mirage		
army	harbor	sharpen	plaza		
artist	harden	sharply	rather		
barber	hardly	sparkle	saga		
bargain	hardship	sparkling	sari		
barking	hardy	starchy	slalom		
barley	harmless	stardom			**ser**geant
carbon	harvest	starfish			
carcass	jargon	starlight			
cardboard	larder	started			
cargo	largely	starter			**aar**dvark
carpet	larger	starting			bazaar
carton	largest	startle			
cartoon	larva	starving			
carving	marble	target			
charcoal	marching	tarnish			**bizarre**
charging	margin	tartan			
charming	market	varnish			
charter	marking	yardstick			
cigar	marshal				ca**tarrh**
darker	martyr				

This activity results in the child rediscovering all the sound spellings for this sound in the context of 2 syllable words.

Support the child to read the words one by one. Ask the child to say the word again in their head or with their 'thinking voice' and notice how they split up each word into two chunks of sounds, or syllables, as they say it.

For each word support the child to work out the sound spelling corresponding to the sound 'ar'.

Words are sorted into lists according to their 'ar' sound spelling.

There are many sound spellings to find; some are less common than others: **ar, a, al** and **ear**.

Encourage the child to say each sound as they write each sound spelling in sequence, *syllable by syllable*, in this way:

e.g.

      sees: d r a   m a

drama

      says: 'd'>'r'>'ar' = 'drar'   'm'>'a' = 'ma'   'drar>ma'   **'drama'**

Remind the child to watch out for schwas! There is a schwa in the second syllable of 'drama'.

Break this task into a number of shorter tasks over a number of lessons if necessary.

Activity 2 Thinking about the sound 'ar'

drama	artist	saga
calmly	father	hearty
heartbeat	darkness	lava
sparkling	behalf	pardon
sari	starfish	balmy

This set of cards is made up of 2 syllable words containing the sound 'ar'. Copy onto card and cut out. Practise the dynamic blending – syllable by syllable reading strategy, as described in the 'Working through the programme' section, to read the words on these cards. Model this process for the child if necessary.

Activity 3 Sorting word cards	ar
apart	garden
started	carpet
market	sparkle
party	lava
drama	rather
behalf	calmly
hearty	heartbeat

Support the child to read each word. To help, the words have been split into two chunks of sounds, or syllables, as indicated by the asterisk *.

Direct the child to blend the sounds within the first syllable and say the syllable chunk, then blend the sounds within the second syllable and say the syllable chunk. Remind the child to watch out for schwas!

Finally push both syllable chunks together to hear the word forming.

e.g.

sees: g ar   d e n

garden

says: 'g'>'ar' = 'gar'   'd'>'e'>'n' = 'den'   'gar>den'   **'garden'**

Activity 4 Reading 2 syllable words   ar

garden	g ar * d e n
drama	d r a * m a
heartbeat	h ear t * b ea t
starfish	s t ar * f i sh
farmer	f ar * m er
pardon	p ar * d o n
calmly	c al m * l y
depart	d e * p ar t
rather	r a * th er
darkness	d ar k * n e ss

Support the child to read the words one by one. Ask the child to say the word again in their head or with their 'thinking voice' and notice how they split up each word into two chunks of sounds, or syllables, as they say it. For each word support the child to draw a line through the word to show where in the word they split it into two syllables.

It is useful to discuss how they made their choice. Remind the child to watch out for schwas!

The first group of words has some sound spellings highlighted to help, and the first one is split as an example.

Activity 5 Syllable split   ar

e n/l **ar** ge   p **ar** t n er

sh ar p e n   t **ar** g e t

h **ar** d l y   b e h **al** f

h **ear** t b r **ea** k   c **ar** t **oo** n

m **ar** b **le**   s l a l o m

Careful, the next ones do not have any sound spellings highlighted:

rather

charging

darker

calmly

heartbeat

starving

market

Support the child to read the clue on the left and work out what the answer word is.

Ask the child to say the word again in their head or with their 'thinking voice' and notice how they split up each word into two chunks of sounds, or syllables, as they say it.

Ask the child to draw a line from the clue to the first syllable of the word and then go on to draw a line to the second syllable of the word.

Finally ask the child to write the whole word on the line at the end indicated by the arrow and read the word out loud.

Activity 6 Join the syllables   ar

Clue	1st	2nd	→	Word
Shock	s c **ar**	c **el**	→	
Package	s t **ar**	l e t	→	
Vivid red	b **ar**	t le	→	*startle*
Pulse	p **ar**	k i **ng**	→	
Dogs noise	l a	b **ea** t	→	
Soapy froth	h **ear** t	f u l	→	
Dangerous	d e	**th er**	→	
Funny drawing	h **ar** m	t **oo** n	→	
Leave to travel	**ar**	p **ar** t	→	
A painter	c **ar**	t i s t	→	

Ask the child to choose a picture and discuss what the matching word might be.
Then ask the child to think about how that word might be split into two syllables.
The child then finds the first syllable and then the second, drawing a line from picture to syllable to syllable.
The child then writes the complete word on one of the lines in the box at the bottom of the page.
Encourage the child to write the word using the sequential segmenting – syllable by syllable spelling strategy.

Activity 7 Match to a picture   ar

tar

fa

get

par

par

ther

ther

cel

ty

gui

tar

la

Support the child to read the words one by one. Ask the child to say the word again in their head or with their 'thinking voice' and notice how they split up the word into two chunks of sounds, or syllables, as they say it.

Then ask the child to show where they split the word up into two syllables by drawing a line through it.

Next ask the child to put a ring round each of the sound spellings.

Finally ask the child to highlight any schwas in the word.

Activity 8 Two syllable word tech   ar

largest

behalf

drama

cardboard

partner

garlic

armpit

market

starlight

hearty

Support the child to read the words one by one. Ask the child to say the word again in their head or with their 'thinking voice' and notice how they split up each word into two chunks of sounds, or syllables, as they say it. For each word, ask the child to work out where they split it into two syllables and then draw a line through the word.

Then ask the child to work out how many sounds there are in each syllable. They could write the number next to each syllable.

Support the child to look at the grid underneath and choose the row that contains the right number of lines in the first box (to match the number of sounds in the first syllable) and the right number of lines in the second box (to match the number of sounds in the second syllable). Ask the child to write the word in the grid on the chosen row, writing a sound spelling on each line.

An example is done to help you.

Activity 9 Syllable trap ar

1 sound | 2 sounds

a|far   market

guitar   artist

starter   alarm

heartbeat   sparkling

a	f ar
—	— — —
—	— — — —
— — —	— — —
— — —	— — — —
— — — —	— — —
— — — —	— — — —
— — — — —	— — — — —

Support the child to read the clue on the left and work out what the word is.

Ask the child to say the word in their head or with their 'thinking voice' and notice how they split up each word into two chunks of sounds, or syllables, as they say it.

Support the child to write the first syllable, sound by sound, in the first boxes and the second syllable, sound by sound, in the second boxes, noticing that there is a box for each sound within the syllables.

Remind them to be careful with split sound spellings!

Then, covering the boxes, ask the child to write out the word from memory in the box at the end, thinking about the syllables and the sounds in them.

The first one is done for you as an example.

Activity 10 Sounds like a syllable   ar

Clue	1st syllable			2nd syllable			Word
Make bigger	e	n		l	ar	ge	enlarge
No light							
Very hungry							
Soft floor covering							
Leave to travel							
A play							
Someone to work with							
Sorry							
Scottish checks							

Support the child to read the clue on the left and work out what the answer word is.
The word has been split into two syllables and the sound spellings in each syllable have been mixed up.
Encourage the child to write the fist syllable, sound by sound, then the second syllable, sound by sound, on the line on the right.
Ask the child to say the word.

Activity 11 Two syllable anagrams   ar

Clue	1st syllable	2nd syllable	Word
Dad	a f	**er th**	_____
Scottish check fabric	**ar** t	n t a	_____
Cheap	**ar** b	**ai** g n	_____
Aim for this	**ar** t	e t g	_____
From a volcano	a l	v a	_____
Beginning	**ar** t s	**ng** i t	_____
Pulse	**ear** t h	**ea** t b	_____
Someone to work with	**ar** p t	n **er**	_____
Excuse me	**ar** p	o d n	_____
e.g. painter, sculptor	**ar**	t t s i	_____
Bicker	**ar**	**ue** g	_____
Relaxing	**al** c	i m **ng**	_____
Soft floor covering	**ar** c	t p e	_____
Dangerous	**ar** h m	l u f	_____
Alert to danger	a	m l **ar**	_____

Support the child to read the clue on the left and work out what the word is.

Ask the child to say the answer word again in their head or with their 'thinking voice' and notice how they split up each word into two chunks of sounds, or syllables, as they say it.

The words have been split into two 'syllable boxes' but are not complete.

Ask the child to finish the word by writing in either the first or second syllable as required in the grey box.

Then ask the child to write out the word in full on the line at the end.

The first one is done for you as an example.

Activity 12 Syllable jigsaw   ar

Clue	1ˢᵗ syllable	2ⁿᵈ syllable	Word
Epic story	sa	ga	_saga_
Bright red		let	_____
Very hungry		ving	_____
Stringed instrument	gui		_____
Aim for this		get	_____
After July		vest	_____
Separate	a		_____
Funny drawing		toon	_____
Package		cel	_____

ar

Activity 13 Spelling challenge

	ar		
garden	g ar / d e n	*	||
bargain	b ar / g ai n	*	||
carpet	c ar / p e t	*	||
parking	p ar / k i ng	*	||
started	s t ar / t e d	*	
father	f a / th er	*	||
calmly	c a l m / l y	*	||
behalf	b e / h al f	*	||

Support the child to read each sentence one by one.

Ask the child to re-read the sentence, several times if necessary, and try to remember it.

Then cover the sentence and ask the child to recall the sentence verbally.

Once they can do this confidently, ask the child to write out the sentence from memory.

The child might find it helpful to think about the individual syllables in the words and say the sounds within each as they write. When the sentence is complete, the child reads out their sentence and then compares it to the original.

Break this task into smaller ones as necessary.

Alternatively, using text to speech software, the child could type the sentence, with the computer reading back each word and then the completed sentence.

Activity 14 Writing challenge   ar

The **carniv**o**re** was st**ar**ting to **ea**t the c**ar**pet.

There are h**ar**dly any sc**ar**let fl**ow**e**r**s in the f**ar**m**er**'s g**ar**den.

I h**ea**ted up my banana on the hot lava.

I **woul**d **rather** go to the drama class with **father**.

Support the child to read the word on the left.

Then look at how the word has been split into three chunks of sounds, or syllables, as indicated by the asterisk * and red, blue and green colour coding.

Then ask the child to work through the word syllable by syllable, writing over each grey sound spelling and saying the corresponding sounds. At the end of each syllable the child says the chunk of sounds and at the end of the word the child says the whole word.

Cover the words and ask the child to write the word syllable by syllable and sound by sound on the three lines, saying the sounds as they write the corresponding sound spellings. The child can then check and correct the answer if necessary.

Finally, the child can write the whole word on the single line, but once again work syllable by syllable and sound by sound, saying the sounds as they write the corresponding sound spellings.

Remind the child to watch out for schwas which are highlighted and to take care with split sound spellings. The child could highlight any sound spellings that they think are tricky, to help them recall them when spelling.

Activity 15 Spelling 3 syllable words

ar

argument	ar*gu*ment	ar*gu*ment	* ____ * ____ * ____
artistic	ar*tis*tic	ar*tis*tic	* ____ * ____ * ____
partnership	part*ner*ship	part*ner*ship	* ____ * ____ * ____
alarming	a*lar*ming	a*lar*ming	* ____ * ____ * ____
gardener	gar*de*ner	gar*de*ner	* ____ * ____ * ____

Answers

ar

Page 231
Activity 2 Thinking about the sound 'ar'

a
drama saga father lava
ar
artist darkness sparkling
pardon sari starfish
al
calmly behalf balmy
ear
hearty heartbeat

Page 235
Activity 5 Syllable split

en / large	part / ner
shar / pen	tar / get
hard / ly	be / half
heart / break	car / toon
mar / ble	sla / lom
ra / ther	
char / ging	
dar / ker	
calm / ly	
heart / beat	
star / ving	
mar / ket	

Page 236
Activity 6 Join the syllables

parcel
scarlet
startle
barking
heartbeat
harmful
lather
cartoon
depart
artist

Page 237
Activity 7 Match to a picture

parcel
guitar
party
target
lava
father

Page 238
Activity 8 Two syllable word tech

l ar / g e s t
b e / h a l f
d r a / m a
c ar d / b oar d
p ar t / n er
g ar / l i c
ar m / p i t
m ar / k e t
s t ar / l i gh t
h ear / t y

Page 239
Activity 9 Syllable trap

a	f ar
a	l ar m
ar	t i s t
gu i	t ar
m ar	k e t
s t ar	t er
h ear t	b ea t
s p ar	k l i ng

Page 240	
Activity 10 Sounds like a syllable	
e n	l ar ge
d ar k	n e ss
s t ar	v i ng
c ar	p e t
d e	p ar t
d r a	m a
p ar t	n er
p ar	d o n
t ar	t a n

Page 241
Activity 11 Two syllable anagrams
father
tartan
bargain
target
lava
starting
heartbeat
partner
pardon
artist
argue
calming
carpet
harmful
alarm

Page 242	
Activity 12 Syllable jigsaw	
sa	ga
scar	let
star	ving
gui	tar
tar	get
har	vest
a	part
car	toon
par	cel

Words with an 'o' sound – word list of 2 syllable words

o	o	a	au
across	jogger	balsa	because
along	jolly	Baltic	faultless
belong	jotter	basalt	faulty
beyond	lorry	falcon	laurel
body	model	quarrel	vaulted
bonfire	modest	quarry	
borrow	monster	swaddle	
bother	novel	swapping	
bottle	object	swampy	
collage	offer	waddle	
collar	often	waffle	
collect	oxide	wallet	
comet	polish	wander	
comic	pollen	wanted	
comma	pothole	wanting	
conduct	problem	warrant	
content	proper	watcher	
contrast	robber	watches	
copper	robin		
copy	rocky		
donkey	solid		
hobble	solvent		
hockey	sorry		
hollow	tonic		
holly	toxin		
horrid	wobble		
jockey			

This activity results in the child rediscovering all the sound spellings for this sound in the context of 2 syllable words.

Support the child to read the words one by one. Ask the child to say the word again in their head or with their 'thinking voice' and notice how they split up each word into two chunks of sounds, or syllables, as they say it.

For each word support the child to work out the sound spelling corresponding to the sound 'o'.

Words are sorted into lists according to their 'o' sound spelling.

There are many sound spellings to find; some are less common than others: **o, a** and **au**.

Encourage the child to say each sound as they write each sound spelling in sequence, *syllable by syllable*, in this way:

e.g.

        sees: w a n   t e d

wanted

        says: 'w'>'a'>'n' = 'wan'   't'>'e'>'d' = 'ted'   'wan>ted'   **'wanted'**

Remind the child to watch out for schwas! There is a schwa in the second syllable of 'wanted'.

Break this task into a number of shorter tasks over a number of lessons if necessary.

Activity 2 Thinking about the sound 'o'

wanted	across	faulty
collect	swapping	problem
because	solid	quarrel
offer	vaulted	comic
wander	monster	along

This set of cards is made up of 2 syllable words containing the sound 'o'. Copy onto card and cut out. Practise the dynamic blending – syllable by syllable reading strategy, as described in the 'Working through the programme' section, to read the words on these cards. Model this process for the child if necessary.

Activity 3 Sorting word cards	o

across	collect
model	comic
monster	problem
solid	sorry
swapping	wanted
wander	watches
faulty	because

Support the child to read each word. To help, the words have been split into two chunks of sounds, or syllables, as indicated by the asterisk *.

Direct the child to blend the sounds within the first syllable and say the syllable chunk, then blend the sounds within the second syllable and say the syllable chunk. Remind the child to watch out for schwas!

Finally push both syllable chunks together to hear the word forming.

e.g.

watching

sees: w a   tch i ng

says: 'w'>'o' = 'wo'   'ch'>'i'>'ng' = 'ching'   'wo>ching'   **'watching'**

Activity 4 Reading 2 syllable words   o

watching	w a * tch i ng
collect	c o * ll e c t
faulty	f au l * t y
sorry	s o * rr y
problem	p r o b * l e m
monster	m o n * s t er
quarrel	qu a * rr el
offer	o * ff er
belong	b e * l o ng
because	b e * c au se

Support the child to read the words one by one. Ask the child to say the word again in their head or with their 'thinking voice' and notice how they split up each word into two chunks of sounds, or syllables, as they say it. For each word support the child to draw a line through the word to show where in the word they split it into two syllables.

It is useful to discuss how they made their choice. Remind the child to watch out for schwas!

The first group of words has some sound spellings highlighted to help, and the first one is split as an example.

Activity 5 Syllable split

co/mic   don k**ey**

w a n t e d   b e c **au se**

m o n s t **er**   c o n t e n t s

w a **tch** e s   **qu** a **rr el**

f **au** l t y   o f t e n

Careful, the next ones do not have any sound spellings highlighted:

swapping

wander

collect

bonfire

proper

wallet

hollow

Support the child to read the clue on the left and work out what the answer word is.

Ask the child to say the word again in their head or with their 'thinking voice' and notice how they split up each word into two chunks of sounds, or syllables, as they say it.

Ask the child to draw a line from the clue to the first syllable of the word and then go on to draw a line to the second syllable of the word.

Finally ask the child to write the whole word on the line at the end indicated by the arrow and read the word out loud.

Activity 6 Join the syllables   o

Clue	1ˢᵗ	2ⁿᵈ	→	Word
Compare	j o	t y	→	
Someone who runs	c o n	**gg** er	→	
Needed	s w a	t r a s t	→	*contrast*
Exchanging	f **au** l	t e d	→	
Not working	w a n	v **el**	→	
Long book	r o	**pp** i **ng**	→	
Van	h o	**rr** y	→	
Red breasted bird	n o	b i n	→	
Empty	l o	**rr el**	→	
Argue	**qu** a	**ll ow**	→	

Ask the child to choose a picture and discuss what the matching word might be.
Then ask the child to think about how that word might be split into two syllables.
The child then finds the first syllable and then the second, drawing a line from picture to syllable to syllable.
The child then writes the complete word on one of the lines in the box at the bottom of the page.
Encourage the child to write the word using the sequential segmenting – syllable by syllable spelling strategy.

Activity 7 Match to a picture   o

ffle

don

bon

wa

ster

wa

llet

lau

key

fire

rel

mon

Support the child to read the words one by one. Ask the child to say the word again in their head or with their 'thinking voice' and notice how they split up the word into two chunks of sounds, or syllables, as they say it.
Then ask the child to show where they split the word up into two syllables by drawing a line through it.
Next ask the child to put a ring round each of the sound spellings.
Finally ask the child to highlight any schwas in the word.

Activity 8 Two syllable word tech   o

faulty

wanting

wobble

donkey

watching

jogging

offer

wander

because

contents

problem

Support the child to read the words one by one. Ask the child to say the word again in their head or with their 'thinking voice' and notice how they split up each word into two chunks of sounds, or syllables, as they say it. For each word, ask the child to work out where they split it into two syllables and then draw a line through the word.

Then ask the child to work out how many sounds there are in each syllable. They could write the number next to each syllable.

Support the child to look at the grid underneath and choose the row that contains the right number of lines in the first box (to match the number of sounds in the first syllable) and the right number of lines in the second box (to match the number of sounds in the second syllable). Ask the child to write the word in the grid on the chosen row, writing a sound spelling on each line.

An example is done to help you.

Activity 9 Syllable trap   o

1 sound | 2 sounds

o|ffer   body

wander   because

across   swapping

along   content

_o_	_ff_ _er_
—	— — —
—	— — — —
— — —	— —
— — —	— — — —
— — —	— — —
— — — —	— — — —
— — — —	— — — — —

Support the child to read the clue on the left and work out what the word is.

Ask the child to say the word in their head or with their 'thinking voice' and notice how they split up each word into two chunks of sounds, or syllables, as they say it.

Support the child to write the first syllable, sound by sound, in the first boxes and the second syllable, sound by sound, in the second boxes, noticing that there is a box for each sound within the syllables.

Remind them to be careful with split sound spellings!

Then, covering the boxes, ask the child to write out the word from memory in the box at the end, thinking about the syllables and the sounds in them.

The first one is done for you as an example.

Activity 10 Sounds like a syllable   o

Clue	1st syllable			2nd syllable			Word
Money holder	w	a		ll	e	t	wallet
Regret							
Cartoon book							
Frequently							
Looking at							
Roam around							
Scary creature							
Not working							
Feel part of							

Support the child to read the clue on the left and work out what the answer word is.
The word has been split into two syllables and the sound spellings in each syllable have been mixed up.
Encourage the child to write the first syllable, sound by sound, then the second syllable, sound by sound, on the line on the right.
Ask the child to say the word.

Activity 11 Two syllable anagrams   o

Clue	1st syllable	2nd syllable	Word
Needed	a w n	d t e	_____
Cartoon book	o c	i m c	_____
Happy	n c o	n t e t	_____
Breakfast pancake	a w	le ff	_____
Looks at	a w	s e tch	_____
Not working properly	au l f	y t	_____
Winter shrub	o h	y ll	_____
Scary creature	n m o	t s er	_____
Frequently	f o	e t n	_____
Argue	qu a	el rr	_____
Roam around	n w a	er d	_____
Bird of prey	l f a	n c o	_____
Difficulty	p o r b	m e l	_____
Horse rider	o j	ey ck	_____
Feel part of	e b	o ng l	_____

Support the child to read the clue on the left and work out what the word is.

Ask the child to say the answer word again in their head or with their 'thinking voice' and notice how they split up each word into two chunks of sounds, or syllables, as they say it.

The words have been split into two 'syllable boxes' but are not complete.

Ask the child to finish the word by writing in either the first or second syllable as required in the grey box.

Then ask the child to write out the word in full on the line at the end.

The first one is done for you as an example.

Activity 12 Syllable jigsaw   o

Clue	1st syllable	2nd syllable	Word
Worry	bo	ther	_bother_
Exchanging		pping	___
Roam around		der	___
Large van		rry	___
Argue		rrel	___
Holds money		llet	___
As a result of	be		___
Not working		ty	___
Difficulty		lem	___

Activity 13 Spelling challenge

across	a/c r o ss	* _ _ _
belong	b e/l o ng	* _ _ _
offer	o/ff er	* _ _ _
collect	c o/ll e c t	* _ _ _
sorry	s o/rr y	* _ _ _
wanted	w a n/t e d	* _ _ _
watching	w a/tch i ng	* _ _ _
because	b e/c au se	* _ _ _

Support the child to read each sentence one by one.
Ask the child to re-read the sentence, several times if necessary, and try to remember it.
Then cover the sentence and ask the child to recall the sentence verbally.
Once they can do this confidently, ask the child to write out the sentence from memory.
The child might find it helpful to think about the individual syllables in the words and say the sounds within each as they write. When the sentence is complete, the child reads out their sentence and then compares it to the original.

Break this task into smaller ones as necessary.

Alternatively, using text to speech software, the child could type the sentence, with the computer reading back each word and then the completed sentence.

Activity 14 Writing challenge   o

The problem is difficult to solve.

He is content to collect comics.

Jon was watching Ron because he was swatting the wasps.

The watch didn't work because it was faulty.

Support the child to read the word on the left.

Then look at how the word has been split into three chunks of sounds, or syllables, as indicated by the asterisk * and red, blue and green colour coding.

Then ask the child to work through the word syllable by syllable, writing over each grey sound spelling and saying the corresponding sounds. At the end of each syllable the child says the chunk of sounds and at the end of the word the child says the whole word.

Cover the words and ask the child to write the word syllable by syllable and sound by sound on the three lines, saying the sounds as they write the corresponding sound spellings. The child can then check and correct the answer if necessary.

Finally, the child can write the whole word on the single line, but once again work syllable by syllable and sound by sound, saying the sounds as they write the corresponding sound spellings.

Remind the child to watch out for schwas which are highlighted and to take care with split sound spellings. The child could highlight any sound spellings that they think are tricky, to help them recall them when spelling.

Activity 15 Spelling 3 syllable words

		o

hospital   h o s * p i * t a l   h o s * p i * t a l   ___ * ___ * ___

occupy   o cc * u * p y   o cc * u * p y   ___ * ___ * ___

collector   c o * ll e c * t or   c o * ll e c * t or   ___ * ___ * ___

consider   c o n * s i * d er   c o n * s i * d er   ___ * ___ * ___

holiday   h o * l i * d ay   h o * l i * d ay   ___ * ___ * ___

Answers   o

Page 249

Activity 2 Thinking about the sound 'o'

a

wanted swapping quarrel
wander

o

across collect problem solid
offer comic monster along

au

faulty because vaulted

Page 253

Activity 5 Syllable split

co / mic   don / key
wan / ted   be / cause
mon / ster   con / tents
wa / tch e s   qu a / rr el
faul / ty   of / te n
s w a / pp i ng
w a n / d er
co / ll e ct
b o n / f i r e
pro / p er
w a / ll e t
h o / ll ow

Page 254

Activity 6 Join the syllables

faulty
jogger
contrast
wanted
novel
swapping
lorry
robin
quarrel
hollow

Page 255

Activity 7 Match to a picture

monster
wallet
lorry
comic
waffle
body

Page 256

Activity 8 Two syllable word tech

w a n / t i ng
w o / bb le
d o n / k ey
w a / tch i ng
j o / gg i ng
o / ff er
w a n / d er
b e / c au se
c o n / t e n ts
p r o b / l em

Page 257

Activity 9 Syllable trap

o	ff er
a	l o ng
a	c r o ss
b o	d y
b e	c au se
w a n	d er
s w a	pp i ng
c o n	t e n t

Page 258	Page 259	Page 260
Activity 10 Sounds like a syllable	**Activity 11 Two syllable anagrams**	**Activity 12 Syllable jigsaw**

Page 258

Activity 10 Sounds like a syllable

w a   ll e t
s o   rr y
c o   m i c
o f   t e n
w a   tch i ng
w a n   d er
m o n   s t er
f au l   t y
b e   l o ng

Page 259

Activity 11 Two syllable anagrams

wanted
comic
content
waffle
watches
faulty
holly
monster
often
quarrel
wander
falcon
problem
jockey
belong

Page 260

Activity 12 Syllable jigsaw

bo   ther
swa   pping
wan   der
lo   rry
qua   rrel
wa   llet
be   cause
faul   ty
prob   lem

Words with an 'i' sound – word list of 2 syllable words

i	i	i	i	i	i	y
addict	dislike	impulse	kidnap	prism	trickle	abyss
adrift	dismay	include	kidney	prison	trigger	crystal
affix	dismiss	income	kingdom	quickly	triple	cygnet
amid	display	increase	kitchen	quiver	twinkle	gymnast
assist	dispose	indeed	kitten	ribbon	until	gypsy
bicker	disrupt	index	limit	riddle	vicar	mystic
bigger	dissolve	indoors	liquid	ripple	victim	physics
bigger	distance	inert	listen	river	victor	pygmy
biggest	distant	infant	litmus	scribble	villa	rhythm
bishop	distil	infect	litter	shingle	village	rhythmic
bitter	distinct	inflate	little	shiver	villain	syrup
blister	distress	inflict	liver	signal	visit	system
brigade	distract	inhale	lizard	silly	vivid	
chicken	district	inject	middle	silver	vixen	
children	disturb	injure	midday	simmer	whisker	**i-e**
chimney	divide	inner	midnight	simple	whisper	
chisel	dribble	input	mimic	sincere	whistle	active
cigar	driven	insect	mirror	single	wiggle	cursive
cinder	fiddle	insert	mischief	sister	willing	forgive
citrus	fidget	insist	mislay	sixteen	willow	massive
city	fifteen	inspect	mislead	sixty	winner	motive
civic	figure	instant	missile	sizzle	winter	notice
civil	filter	instead	nibble	skinny	windmill	passive
clinic	finger	instinct	nimble	skipper	window	service
conflict	flicker	instruct	omit	slipper	wisdom	
consist	flipper	insult	permit	slither	without	
convict	forbid	intact	persist	sniffle	witness	**Misc**
cricket	giggle	intend	pickle	spinach	wizard	
crinkle	ginger	into	picnic	spirit	wriggle	busy
critic	glimmer	intrude	pigeon	sprinkle	wrinkle	
didn't	glitter	invade	piglet	squirrel	zigzag	women
differ	illness	invent	pigment	submit		
dimple	igloo	invert	pilgrim	swimming		
dinner	ignite	invest	pillar	swimmer		
discard	ignore	invite	pillow	thimble		
disco	impact	involve	pimple	thistle		
discount	imply	issue	pistol	tickle		
discuss	import	itself	pivot	tinkle		
disease	imprint	jigsaw	predict	tinsel		
disgrace	improve	jingle	printer	tissue		

This activity results in the child rediscovering all the sound spellings for this sound in the context of 2 syllable words.

Support the child to read the words one by one. Ask the child to say the word again in their head or with their 'thinking voice' and notice how they split up each word into two chunks of sounds, or syllables, as they say it.

For each word support the child to work out the sound spelling corresponding to the sound 'i'.

Words are sorted into lists according to their 'i' sound spelling.

There are many sound spellings to find; some are less common than others: **i, y** and **i-e**.

Encourage the child to say each sound as they write each sound spelling in sequence, *syllable by syllable*, in this way:

e.g.

	sees:	c r y	s t al		
crystal					
	says:	'c'>'r'>'i' = 'cri'	's'>'t'>'l' = 'stl'	'cri>stl'	**'crystal'**

Remind the child to watch out for schwas!

Break this task into a number of shorter tasks over a number of lessons if necessary.

Activity 2 Thinking about the sound 'i'

crystal	limit	kidnap
active	physics	insect
children	invest	massive
intend	forgive	system
gymnast	kitten	instruct

This set of cards is made up of 2 syllable words containing the sound 'i'. Copy onto card and cut out. Practise the dynamic blending – syllable by syllable reading strategy, as described in the 'Working through the programme' section, to read the words on these cards. Model this process for the child if necessary.

Activity 3 Sorting word cards   i

assist	discuss
limit	intend
predict	inspect
invent	instruct
system	crystal
forgive	notice
women	busy

Support the child to read each word. To help, the words have been split into two chunks of sounds, or syllables, as indicated by the asterisk *.

Direct the child to blend the sounds within the first syllable and say the syllable chunk, then blend the sounds within the second syllable and say the syllable chunk. Remind the child to watch out for schwas!

Finally push both syllable chunks together to hear the word forming.

e.g.

	sees:	wh i s	p er		
whisper					
	says:	'w'>'i'>'s' = 'wis'	'p'>'er' = 'per'	'wis>per'	**'whisper'**

Activity 4 Reading 2 syllable words   i

whisper	wh i s * p er
sixteen	s i x * t ee n
active	a c * t i v e
winter	w i n * t er
gymnast	g y m * n a s t
insect	i n * s e c t
massive	m a * ss i v e
instead	i n * s t ea d
rhythm	rh y * th m
discuss	d i s * c u ss

Support the child to read the words one by one. Ask the child to say the word again in their head or with their 'thinking voice' and notice how they split up each word into two chunks of sounds, or syllables, as they say it. For each word support the child to draw a line through the word to show where in the word they split it into two syllables.

It is useful to discuss how they made their choice. Remind the child to watch out for schwas!

The first group of words has some sound spellings highlighted to help, and the first one is split as an example.

Activity 5 Syllable split   i

in/sect	discu**ss**
notic**e**	sist**er**
rh y **th** m	invent
cri**ck**et	li z **ar** d
li **st** en	distan**ce**

Careful, the next ones do not have any sound spellings highlighted:

pickle

winter

massive

instead

infect

service

itself

Support the child to read the clue on the left and work out what the answer word is.

Ask the child to say the word again in their head or with their 'thinking voice' and notice how they split up each word into two chunks of sounds, or syllables, as they say it.

Ask the child to draw a line from the clue to the first syllable of the word and then go on to draw a line to the second syllable of the word.

Finally ask the child to write the whole word on the line at the end indicated by the arrow and read the word out loud.

Activity 6 Join the syllables   i

Clue	1st	2nd	→	Word
Female fox	w i n	**th** m	→	
Coldest season	**rh** y	e n	→	*vixen*
Beat	v i x	t **er**	→	
Baby swan	l i	t i v **e**	→	
Reptile	a c	l **oo**	→	
Moves a lot	c y g	z **ar** d	→	
Very big	i g	n e t	→	
Inuit house	i n	**ss** i v **e**	→	
Six-legged mini-beast	m a	s e c t	→	
Ask to a party	i n	v i t **e**	→	

Ask the child to choose a picture and discuss what the matching word might be.

Then ask the child to think about how that word might be split into two syllables.

The child then finds the first syllable and then the second, drawing a line from picture to syllable to syllable.

The child then writes the complete word on one of the lines in the box at the bottom of the page.

Encourage the child to write the word using the sequential segmenting – syllable by syllable spelling strategy.

Activity 7 Match to a picture   i

li

cri

cry

fif

vix

zard

teen

dren

chil

cket

stal

en

Support the child to read the words one by one. Ask the child to say the word again in their head or their 'thinking voice' and notice how they split up the word into two chunks of sounds, or syllables, as they say it.
Then ask the child to show where they split the word up into two syllables by drawing a line through it.
Next ask the child to put a ring round each of the sound spellings.
Finally ask the child to highlight any schwas in the word.

Activity 8 Two syllable word tech i

women

finger

dinner

active

crystal

persist

service

gymnast

invest

scribble

system

Support the child to read the words one by one. Ask the child to say the word again in their head or with their 'thinking voice' and notice how they split up each word into two chunks of sounds, or syllables, as they say it. For each word, ask the child to work out where they split it into two syllables and then draw a line through the word.

Then ask the child to work out how many sounds there are in each syllable. They could write the number next to each syllable.

Support the child to look at the grid underneath and choose the row that contains the right number of lines in the first box (to match the number of sounds in the first syllable) and the right number of lines in the second box (to match the number of sounds in the second syllable). Ask the child to write the word in the grid on the chosen row, writing a sound spelling on each line.

An example is done to help you.

Activity 9 Syllable trap   i

2 sounds   4 sounds

in|stead   forgive

assist   silly

winter   driven

consist   amid

—	— — — —
—	— — — — —
— —	— — —
— — —	— — — —
i n	s t ea d
— — — —	— — —
— — — —	— — — —
— — — — —	— — — — —

Support the child to read the clue on the left and work out what the word is.
Ask the child to say the word in their head or with their 'thinking voice' and notice how they split up each word into two chunks of sounds, or syllables, as they say it.
Support the child to write the first syllable, sound by sound, in the first boxes and the second syllable, sound by sound, in the second boxes, noticing that there is a box for each sound within the syllables.
Remind them to be careful with split sound spellings!
Then, covering the boxes, ask the child to write out the word from memory in the box at the end, thinking about the syllables and the sounds in them.
The first one is done for you as an example.

Activity 10 Sounds like a syllable   i

Clue	1st syllable		2nd syllable			Word
Allow	p	er	m	i	t	permit
Baby cat						
Moves a lot						
Mum's other daughter						
Use your ears						
Outdoor meal						
Baby swan						
Very big						
Go and see						

Support the child to read the clue on the left and work out what the answer word is.
The word has been split into two syllables and the sound spellings in each syllable have been mixed up.
Encourage the child to write the first syllable, sound by sound, then the second syllable, sound by sound, on the line on the right.
Ask the child to say the word.

Activity 11 Two syllable anagrams   i

Clue	1st syllable	2nd syllable	Word
How far	d s i	t **ce** a n	_____
Breathe in	n i	**a-e** l h	_____
Beat	y **rh**	m **th**	_____
Talk quietly	s **wh** i	**er** p	_____
Moves a lot	c a	**i-e** t v	_____
Split up	i d	**i-e** d v	_____
Female fox	i v x	n e	_____
Excuse	**or** f	v **i-e** g	_____
Mini-beast with six legs	n i	e t s c	_____
Gooey and sweet	y s	p r u	_____
Great knowledge	i s w	m o d	_____
Straightaway	n i	t s n a t	_____
Aware of	o n	c **i-e** t	_____
Stars do this	i w n t	**le** k	_____
Allow	**er** p	t m i	_____

Support the child to read the clue on the left and work out what the word is.
Ask the child to say the answer word again in their head or with their 'thinking voice' and notice how they split up each word into two chunks of sounds, or syllables, as they say it.
The words have been split into two 'syllable boxes' but are not complete.
Ask the child to finish the word by writing in either the first or second syllable as required in the grey box.
Then ask the child to write out the word in full on the line at the end.
The first one is done for you as an example.

Activity 12 Syllable jigsaw　　　　　　i

Clue	1st syllable	2nd syllable	Word
Writing style	cur	sive	*cursive*
Set on fire		nite	
Teach		struct	
Way things work		tem	
e.g. water, milk		quid	
Mum's daughter		ter	
Excuse	for		
Word puzzle		ddle	
Females		men	

Activity 13 Spelling challenge

i

discuss	d i s / c u s s	*	*
divide	d i / v i d e	*	*
listen	l i / s t e n	*	*
insect	i n / s e c t	*	*
invent	i n / v e n t	*	*
notice	n o / t i c e	*	*
forgive	f o r / g i v e	*	*
system	s y s / t e m	*	*

Support the child to read each sentence one by one.
Ask the child to re-read the sentence, several times if necessary, and try to remember it.
Then cover the sentence and ask the child to recall the sentence verbally.
Once they can do this confidently, ask the child to write out the sentence from memory.
The child might find it helpful to think about the individual syllables in the words and say the sounds within each as they write. When the sentence is complete, the child reads out their sentence and then compares it to the original.

Break this task into smaller ones as necessary.

Alternatively, using text to speech software, the child could type the sentence, with the computer reading back each word and then the completed sentence.

Activity 14 Writing challenge   i

Instantly the litmus indicated acid.

The **boy** is **int**e**r**ested in insects.

I f**ou**nd a **cry**stal in the crypt.

We **used** the cyli**nd**e**r** in the **phy**sics lesson.

The **mass**ive notice **said** the **ser**vice was clo**s**ed.

Support the child to read the word on the left.

Then look at how the word has been split into three chunks of sounds, or syllables, as indicated by the asterisk * and red, blue and green colour coding.

Then ask the child to work through the word syllable by syllable, writing over each grey sound spelling and saying the corresponding sounds. At the end of each syllable the child says the chunk of sounds and at the end of the word the child says the whole word.

Cover the words and ask the child to write the word syllable by syllable and sound by sound on the three lines, saying the sounds as they write the corresponding sound spellings. The child can then check and correct the answer if necessary.

Finally, the child can write the whole word on the single line, but once again work syllable by syllable and sound by sound, saying the sounds as they write the corresponding sound spellings.

Remind the child to watch out for schwas which are highlighted and to take care with split sound spellings. The child could highlight any sound spellings that they think are tricky, to help them recall them when spelling.

Activity 15 Spelling 3 syllable words

difference	d i * ff er * ence	d i * ff er * ence	___ * ___ * ___
discover	d i s * c o * v er	d i s * c o * v er	___ * ___ * ___
objective	o b * j e c * t i v e	o b * j e c * t i v e	___ * ___ * ___
mystery	m y s * t er * y	m y s * t er * y	___ * ___ * ___
cylinder	c y l * i n * d er	c y l * i n * d er	___ * ___ * ___

Answers

Page 267
Activity 2 Thinking about the sound 'i'

y
crystal physics system
gymnast
i
limit kidnap insect children
invest intend kitten
i-e
active massive forgive
o
women

Page 272
Activity 5 Syllable split

in / sect	dis / cuss
no / tice	sis / ter
rhy / thm	in / vent
cri / cket	li / zard
li / sten	dis / tance
pi / ckle	
win / ter	
ma / ssive	
in / stead	
in / fect	
ser / vice	
its / elf	

Page 273
Activity 6 Join the syllables

rhythm
vixen
winter
active
igloo
lizard
cygnet
massive
insect
invite

Page 274
Activity 7 Match to a picture

lizard
children
vixen
fifteen
crystal
cricket

Page 275
Activity 8 Two syllable word tech

f in / g er
d i / nn er
a c / t i v e
c r y s / t al
per / s i s t
s er / v i c e
g y m / n a s t
in / v e s t
s c r i / bb le
s y s / t e m

Page 276
Activity 9 Syllable trap

a	mid
a	ssist
si	lly
for	give
in	stead
win	ter
dri	ven
con	sist

Page 277	Page 278	Page 279
Activity 10 Sounds like a syllable	**Activity 11 Two syllable anagrams**	**Activity 12 Syllable jigsaw**

Page 277

Activity 10 Sounds like a syllable

p er   m i t
k i   tt e n
a c   t i v e
s i s   t er
l i   st e n
p i c   n i c
c y g   n e t
m a   ss i v e
v i   s i t

Page 278

Activity 11 Two syllable anagrams

distance
inhale
rhythm
whisper
active
divide
vixen
forgive
insect
syrup
wisdom
instant
notice
twinkle
permit

Page 279

Activity 12 Syllable jigsaw

cur   sive
ig   nite
in   struct
sys   tem
li   quid
sis   ter
for   give
ri   ddle
wo   men

Words with an 'u-e' sound – word list of 2 syllable words

u	u-e	ue	ew
cubic	abuse	muesli	fewer
cuboid	accuse	pursue	pewter
dual	acute	revue	
duel	amuse		
duet	assume		
duty	commute		
fuel	compute		
futile	confuse		
humid	consume		
humour	dispute		
mucous	immune		
mucus	induce		
music	obtuse		
puny			
putrid			
stupid			
student			
Stuart			
tuba			
tuber			
tulip			
tunic			
tutor			
unique			
unit			
unite			

This activity results in the child rediscovering all the sound spellings for this sound in the context of 2 syllable words.

Support the child to read the words one by one. Ask the child to say the word again in their head or with their 'thinking voice' and notice how they split up each word into two chunks of sounds, or syllables, as they say it.

For each word support the child to work out the sound spelling corresponding to the sound 'u-e'.

Words are sorted into lists according to their 'u-e' sound spelling.

There are many sound spellings to find; some are less common than others: **u, u-e, ue** and **ew**.

Encourage the child to say each sound as they write each sound spelling in sequence, *syllable by syllable*, in this way:

e.g.

        sees: m   u   s i c

music

        says: 'm'>'u-e' = 'mu-e'   'z'>'i'>'k' = 'zik'   'mu-e>zik'   **'music'**

Remind the child to watch out for schwas!

Break this task into a number of shorter tasks over a number of lessons if necessary.

Activity 2 Thinking about the sound 'u-e'

music	amuse	cubic
compute	stupid	fewer
fewest	humour	pursue
student	consume	unit
muesli	tuna	immune

_____	_____
_____	_____
_____	_____
_____	_____
_____	_____

This set of cards is made up of 2 syllable words containing the sound 'u-e'. Copy onto card and cut out. Practise the dynamic blending – syllable by syllable reading strategy, as described in the 'Working through the programme' section, to read the words on these cards. Model this process for the child if necessary.

Activity 3 Sorting word cards	u-e
cubic	duty
music	student
unite	stupid
commute	confuse
accuse	amuse
muesli	pursue
fewer	pewter

Support the child to read each word. To help, the words have been split into two chunks of sounds, or syllables, as indicated by the asterisk *.

Direct the child to blend the sounds within the first syllable and say the syllable chunk, then blend the sounds within the second syllable and say the syllable chunk. Remind the child to watch out for schwas!

Finally push both syllable chunks together to hear the word forming.

e.g.

student

sees: s t u   d e n t

says: 's'>'t'>'u-e' = 'stu-e'   'd'>'e'>'n'>'t' = 'dent'   'stu-e>dent'   **'student'**

Activity 4 Reading 2 syllable words   u-e

student	s t u * d e n t
compute	c o m * p u t e
fewer	f ew * er
tuna	t u * n a
accuse	a * cc u s e
music	m u * s i c
pursue	p ur * s ue
consume	c o n * s u m e
duty	d u * t y
tulip	t u * l i p

Support the child to read the words one by one. Ask the child to say the word again in their head or with their 'thinking voice' and notice how they split up each word into two chunks of sounds, or syllables, as they say it.
For each word support the child to draw a line through the word to show where in the word they split it into two syllables.
It is useful to discuss how they made their choice. Remind the child to watch out for schwas!
The first group of words has some sound spellings highlighted to help, and the first one is split as an example.

Activity 5 Syllable split   u-e

con/sume   immune

few er   stupid

unite   muesli

amuse   compute

tutor   humid

Careful, the next ones do not have any sound spellings highlighted:

accuse

confuse

obtuse

humour

student

unit

tuna

Support the child to read the clue on the left and work out what the answer word is.

Ask the child to say the word again in their head or with their 'thinking voice' and notice how they split up each word into two chunks of sounds, or syllables, as they say it.

Ask the child to draw a line from the clue to the first syllable of the word and then go on to draw a line to the second syllable of the word.

Finally ask the child to write the whole word on the line at the end indicated by the arrow and read the word out loud.

Activity 6 Join the syllables   u-e

Clue	1st	2nd	→	Word
Mix up	s t u	t **or**	→	
Pupil	t u	f u s e	→	*confuse*
Teacher	c o n	m i d	→	
Songs and tunes	h u	d e n t	→	
Hot and wet	c o m	b **oi** d	→	
Make laugh	m u	m u s e	→	
Calculate	c u	p u t e	→	
Like a box	a	s i c	→	
One of a kind	c o n	n i **que**	→	
Eat	u	s u m e	→	

Ask the child to choose a picture and discuss what the matching word might be.

Then ask the child to think about how that word might be split into two syllables.

The child then finds the first syllable and then the second, drawing a line from picture to syllable to syllable.

The child then writes the complete word on one of the lines in the box at the bottom of the page.

Encourage the child to write the word using the sequential segmenting – syllable by syllable spelling strategy.

Activity 7 Match to a picture   u-e

mue

stu

com

tu

sli

lip

dent

pute

mu

tor

tu

sic

Support the child to read the words one by one. Ask the child to say the word again in their head or with their 'thinking voice' and notice how they split up the word into two chunks of sounds, or syllables, as they say it.
Then ask the child to show where they split the word up into two syllables by drawing a line through it.
Next ask the child to put a ring round each of the sound spellings.
Finally ask the child to highlight any schwas in the word.

Activity 8 Two syllable word tech   u-e

confuse

student

dispute

fewest

pursue

accuse

immune

tunic

puny

futile

Support the child to read the words one by one. Ask the child to say the word again in their head or with their 'thinking voice' and notice how they split up each word into two chunks of sounds, or syllables, as they say it. For each word, ask the child to work out where they split it into two syllables and then draw a line through the word.

Then ask the child to work out how many sounds there are in each syllable. They could write the number next to each syllable.

Support the child to look at the grid underneath and choose the row that contains the right number of lines in the first box (to match the number of sounds in the first syllable) and the right number of lines in the second box (to match the number of sounds in the second syllable). Ask the child to write the word in the grid on the chosen row, writing a sound spelling on each line.

An example is done to help you.

Activity 9 Syllable trap   u-e

2 sounds   2 sounds

tu|na   amuse

student   putrid

fewer   music

duty   stupid

___	___ ___ ___
___ ___	___
_t_ _u_	_n_ _a_
___ ___	___ ___
___ ___	___ ___ ___
___ ___	___ ___ ___
___ ___ ___	___ ___ ___
___ ___ ___	___ ___ ___

Support the child to read the clue on the left and work out what the word is.

Ask the child to say the word in their head or with their 'thinking voice' and notice how they split up each word into two chunks of sounds, or syllables, as they say it.

Support the child to write the first syllable, sound by sound, in the first boxes and the second syllable, sound by sound, in the second boxes, noticing that there is a box for each sound within the syllables.

Remind them to be careful with split sound spellings!

Then, covering the boxes, ask the child to write out the word from memory in the box at the end, thinking about the syllables and the sounds in them.

The first one is done for you as an example.

Activity 10 Sounds like a syllable   u-e

Clue	1st syllable			2nd syllable			Word
Breakfast cereal	m	ue		s	l	i	muesli
Hot and wet							
Eat							
Kind of fish							
Song for two people							
Songs and tunes							
Bring together							
Argument							
Kind of flower							

Support the child to read the clue on the left and work out what the answer word is.
The word has been split into two syllables and the sound spellings in each syllable have been mixed up.
Encourage the child to write the first syllable, sound by sound, then the second syllable, sound by sound, on the line on the right.
Ask the child to say the word.

Activity 11 Two syllable anagrams   u-e

Clue	1st syllable	2nd syllable	Word
Make someone laugh	a	s m **u-e**	_____
Kind of fish	u t	a n	_____
Even less	**ew** f	**er**	_____
Mix up	o n c	**u-e** s f	_____
Flower	u t	p l i	_____
Slime	u m	u s c	_____
Argument	s d i	t **u-e** p	_____
Songs and tunes	u m	i s c	_____
Run after	**ur** p	**ue** s	_____
Calculate	m c o	p t **u-e**	_____
One of a kind	u	i n **que**	_____
Take for granted	a	m **ss** **u-e**	_____
Teacher	u t	**or** t	_____
Pupil	u t s	n d t e	_____
Eat	c n o	**u-e** m s	_____

Support the child to read the clue on the left and work out what the word is.
Ask the child to say the answer word again in their head or with their 'thinking voice' and notice how they split up each word into two chunks of sounds, or syllables, as they say it.
The words have been split into two 'syllable boxes' but are not complete.
Ask the child to finish the word by writing in either the first or second syllable as required in the grey box.
Then ask the child to write out the word in full on the line at the end.
The first one is done for you as an example.

Activity 12 Syllable jigsaw   u-e

Clue	1st syllable	2nd syllable	Word
Travel to work	co	**mmute**	_commute_
Teacher		tor	_____
Brass instrument		ba	_____
One of a kind		nique	_____
Slime		cus	_____
Two people singing		et	_____
Mix up	con		_____
Even less		er	_____
Get together		nite	_____

Activity 13 Spelling challenge

u-e

music   mu/sic   *   *

student   stu/dent   *   *

tutor   tu/tor   *   *

accuse   a/cc use   *   *

amuse   a/muse   *   *

commute   co/mmute   *   *

compute   co/mpute   *   *

consume   con/sume   *   *

Support the child to read each sentence one by one.
Ask the child to re-read the sentence, several times if necessary, and try to remember it.
Then cover the sentence and ask the child to recall the sentence verbally.
Once they can do this confidently, ask the child to write out the sentence from memory.
The child might find it helpful to think about the individual syllables in the words and say the sounds within each as they write. When the sentence is complete, the child reads out their sentence and then compares it to the original.

Break this task into smaller ones as necessary.

Alternatively, using text to speech software, the child could type the sentence, with the computer reading back each word and then the completed sentence

Activity 14 Writing challenge   u-e

At m**u**seums we find **ou**t ab**ou**t h**u**man hist**or**y.

Us**u**ally p**u**mas don't **ea**t t**u**na.

She a**cc**u**s**ed him of ge**tt**ing h**er** conf**u**sed.

I cons**u**me h**u**ge am**ou**nts of wat**er**.

Support the child to read the word on the left.

Then look at how the word has been split into three chunks of sounds, or syllables, as indicated by the asterisk * and red, blue and green colour coding.

Then ask the child to work through the word syllable by syllable, writing over each grey sound spelling and saying the corresponding sounds. At the end of each syllable the child says the chunk of sounds and at the end of the word the child says the whole word.

Cover the words and ask the child to write the word syllable by syllable and sound by sound on the three lines, saying the sounds as they write the corresponding sound spellings. The child can then check and correct the answer if necessary.

Finally, the child can write the whole word on the single line, but once again work syllable by syllable and sound by sound, saying the sounds as they write the corresponding sound spellings.

Remind the child to watch out for schwas which are highlighted and to take care with split sound spellings. The child could highlight any sound spellings that they think are tricky, to help them recall them when spelling.

Activity 15 Spelling 3 syllable words

u-e

continue	con*tin*ue	con*tin*ue	___*___ ___*___
musical	mu*si*cal	mu*si*cal	___*___ ___*___
calculate	cal*cu*late	cal*cu*late	___*___ ___*___
argument	ar*gu*ment	ar*gu*ment	___*___ ___*___
gradual	gra*du*al	gra*du*al	___*___ ___*___

Answers

Page 286
Activity 2 Thinking about the sound 'u-e'

u
music cubic stupid humour
student unit tuna

u-e
amuse compute consume
immune

ew
fewer fewest

ue
pursue muesli

Page 290
Activity 5 Syllable split

con / sume   i / mmune
few / er   stu / pid
u / nite   mue /sli
a / muse   com / pute
tu / tor   hu / mid
a / ccuse
con / fuse
ob / tuse
hu / mour
stu / dent
u / nit
tu / na

Page 291
Activity 6 Join the syllables

tutor
confuse
humid
student
cuboid
amuse
compute
music
unique
consume

Page 292
Activity 7 Match to a picture

student
compute
muesli
tutor
music
tulip

Page 293
Activity 8 Two syllable word tech

con / f u s e
stu / d e n t
dis / p u t e
few / e s t
pur / s ue
a / cc u s e
i / mm u n e
tu / n i c
pu / n y
fu / t i l e

Page 294
Activity 9 Syllable trap

a   m u s e
few   er
tu   n a
m u   s i c
p u   t r i d
stu   p i d
stu   d e n t

Page 295	Page 296	Page 297
Activity 10 Sounds like a syllable	**Activity 11 Two syllable anagrams**	**Activity 12 Syllable jigsaw**

Page 295

Activity 10 Sounds like a syllable

m ue	s l i
h u	m i d
c o n	s u m e
t u	n a
d u	e t
m u	s i c
u	n i t e
d i s	p u t e
t u	l i p

Page 296

Activity 11 Two syllable anagrams

amuse
tuna
fewer
confuse
tulip
mucus
dispute
music
pursue
compute
unique
assume
tutor
student
consume

Page 297

Activity 12 Syllable jigsaw

co	mmute
tu	tor
tu	ba
u	nique
mu	cus
du	et
con	fuse
few	er
u	nite
du	ty

PART 2

Teacher word list　　　Set 1: 3 syllable words

Simple sound to sound spelling relationship without a schwa

abacus
abolish
astonish
bonanza
Celsius
cinema
concentric
contradict
difficult
discontent
discredit
disinfect
finishing
habitat
handicraft
historic
italic
indirect
indistinct
inhabit

insulting
intrepid
Islamic
kinetic
limiting
lollipop
melodic
origin
platinum
plentiful
stamina
statistics
tetanus
unhelpful

This set of cards is made up of 3 syllable words. The syllables are indicated by an asterisk to aid reading. Copy onto card and cut out. Practise the dynamic blending – syllable by syllable reading strategy, as described in the 'Working through the programme' section, to read the words on these cards.

Activity 1 Reading 3 syllable words highlighted	Multisyllable set 1

a * bo * lish
con * tra * dict
ha * bi * tat
in * tre * pid
un * help * ful
fi * ni * shing
lo * lli * pop
pla * ti * num

This set of cards is made up of 3 syllable words. Copy onto card and cut out.
Practise the dynamic blending – syllable by syllable reading strategy, as described in the 'Working through the programme' section, to read the words on these cards.

Activity 1 Reading 3 syllable words	Multisyllable set 1

cinema
inhabit
indirect
insulting
melodic
origin
historic
Islamic

Support the child to read the words one by one.

Ask the child to say the word again in their head or with their 'thinking voice' and notice how they split up each word into three chunks of sounds, or syllables, as they say it.

For each word support the child to draw two lines through the word to show where in the word they split it into three syllables.

It is useful to discuss how they made their choice.

The first group of words has some sound spellings highlighted to help, and the first one is split as an example.

Activity 2 Syllable split	Multisyllable set 1
dis/in/fect	cinema
limiti**ng**	melodic
fini**sh**i**ng**	historic
origin	lo**ll**ipop
platinum	aboli**sh**

Careful, the next ones do not have any sound spellings highlighted:

insulting

difficult

Celsius

Islamic

plentiful

unhelpful

italic

Support the child to read the word.
Ask the child to say the word again in their head or with their 'thinking voice' and notice how they split up the word into three chunks of sounds, or syllables, as they say it.
Ask the child to show where they split the word up into three syllables by drawing two lines through it.
Next ask the child to put a ring round each sound spelling.
Finally ask the child to identify any schwas by highlighting them.
The word is written twice so that the child can refer to an uncluttered version of the word.

Activity 3 Advanced word tech	Multisyllable set 1

astonish   astonish

difficult   difficult

contradict   contradict

disinfect   disinfect

lollipop   lollipop

origin   origin

finishing   finishing

unhelpful   unhelpful

statistics   statistics

Ask the child to look at the word strings, each of which contains lots of words written with no gaps between.
Ask the child to track through the string and read each word.
At the end of the string the child writes down how many words are in that string.
Note that strings are written in a variety of styles.

Activity 4 Word strings	Multisyllable set 1

abolishcinemalimitingdifficultlollipop

disinfecthistoricinhabitplentifulinsulting

finishinghabitatastonish

contradictstaminaitalicdiscredit

Support the child to read the words by giving information about sounds, supporting blending and syllable splitting, but do not supply the whole word.

Count how many words the child can read in one minute and record on the sheet. Repeat at a later time and see if the child can beat their own record.

Activity 5 Speeding fine   Multisyllable set 1

- ☐ difficult
- ☐ finishing
- ☐ habitat
- ☐ finishing
- ☐ historic
- ☐ inhabit
- ☐ lollipop
- ☐ limiting
- ☐ platinum
- ☐ plentiful
- ☐ unhelpful
- ☐ disinfect
- ☐ stamina
- ☐ melodic
- ☐ discontent
- ☐ handicraft
- ☐ italic
- ☐ indirect
- ☐ intrepid

Number of words:

1.

2.

3.

Support the child to read the words one by one. Ask the child to say the word again in their head or with their 'thinking voice' and notice how they split up each word into three chunks of sounds, or syllables, as they say it. For each word, ask the child to work out where they split it into three syllables and draw lines through the word.

Then ask the child to work out how many sounds there are in each syllable. They could write the number next to each syllable.

Support the child to look at the grid underneath and choose the row that contains the right number of lines which match the number of sounds in the first syllable, the right number in the second syllable and the right number in the third syllable.

Ask the child to write the word in the grid, trapping the words, by writing the words in the boxes on the row that has the matching number of sounds in each syllable. Remind the child to think carefully about any split sound spellings.

An example is done to help you.

Activity 6 Syllable trap   Multisyllable set 1

2 sounds	2 sounds	3 sounds

in\ha\bit   historic

abacus   intrepid

plentiful   astonish

indistinct   contradict

—	— —	— — —
—	— — —	— — —
i n	*h a*	*b i t*
— —	— —	— — —
— —	— —	— — — — —
— — —	— —	— — —
— — —	— —	— — —
— — — —	— — —	— — —

Support the child to read these nonsense words, thinking about sound spellings and sounds and applying the dynamic blending strategy sequentially syllable by syllable.

These words follow the orthography of English, that is the conventions for spelling and writing, so all of these words *could* be genuine!

It is good to point out to the child that if they can read these, they can read anything!

Activity 7 Nonsense word fun   Multisyllable set 1

inslumping

condripic

antropod

ondrostic

mostican

merriac

discomfect

tripandin

stundifact

Support the child to read the clue on the left and work out what the word is. To help the child, two of the syllables have been written in.
Ask the child to say the word in their head or with their 'thinking voice' and notice how they split up each word into three chunks of sounds, or syllables, as they say it.
Support the child to write in the missing syllable, sound by sound, in the appropriate box.
Then, covering the boxes, ask the child to write out the word from memory on the line at the end, thinking about the syllables and the sounds in them.

Activity 8 Syllable jigsaw

Multisyllable set 1

Clue	Box 1	Box 2	Box 3	Word
	a	*sto*	nish	*astonish*
Amaze	a			___
Not giving assistance	in	help	ful	___
Very brave			pid	___
Precious metal	pla		num	___
Opposing ideas		tra	dict	___
Place to see films		ne	ma	___
Clean thoroughly	dis	in		___

Support the child to read the words in the box on the left. This is the definition of a word.
Then ask the child to choose which of the words in the box on the right is the accepted spelling of the word, and tick to indicate.

Activity 9 Meaning & spelling   Multisyllable set 1

Definition	Which is the accepted spelling?	Tick
To say something is true and then say the opposite, as if that is true also	contradict	
	contradyct	
This describes something that is not easy to do or is hard to understand	dificult	
	difficult	
Describes someone who is brave and fearless	intrepid	
	intreppid	
The natural place an animal can be found in; it's usual home	habitat	
	habbitat	

Support the child to read each word. To help, the words have been split into three chunks of sounds, or syllables, as indicated by the asterisk * and red, blue and green colour coding.

Direct the child to blend the sounds within the first syllable and say the syllable chunk, then blend the sounds within the second syllable and say the syllable chunk and finally blend the sounds within the third syllable and say the syllable chunk.

Finally push the three syllable chunks together to hear the word forming.

At this stage in the programme the child may be meeting vocabulary which is unfamiliar, so discuss meaning, as appropriate.

Once the child has read the word, then they can write it on the lines.

For each syllable, encourage the child to say each sound as they write the matching sound spelling and blend the sounds together at the end of each chunk as well as the complete word at the end.

Activity 10 Spelling challenge

Multisyllable set 1

historic	h i * s t o * r i c	_____ *	_____ *
difficult	d i * f f i * c u l t	_____ *	_____ *
indirect	i n * d i * r e c t	_____ *	_____ *
lollipop	l o * l l i * p o p	_____ *	_____ *
unhelpful	u n * h e l p * f u l	_____ *	_____ *

Answers   Multisyllable set 1

Page 307
Activity 2 Syllable split

dis/in/fect   ci/ne/ma
li/mi/ting   me/lo/dic
fi/ni/shing   hi/sto/ric
o/ri/gin   lo/lli/pop
pla/ti/num   a/bo/lish
in/sul/ting
di/ffi/cult
Cel/si/us
Is/la/mic
plen/ti/ful
un/help/ful
i/tal/ic

Page 308
Activity 3 Advanced word tech

di/ffi/cult
con/tra/dict
dis/in/fect
lo/lli/pop
o/ri/gin
fi/ni/shing
un/help/ful
sta/tis/tics

Page 309
Activity 4 Word strings

abolish cinema limiting difficult lollipop

disinfect historic inhabit plentiful insulting

finishing habitat astonish

contradict stamina italic discredit

Page 311
Activity 6 Syllable trap

a/ba/cus
a/sto/nish
in/ha/bit
in/tre/pid
in/dis/tinct
his/to/ric
con/tra/dict
plen/ti/ful

Page 313
Activity 8 Syllable jigsaw

a / sto / nish
un / help / ful
in / tre / pid
pla / ti / num
con / tra / dict
ci / ne / ma
dis / in / fect

Page 314
Activity 9 Meaning & spelling

contradict

difficult

intrepid

habitat

Teacher word list   Set 2: 3 syllable words
Simple sound to sound spelling relationship with schwas

abandon	limited
addicted	luckiest
Africa	obstructed
anagram	optimist
attended	pelican
badminton	penniless
cabinet	pessimist
caravan	politics
confident	profiting
continent	prominent
consistent	punishment
corrected	recollect
derelict	recommend
diminish	sediment
dominant	silicon
embarrass	suspected
emptiness	ugliest
existed	ugliness
expectant	unfinished
expected	vanilla
extended	visited
gorilla	vitamin
incorrect	
indented	
insisted	
invented	

This set of cards is made up of 3 syllable words. The syllables are indicated by an asterisk to aid reading. Copy onto card and cut out. Practise the dynamic blending – syllable by syllable reading strategy, as described in the 'Working through the programme' section, to read the words on these cards.

Activity 1 Reading 3 syllable words highlighted	Multisyllable set 2

a * b a n * d o n
c o n * s i s * t e n t
e m p * t i * n e s s
i n * c o * r r e c t
u n * f i * n i sh ed
c a * r a * v a n
l u * c k i * e s t
e x * p e c * t e d

This set of cards is made up of 3 syllable words. Copy onto card and cut out.
Practise the dynamic blending – syllable by syllable reading strategy as described in the 'Working through the programme' section, to read the words on these cards.

Activity 1 Reading 3 syllable words	Multisyllable set 2

attended
insisted
embarrass
invented
suspected
vitamin
recommend
visited

Support the child to read the words one by one.

Ask the child to say the word again in their head or with their 'thinking voice' and notice how they split up each word into three chunks of sounds, or syllables, as they say it.

For each word support the child to draw two lines through the word to show where in the word they split it into three syllables.

It is useful to discuss how they made their choice.

The first group of words some sound spellings highlighted to help, and the first one is split as an example.

Activity 2 Syllable split	Multisyllable set 2

c a / b i / n e t   v a n i ll a

e x i s t e d   s u s p e c t e d

c o n f i d e n t   i n s i s t e d

d o m i n a n t   e m b a **rr** a **ss**

g o r i ll a   b a d m i n t o n

Careful, the next ones do not have any sound spellings highlighted:

emptiness

derelict

anagram

Africa

punishment

recommend

incorrect

Support the child to read a word. Ask the child to say the word again in their head or with their 'thinking voice' and notice how they split up the word into three chunks of sounds, or syllables, as they say it.

Ask the child to show where they split the word up into three syllables by drawing two lines through it.

Next ask the child to put a ring round each sound spelling.

Finally ask the child to identify any schwas by highlighting them.

The word is written twice so that the child can refer to an uncluttered version of the word.

Activity 3 Advanced word tech	**Multisyllable set 2**

embarrass

vitamin

expected

penniless

confident

caravan

attended

corrected

visited

Ask the child to look at the word strings, each of which contains lots of words written with no gaps between.

Ask the child to track through the string and read each word.

At the end of the string the child writes down how many words are in that string.

Note that strings are written in a variety of styles.

| **Activity 4 Word strings** | **Multisyllable set 2** |

visitedgorillabadmintonpelicancaravan

embarrassvitaminafricanvanilla

abandonrecommendinvented

luckiestsuspectedexpectedpunishment

Support the child to read the words by giving information about sounds, supporting blending and syllable splitting but do not supply the whole word.

Count how many words the child can read in one minute and record on the sheet. Repeat at a later time and see if the child can beat their own record.

Activity 5 Speeding fine	Multisyllable set 2

☐ African
☐ confident
☐ vitamin
☐ invented
☐ luckiest
☐ embarrass
☐ visited
☐ suspected
☐ recommend
☐ politics
☐ punishment
☐ consistent
☐ badminton
☐ caravan
☐ abandon
☐ incorrect
☐ gorilla
☐ expected
☐ unfinished

Number of words:

1.

2.

3.

323

Support the child to read the words one by one. Ask the child to say the word again in their head or with their 'thinking voice' and notice how they split up each word into three chunks of sounds, or syllables, as they say it. Remind the child to watch out for schwas!

For each word, ask the child to work out where they split it into three syllables and draw lines through the word.

Then ask the child to work out how many sounds there are in each syllable. They could write the number next to each syllable.

Support the child to look at the grid underneath and choose the row that contains the right number of lines which match the number of sounds in the first syllable, the right number in the second syllable and the right number in the third syllable.

Ask the child to write the word in the grid, trapping the words, by writing the words in the boxes on the row that has the matching number of sounds in each syllable. Remind the child to think carefully about any split sound spellings.

Activity 6 Syllable trap   Multisyllable set 2

2 sounds   3 sounds
em\ba\rrass   punishment
2 sounds

confident   abandon

insisted   vanilla

anagram   consistent

—	— — —	— — —
— — —	—	— — — — —
— — —	— —	— — —
— — —	— — —	— — —
— — —	— — —	— — —
— — —	— — —	— — — —
— — — —	— — —	— — — —
— — — —	— — —	— — — —

Support the child to read these nonsense words, thinking about sound spellings and sounds and applying the dynamic blending strategy sequentially syllable by syllable. Remind the child to think about schwas!
These words follow the orthography of English, that is the conventions for spelling and writing, so all of these words *could* be genuine!
It is good to point out to the child that if they can read these, they can read anything!

Activity 7 Nonsense word fun	Multisyllable set 2

mantrickle

drangustle

zonilla

birrected

inbrifted

bonibet

opliest

allended

havishment

Support the child to read the clue on the left and work out what the word is. To help the child, two of the syllables have been written in.

Ask the child to say the word in their head or with their 'thinking voice' and notice how they split up each word into three chunks of sounds, or syllables, as they say it.

Support the child to write in the missing syllable, sound by sound, in the appropriate box.

Then, covering the boxes, ask the child to write out the word from memory on the line at the end, thinking about the syllables and the sounds in them.

Activity 8 Syllable jigsaw   Multisyllable set 2

Clue				Word
Become smaller	di	*min*	nish	*diminish*
Self assured	con	fi		
Wrong	in		rrect	
Went to see	si	ted		
A continent	A	ca		
Tell friends about something	re	co		
Leave all alone	a	ban		

Support the child to read the words in the box on the left. This is the definition of a word.
Then ask the child to choose which of the words in the box on the right is the accepted spelling of the word,
and tick to indicate.

Activity 9 Meaning & spelling   Multisyllable set 2

Definition	Which is the accepted spelling?	Tick
To say something or someone is good and worthy of mention	recomend	
	recommend	
To make something smaller	diminish	
	dimminish	
To make someone feel ashamed or uncomfortable	embarass	
	embarrass	
To be sure of yourself and be certain of your abilities	confident	
	confidant	

Support the child to read each word. To help, the words have been split into three chunks of sounds, or syllables, as indicated by the asterisk * and red, blue and green colour coding.

Direct the child to blend the sounds within the first syllable and say the syllable chunk, then blend the sounds within the second syllable and say the syllable chunk and finally blend the sounds within the third syllable and say the syllable chunk.

Finally push the three syllable chunks together to hear the word forming.

At this stage in the programme the child may be meeting vocabulary which is unfamiliar, so discuss meaning, as appropriate.

Once the child has read the word, then they can write it on the lines.

For each syllable, encourage the child to say each sound as they write the matching sound spelling and blend the sounds together at the end of each chunk as well as the complete word at the end.

Activity 10 Spelling challenge

Multisyllable set 2

abandon	a * b a n * d o n	_____ * _____	_____ * _____
confident	c o n * f i * d e n t	_____ * _____	_____ * _____
incorrect	i n * c o * rr e c t	_____ * _____	_____ * _____
embarrass	e m * b a * rr a ss	_____ * _____	_____ * _____
recommend	r e * c o * mm e n d	_____ * _____	_____ * _____

Answers

Page 320
Activity 2 Syllable split

ca / bi / net
ex / is / ted
con / fi / dent
do / mi / nant
go / ri / lla
emp / ti / ness
de / re / lict
a / na / gram
A / fri / ca
pu / nish / ment
re / co / mmend
in / co / rrect

va / ni / lla
su / spec / ted
in / sis / ted
em / ba / rrass
bad / min / ton

Page 321
Activity 3 Advanced word tech

vi / ta / min
ex / pec / ted
pe / nni / less
con / fi / dent
ca / ra / van
a / tten / ded
co / rrec / ted
vi / si / ted

Page 322
Activity 4 Word strings

visited gorilla badminton pelican caravan

embarrass vitamin African vanilla

abandon recommend invented

luckiest suspected expected punishment

Page 324
Activity 6 Syllable trap

a / ban / don
an / a / gram
va / ni / lla
em / bar / rass
in / sis / ted
pu / nish / ment
con / fi / dent
con / sis / tent

Page 326
Activity 8 Syllable jigsaw

di / min / ish
con / fi / dent
in / co / rrect
vi / si / ted
A / fri / ca
re / co / mmend
a / ban / don

Page 327
Activity 9 Meaning & spelling

recommend

diminish

embarrass

confident

Teacher word list
Advanced sound to sound spelling relationships with schwas

Set 3: 3 syllable words

abundance	commitment	envelope	loneliness	progressing
advantage	computer	equator	magnify	prosecute
activate	concealing	equipment	mechanic	publicly
aggravate	concerning	escalate	microscope	quality
altitude	consider	escapade	monument	quantity
amendment	container	establish	motivate	radiate
animate	contemplate	example	multiple	rectify
antidote	continue	external	multiply	reflective
apparent	cordial	family	musical	refreshment
appendix	cranberry	fellowship	narrator	register
aqueous	cucumber	follower	navigate	reinforce
argument	cylinder	following	nitrogen	relative
attitude	defeated	friendliness	nursery	reluctant
audience	deliver	gallery	observer	remainder
bakery	dependent	gigantic	obstacle	remember
beautiful	deposit	gossiping	obstinate	revolving
bountiful	descending	gradual	occupy	separate
calculate	desperate	happening	occurrence	simplify
capital	detaining	happiness	operate	soluble
carefully	detective	hesitate	organise	suddenly
cardinal	devouring	horrible	overdraft	symbolic
carnival	diagram	hospital	overflow	tablecloth
carpenter	different	included	oxygen	telescope
catalogue	diploma	incomplete	particle	terrible
celebrate	disgusting	increasing	poisonous	tournament
centigrade	document	imitate	possible	tropical
certainly	elastic	immobile	potato	uneasy
champion	elephant	imploring	potatoes	unpleasant
character	elevate	injury	president	various
cheerfully	ellipsoid	innocent	principal	vegetable
chemistry	emulate	irrigate	principle	verify
chimpanzee	enjoyment	institute	prisoner	virtual
citizen	enormous	internal	professor	wonderful

This set of cards is made up of 3 syllable words. The syllables are indicated by an asterisk to aid reading. Copy onto card and cut out. Practise the dynamic blending – syllable by syllable reading strategy, as described in the 'Working through the programme' section, to read the words on these cards.

Activity 1 Reading 3 syllable words highlighted	Multisyllable set 3

c o n * s i * d e r
f a * m i * l y
s u * d d e n * l y
d e s * p e r * a t e
s e * p a r * a t e
r e * m e m * b e r
e * n o r * m o u s
b e a u * t i * f u l

This set of cards is made up of 3 syllable words. Copy onto card and cut out.
Practise the dynamic blending – syllable by syllable reading strategy, as described in the 'Working through the programme' section, to read the words on these cards.

Activity 1 Reading 3 syllable words	**Multisyllable set 3**

audience
narrator
happening
example
celebrate
incomplete
computer
consider

Support the child to read the words one by one.
Ask the child to say the word again in their head or with their 'thinking voice' and notice how they split up each word into three chunks of sounds or syllables as they say it.
For each word support the child to draw two lines through the word to show where in the word they split it into three syllables.
It is useful to discuss how they made their choice.
The first group of words has some sound spellings highlighted to help, and the first one is split as an example.

Activity 2 Syllable split   Multisyllable set 3

d e s/p **er**/**a** t e   i n c l u d e d

a c t i v a t e   r e m e m b **er**

r e g i s t **er**   **ch** a r a c t **er**

d e l i v **er**   c **er** t a i n l y

s u **dd** e n l y   m i c r o s c **o** p e

Careful, the next ones do not have any sound spellings highlighted:

chimpanzee

equipment

reluctant

wonderful

reinforce

different

president

Support the child to read a word. Ask the child to say the word again in their head or with their 'thinking voice' and notice how they split up the word into three chunks of sounds, or syllables, as they say it.

Ask the child to show where they split the word up into three syllables by drawing two lines through it.

Next ask the child to put a ring round each sound spelling.

Finally ask the child to identify any schwas by highlighting them.

The word is written twice so that the child can refer to an uncluttered version of the word.

Activity 3 Advanced word tech	Multisyllable set 3

different	d i ff er ent
audience	audience
reluctant	reluctant
diagram	diagram
enjoyment	enjoyment
organise	organise
simplify	simplify
computer	computer
deliver	deliver

Ask the child to look at the word strings, each of which contains lots of words written with no gaps between.
Ask the child to track through the string and read each word.
At the end of the string the child writes down how many words are in that string.
Note that strings are written in a variety of styles.

Activity 4 Word strings	Multisyllable set 3

registercitizenmultiplyvegetablebakery

enormouscarefullymicroscopesuddenly

considercapitalattitudeexampleuneasy

familyrefreshmentbeautiful

Support the child to read the words by giving information about sounds, supporting blending and syllable splitting, but do not supply the whole word.

Count how many words the child can read in one minute and record on the sheet. Repeat at a later time and see if the child can beat their own record.

Activity 5 Speeding fine   Multisyllable set 3

☐ desperate
☐ increasing
☐ celebrate
☐ remember
☐ reinforce
☐ argument
☐ reluctant
☐ gradual
☐ wonderful
☐ vegetable
☐ narrator
☐ chemistry
☐ concerning
☐ friendliness
☐ contemplate
☐ advantage
☐ professor
☐ relative
☐ separate

Number of words:

1.

2.

3.

Support the child to read the words one by one. Ask the child to say the word again in their head or with their 'thinking voice' and notice how they split up each word into three chunks of sounds, or syllables, as they say it. Remind the child to watch out for schwas!

For each word, ask the child to work out where they split it into three syllables and draw lines through the word.

Then ask the child to work out how many sounds there are in each syllable. They could write the number next to each syllable.

Support the child to look at the grid underneath and choose the row that contains the right number of lines which match the number of sounds in the first syllable, the right number in the second syllable and the right number in the third syllable.

Ask the child to write the word in the grid, trapping the words, by writing the words in the boxes on the row that has the matching number of sounds in each syllable. Remind the child to think carefully about any split sound spellings.

Activity 6 Syllable trap   Multisyllable set 3

2 sounds 2 sounds 2 sounds
de\li\ver   elastic

remember   nitrogen

chimpanzee   computer

enjoyment   overflow

—	— —	— — —
—	— —	— — — — —
— —	— —	— —
— —	— —	— —
— —	— — —	— —
— —	— — —	— — —
— — —	— —	— —
— — —	— —	— —

Support the child to read these nonsense words, thinking about sound spellings and sounds and applying the dynamic blending strategy sequentially syllable by syllable. Remind the child to think about schwas!

These words follow the orthography of English, that is the conventions for spelling and writing, so all of these words *could* be genuine!

It is good to point out to the child that if they can read these, they can read anything!

Activity 7 Nonsense word fun   Multisyllable set 3

blindering

shamperly

convorcing

inflaunting

enflibbing

plutterly

moscurdling

conflounder

dismulching

Support the child to read the clue on the left and work out what the word is. To help the child, two of the syllables have been written in.
Ask the child to say the word in their head or with their 'thinking voice' and notice how they split up each word into three chunks of sounds, or syllables, as they say it.
Support the child to write in the missing syllable, sound by sound, in the appropriate box.
Then, covering the boxes, ask the child to write out the word from memory on the line at the end, thinking about the syllables and the sounds in them.

Multisyllable set 3

Activity 8 Syllable jigsaw

Clue				Word
Do sums	cal		late	_____
Root vegetable	po	ta		_____
Not the same	di		ent	_____
Think about		si	der	_____
Make things easier	sim	pli		_____
Use to see the stars	te	le		_____
Beaten		fea	ted	_____

Support the child to read the words in the box on the left. This is the definition of a word.
Then ask the child to choose which of the words in the box on the right is the accepted spelling of the word, and tick to indicate.

Activity 9 Meaning & spelling   Multisyllable set 3

Definition	Which is the accepted spelling?	Tick
Not the same	different	
	diffrent	
A person's manner and being	atitude	
	attitude	
To keep apart or divide	separate	
	seperate	
To have an urgent need to do something	desparate	
	desperate	

Support the child to read each word. To help, the words have been split into three chunks of sounds, or syllables, as indicated by the asterisk * and red, blue and green colour coding.

Direct the child to blend the sounds within the first syllable and say the syllable chunk, then blend the sounds within the second syllable and say the syllable chunk and finally blend the sounds within the third syllable and say the syllable chunk.

Finally push the three syllable chunks together to hear the word forming.

At this stage in the programme the child may be meeting vocabulary which is unfamiliar, so discuss meaning, as appropriate.

Once the child has read the word, then they can write it on the lines.

For each syllable, encourage the child to say each sound as they write the matching sound spelling and blend the sounds together at the end of each chunk as well as the complete word at the end.

Activity 10 Spelling challenge

Multisyllable set 3

consider	con * si * d er	_____ * _____ * _____
remember	re * mem * ber	_____ * _____ * _____
included	in * co * rrect	_____ * _____ * _____
family	fa * mi * ly	_____ * _____ * _____
organise	or * ga * nise	_____ * _____ * _____

Answers   Multisyllable set 3

Page 333
Activity 2 Syllable split

des / per / ate   in / clu / ded
ac / ti / vate   re / mem / ber
re / gi / ster   cha / rac / ter
de / li / ver   cer / tain / ly
su / dden / ly   mi / cro / scope
chim / pan / zee
e / quip / ment
re / luc / tant
won / der / ful
re / in / force
di / ffer / ent
pre / si / dent

Page 334
Activity 3 Advanced word tech

au / di / en ce
re / luc / tant
di / a / gram
en / joy / ment
or / ga / nise
sim / pli / fy
com / pu / ter
de / li / v er

Page 335
Activity 4 Word strings

register citizen multiply
vegetable bakery

enormous carefully
microscope suddenly

consider capital attitude
example uneasy

family refreshment beautiful

Page 337
Activity 6 Syllable trap

o / v er / flow
e / la / stic
de / li / v er
en / joy / ment
re / mem / ber
ni / tro / gen
com / pu / ter
chim / pan / zee

Page 339
Activity 8 Syllable jigsaw

cal / cu / late
po / ta / to
di / ffer / ent
con / si / der
sim / pli / fy
te / le / scope
de / fea / ted

Page 340
Activity 9 Meaning & spelling

different

attitude

separate

desperate

Teacher word list   set 4: 4 syllable words
Advanced sound to sound spelling relationships with schwas

ability

accommodate

accompany

activity

administer

advertisement

alternative

anticipate

bacteria

believable

binoculars

biology

calculator

caterpillar

certificate

communicate

community

curriculum

disappointment

discovery

emergency

environment

experiment

identify

identity

independent

ingredient

investigate

material

occupancy

participate

recovery

secretary

security

significance

society

stability

technology

territory

uncertainty

understanding

variable

variety

This set of cards is made up of 4 syllable words. The syllables are indicated by an asterisk to aid reading. Copy onto card and cut out. Practise the dynamic blending – syllable by syllable reading strategy, as described in the 'Working through the programme' section, to read the words on these cards.

Activity 1 Reading 4 syllable words highlighted	Multisyllable Set 4

a * b i * l i * t y
d i s * c o * v e r * y
e * m e r * g e n * c y
e x * p e * r i * m e n t
i n * g r e * d i * e n t
t e c h * n o * l o * g y
i * d e n * t i * f y
a * c c o * m m o * d a t e

This set of cards is made up of 4 syllable words. Copy onto card and cut out.
Practise the dynamic blending – syllable by syllable reading strategy, as described in the 'Working through the programme' section, to read the words on these cards.

Activity 1 Reading 4 syllable words	Multisyllable Set 4

bacteria
certificate
independent
understanding
society
activity
communicate
calculator

Support the child to read the words one by one.

Ask the child to say the word again in their head or with their 'thinking voice' and notice how they split up each word into three chunks of sounds or syllables as they say it.

For each word support the child to draw two lines through the word to show where in the word they split it into three syllables.

It is useful to discuss how they made their choice.

The first group of words has some sound spellings highlighted to help, and the first one is split as an example.

Activity 2 Syllable split	Multisyllable set 4

c a l/c u/l a/t **or**   i d e n t i f y

a **cc** o **mm** o d a t e   i n d e p e n d e n t

a n t i c i p **a** t **e**   b e l **ie** v a b **le**

e x p e r i m e n t   e m **er** g e n c y

d i s c o v **er** y   u n d **er** s t a n d i **ng**

Careful, the next ones do not have any sound spellings highlighted:

disappointment

ingredient

biology

administer

variety

significance

technology

Support the child to read a word. Ask the child to say the word again in their head or with their 'thinking voice' and notice how they split up the word into four chunks of sounds, or syllables, as they say it.

Ask the child to show where they split the word up into four syllables by drawing three lines through it.

Next ask the child to put a ring round each sound spelling.

Finally ask the child to identify any schwas by highlighting them.

The word is written twice so that the child can refer to an uncluttered version of the word.

Activity 3 Advanced word tech   Multisyllable set 4

certificate   certificate

accommodate   accommodate

caterpillar   caterpillar

recovery   recovery

identify   identify

ability   ability

experiment   experiment

Ask the child to look at the word strings, each of which contains lots of words written with no gaps between.
Ask the child to track through the string and read each word.
At the end of the string the child writes down how many words are in that string.
Note that strings are written in a variety of styles.

Activity 4 Word strings	Multisyllable set 4

abilityemergencyingredienttechnologybiology

activitycertificatecommunicate

understandingexperimentindependent

recoveryidentifystability

Support the child to read the words by giving information about sounds, supporting blending and syllable splitting, but do not supply the whole word.

Count how many words the child can read in one minute and record on the sheet. Repeat at a later time and see if the child can beat their own record.

Activity 5 Speeding fine   Multisyllable set 4

- ☐ ability
- ☐ understanding
- ☐ investigate
- ☐ disappointment
- ☐ alternative
- ☐ community
- ☐ material
- ☐ security
- ☐ variety
- ☐ ingredient
- ☐ bacteria
- ☐ binoculars
- ☐ participate
- ☐ emergency
- ☐ curriculum
- ☐ technology
- ☐ significance
- ☐ accommodate
- ☐ advertisement

Number of words:

1.

2.

3.

Support the child to read the words one by one. Ask the child to say the word again in their head or with their 'thinking voice' and notice how they split up each word into four chunks of sounds, or syllables, as they say it. Remind the child to watch out for schwas!

For each word, ask the child to work out where they split it into four syllables and draw lines through the word. Then ask the child to work out how many sounds there are in each syllable. They could write the number next to each syllable.

Support the child to look at the grid underneath and choose the row that contains the right number of lines which match the number of sounds in the first syllable, the right number in the second syllable and so on. Ask the child to write the word in the grid, trapping the words, by writing the words in the boxes on the row that has the matching number of sounds in each syllable. Remind the child to think carefully about any split sound spellings.

Activity 6 Syllable trap			Multisyllable set 4

2 sounds an\ti\ci\pate 3 sounds
2
2

discovery

believable

understanding

independent

accommodate

identify

stability

Support the child to read these nonsense words, thinking about sound spellings and sounds and applying the dynamic blending strategy sequentially syllable by syllable. Remind the child to think about schwas!
These words follow the orthography of English, that is the conventions for spelling and writing, so all of these words *could* be genuine!
It is good to point out to the child that if they can read these, they can read anything!

Activity 7 Nonsense word fun	Multisyllable set 4

disimpartent

indobnity

reglovering

occimpancy

pymology

elathative

emarnancy

carditory

sprondanticle

Support the child to read the clue on the left and work out what the word is. To help the child, two of the syllables have been written in.

Ask the child to say the word in their head or with their 'thinking voice' and notice how they split up each word into four chunks of sounds, or syllables, as they say it.

Support the child to write in the missing syllables, sound by sound, in the appropriate boxes.

Then, covering the boxes, ask the child to write out the word from memory on the line at the end, thinking about the syllables and the sounds in them.

Activity 8 Syllable jigsaw   Multisyllable set 4

Clue					
Does sums for you	cal		la		_____
Look into e.g. crime		ve	sti		_____
Talk to each other	co			cate	_____
Call 999!		mer		cy	_____
Local residents	co	mu			_____
Turns into a butterfly			pi	llar	_____
Computers and phones		no		gy	_____

Support the child to read the words in the box on the left. This is the definition of a word.
Then ask the child to choose which of the words in the box on the right is the accepted spelling of the word, and tick to indicate.

Activity 9 Meaning & spelling   Multisyllable set 4

Definition	Which is the accepted spelling?	Tick
Paper qualification	certificat	
	certificate	
Confident that something is true	beleivable	
	believable	
A machine that does sums for you	calculator	
	calculater	
A test or trial of something	experiment	
	experimunt	

Support the child to read each word. To help, the words have been split into four chunks of sounds, or syllables, as indicated by the asterisk * and red, blue, green and purple colour coding.

Direct the child to blend the sounds within the first syllable and say the syllable chunk, then blend the sounds within the second syllable and say the syllable chunk and finally blend the sounds within the third and fourth syllables and say the syllable chunks.

Finally push the four syllable chunks together to hear the word forming.

At this stage in the programme the child may be meeting vocabulary which is unfamiliar, so discuss meaning, as appropriate.

Once the child has read the word then they can write it on the lines.

For each syllable, encourage the child to say each sound as they write the matching sound spelling and blend the sounds together at the end of each chunk as well as the complete word at the end.

Multisyllable set 4

Activity 10 Spelling challenge

ability	a * bi * li * ty	___ * ___ * ___ * ___
identify	i * den * ti * fy	___ * ___ * ___ * ___
technology	tech * no * lo * gy	___ * ___ * ___ * ___
understanding	un * der * stan * ding	___ * ___ * ___ * ___
emergency	e * mer * gen * cy	___ * ___ * ___ * ___

Answers   Multisyllable set 4

Page 346
Activity 2 Syllable split

cal / cu / la / tor   i / den / ti / fy
a / cco / mmo / date   in / de / pen / dent
an / ti / ci / pate   be / lie / va / ble
ex / pe / ri / ment   e / mer / gen / cy
dis / co / ver / y   un / der /stan / ding
dis / a / ppoint / ment
in / gre / di / ent
bi / o / lo / gy
ad / min / i / ster
va / ri / e / ty
sig / ni / fi / cance
tech / no / lo / gy

Page 347
Activity 3 Advanced word tech

a / cco / mmo / date
ca / ter / pi / llar
re / co / ver / y
i / den / ti / fy
a / bil / i / ty
ex / pe / ri / ment

Page 348
Activity 4 Word strings

ability emergency ingredient
technology biology

activity certificate
communicate

understanding experiment
independent

recovery identify stability

Page 350
Activity 6 Syllable trap

a / cco / mo / date
i / den / ti / fy
be / lie / va / ble
an / ti / ci / pate
in / de / pen / dent
un / der / stan / ding
dis / co / ver / y
sta / bi / li / ty

Page 352
Activity 8 Syllable jigsaw

cal / cu / la / tor
in / ve / sti / gate
co / mu / ni / cate
e / mer / gen / cy
co / mu / ni / ty
ca / ter / pi / llar
tech / no / lo / gy

Page 353
Activity 9 Meaning & spelling

certificate

believable

calculator

experiment

Teacher word list — Suffixes: tion/cian/ssion sion/shion/cion

Advanced sound to sound spelling relationships with schwas

These suffixes represent a group of sounds, 'shun'.

2 Syllables	3 Syllables	4 Syllables	5 Syllables
tion	tion	tion	tion
station	addition	competition	evaluation
action	attention	condensation	imagination
fiction	attraction	contribution	
fraction	completion	conversation	
friction	condition	exploration	
motion	construction	information	
section	correction	introduction	
mention	description	population	
suction	direction	preparation	
	disruption	punctuation	
	instruction	revolution	
	position	satisfaction	
	production	separation	
	reaction		
	relation		
	solution		
	subtraction		
	cian	cian	cian
	beautician	politician	mathematician
	magician	electrician	
	musician		
	optician		
	physician		

2 Syllables	3 Syllables	4 Syllables	5 Syllables
ssion	ssion	ssion	ssion
mission	admission	expressionless	impressionable
passion	expression		
	impression		
	omission		
	permission		
	possession		
	procession		
	progression		

sion
mansion
pension
tension

shion
cushion
fashion

shion
fashionable

cion
suspicion

This set of cards is made up of multisyllable words. The syllables are indicated by an asterisk to aid reading. Copy onto card and cut out. Practise the dynamic blending – syllable by syllable reading strategy, as described in the 'Working through the programme' section, to read the words on these cards.

Activity 1 Reading multisyllable words highlighted	Suffixes: tion/cian/ssion shion/sion/cion

s t a * tion
i n * s t r u c * tion
m u * s i * cian
i * m a * g i * n a * tion
p er * m i * ssion
f a * shion
s u s * p i * cion
p e n * sion

This set of cards is made up of multisyllable. Copy onto card and cut out.
Practise the syllable by syllable/sound by sound reading strategy, as described in the 'Working through the programme' section, to read the words on these cards.

Activity 1 Reading multisyllable words	Suffixes: tion/cian/ssion shio/sion/cion

mention
description
optician
electrician
admission
impression
suspicion
mansion

Support the child to read the words one by one.

Ask the child to say the word again in their head or with their 'thinking voice' and notice how they split up each word into chunks of sounds, or syllables, as they say it.

For each word support the child to draw lines through the word to show where in the word they split it into syllables.

It is useful to discuss how they made their choice.

The first group of words has some sound spellings highlighted to help, and the first one is split as an example.

Activity 2 Syllable split	Suffixes: tion/cian/ssion shion/sion/cion

c o m/p e/t i/tion   m u s i cian

a d m i ssion   s t a tion

f r a c tion   m i ssion

o p t i cian   p o **ss** e ssion

Careful, the next ones do not have any sound spellings highlighted and include the less common suffixes:

tension

electrician

fashion

instructions

suspicion

impression

Support the child to read a word. Ask the child to say the word again in their head or with their 'thinking voice' and notice how they split up the word into chunks of sounds, or syllables, as they say it.

Ask the child to show where they split the word up into syllables by drawing lines through it.

Next ask the child to put a ring round each sound spelling or 'sh' 'u' 'n' suffix.

Finally ask the child to identify any schwas by highlighting them.

The word is written twice so that the child can refer to an uncluttered version of the word.

Activity 3 Advanced word tech	Suffixes: tion/cian/ssion shion/sion/cion
addition	addition
procession	procession
cushion	cushion
magician	magician
construction	construction
pension	pension
optician	optician
suspicion	suspicion

361

Ask the child to look at the word strings, each of which contains lots of words written with no gaps between.
Ask the child to track through the string and read each word.
At the end of the string the child writes down how many words are in that string.
Note that strings are written in a variety of styles.

Activity 4 Word strings	**Suffixes: tion/cian/ssion** **shion/sion/cion**

stationactionmissioncushionfashionmention

musicianopticiandirectionposition

suspicionconditioninstructionsadmission

permissionphysicianpreparationreaction

Support the child to read the words by giving information about sounds, supporting blending and syllable splitting, but do not supply the whole word.

Count how many words the child can read in one minute and record on the sheet. Repeat at a later time and see if the child can beat their own record.

Activity 5 Speeding fine	Suffixes: tion/cian/ssion shion/sion/cion

☐ mention
☐ conversation
☐ possession
☐ mission
☐ mathematician
☐ description
☐ competition
☐ station
☐ suspicion
☐ expression
☐ action
☐ introduction
☐ fashion
☐ pension
☐ progression
☐ construction
☐ preparation
☐ position
☐ subtraction

Number of words:

1.

2.

3.

Support the child to read the clue on the left and work out what the word is. To help the child, some of the syllables have been written in.
Ask the child to say the word in their head or with their 'thinking voice' and notice how they split up each word into chunks of sounds, or syllables, as they say it.
Support the child to write in the missing syllables, sound by sound, in the appropriate boxes.
Then, covering the boxes, ask the child to write out the word from memory on the line at the end, thinking about the syllables and the sounds in them.

Suffixes: tion/cian/ssion shion/sion/cion

Activity 8 Syllable jigsaw

Clue	Syllables	Line
Person who does magic	gi / cian	_____
Something you own	po / ssion	_____
Very big house	man	_____
Say hello and talk about yourself	in / duc	_____
Allow someone to do something	mi	_____
What everyone is wearing!	a / ble	_____
Talking to each other	ver / tion	_____

Support the child to read the words in the box on the left. This is the definition of a word.
Then ask the child to choose which of the words in the box on the right is the accepted spelling of the word, and tick to indicate.

Activity 9 Meaning & spelling	Suffixes: tion/cian/ssion shion/sion/cion	
Definition	**Which is the accepted spelling?**	**Tick**
Knowledge and facts	information	
	infermation	
Person who looks after our eyes and gives glasses	optition	
	optician	
To allow someone to do something	permission	
	permision	
To make sure you are ready for something	preparation	
	preparasion	

Support the child to read each word. To help, the words have been split into chunks of sounds, or syllables, as indicated by the asterisk * and red, blue and green colour coding.

Direct the child to blend the sounds within the first syllable and say the syllable chunk, then blend the sounds within the second syllable and so on.

Finally push the syllable chunks together to hear the word forming.

At this stage in the programme the child may be meeting vocabulary which is unfamiliar so discuss meaning, as appropriate.

Once the child has read the word, then they can write it on the lines.

For each syllable, encourage the child to say each sound as they write the matching sound spelling and blend the sounds together at the end of each chunk as well as the complete word at the end.

Activity 10 Spelling challenge

Suffixes: tion/cian/ssion shion/sion/cion

station	s t a * tion	* ___		* ___
addition	a * dd i * tion	* ___	* ___	
permission	p er * m i * ssion	* ___	* ___	
information	in * f or * m a * tion	* ___	* ___	* ___
competition	c o m * p e * t i * tion	* ___	* ___	* ___

Answers   Suffixes: tion/cian/ssion

Page 360
Activity 2 Syllable split

com / pe / ti / tion   mu /si / cian
ad / mi / ssion   sta / tion
frac / tion   mi / ssion
op / ti / cian   po / sse / ssion
ten / sion
e / lec / tri / cian
fa / shion
in / struc / tions
su / spi / cion
im / pre / ssion

Page 361
Activity 3 Advanced word tech

p r o / c e / ssion
c u / shion
m a / g i / cian
c o n / s t r u c / tion
p e n / sion
o p / t i / cian
s u / s p i / cion

Page 362
Activity 4 Word strings

station action mission
cushion fashion mention

musician optician direction
position

suspicion condition
instructions admission

permission physician
preparation reaction

Page 364
Activity 8 Syllable jigsaw

ma / gi / cian
po / se / ssion
man /sion
in / tro / duc / tion
per / mi / ssion
fa / shion / a / ble
con / ver / sa / tion

Page 365
Activity 9 Meaning & spelling

information

optician

permission

preparation

Teacher word list   Suffixes: sion
Advanced sound to sound spelling relationships with schwas

This suffix represents a group of sounds, 'zjun'

2 Syllables	3 Syllables	4 Syllables	5 Syllables
sion	sion	sion	sion
fusion	abrasion	occasional	occasionally
lesion	adhesion	television	
vision	cohesion		
	collision		
	conclusion		
	confusion		
	conversion		
	corrosion		
	decision		
	diversion		
	division		
	erosion		
	explosion		
	evasion		
	immersion		
	incision		
	inclusion		
	invasion		
	inversion		
	occasion		
	precision		
	revision		

Remember that sion can also be a 'sh' 'ʊ' 'n' suffix e.g. pension

This set of cards is made up of multisyllable words. The syllables are indicated by an asterisk to aid reading. Copy onto card and cut out. Practise the dynamic blending – syllable by syllable reading strategy, as described in the 'Working through the programme' section, to read the words on these cards.

Activity 1 Reading multisyllable words highlighted	Suffixes: sion

v i * sion
d e * c i * sion
e x * p l o * sion
i n * c l u * sion
r e * v i * sion
i n * v a * sion
c o l l * i * sion
t e l * e * v i * sion

This set of cards is made up of multisyllable words. Copy onto card and cut out.
Practise the dynamic blending – syllable by syllable reading strategy, as described in the 'Working through the programme' section, to read the words on these cards.

Activity 1 Reading multisyllable words	Suffixes: sion

fusion
diversion
conversion
erosion
immersion
occasion
precision
occasional

Ask the child to say the word again in their head or with their 'thinking voice' and notice how they split up each word into chunks of sounds, or syllables, as they say it.

For each word support the child to draw lines through the word to show where in the word they split it into syllables.

It is useful to discuss how they made their choice.

The first group of words has some sound spellings highlighted to help, and the first one is split as an example.

Activity 2 Syllable split	Suffixes: sion

i n/v a/sion   t e l e v i sion

c o n f u sion   o **cc** a sion

v i sion   e x p l o sion

i **mm er** sion   p r e c i sion

c o n v **er** sion   r e v i sion

Careful, the next ones do not have any sound spellings highlighted:

conclusion

division

occasional

erosion

corrosion

Remember that sion can also represent a different suffix!

pension

mansion

Support the child to read a word. Ask the child to say the word again in their head or with
their 'thinking voice' and notice how they split up the word into chunks of sounds, or syllables, as they say it.
Ask the child to show where they split the word up into syllables by drawing lines through it.
Next ask the child to put a ring round each sound spelling or 'zj' 'ʊ' 'n' suffix.
Finally ask the child to identify any schwas by highlighting them.
The word is written twice so that the child can refer to an uncluttered version of the word.

Activity 3 Advanced word tech   Suffixes: sion

occasion   occasion

conclusion   conclusion

television   television

revision   revision

vision   vision

confusion   confusion

collision   collision

decision   decision

Ask the child to look at the word strings, each of which contains lots of words written with no gaps between.
Ask the child to track through the string and read each word.
At the end of the string the child writes down how many words are in that string.
Note that strings are written in a variety of styles.

Activity 4 Word strings	Suffixes: sion

televisioncollisiondecisioncorrosion

explosiondivisionoccasionallyconfusion

visioninvasionconversionoccasion

inclusionrevisionconclusion

Support the child to read the words by giving information about sounds, supporting blending and syllable splitting, but do not supply the whole word.

Count how many words the child can read in one minute and record on the sheet. Repeat at a later time and see if the child can beat their own record.

Activity 5 Speeding fine   Suffixes: sion

☐ conclusion
☐ television
☐ collision
☐ conversion
☐ vision
☐ division
☐ explosion
☐ inclusion
☐ erosion
☐ decision
☐ confusion
☐ occasion
☐ invasion
☐ immersion
☐ occasionally
☐ corrosion
☐ revision

Number of words:

1.

2.

3.

Support the child to read the clue on the left and work out what the word is. To help the child, some of the syllables have been written in.
Ask the child to say the word in their head or with their 'thinking voice' and notice how they split up each word into chunks of sounds, or syllables, as they say it.
Support the child to write in the missing syllables, sound by sound, in the appropriate boxes.
Then, covering the boxes, ask the child to write out the word from memory on the line at the end, thinking about the syllables and the sounds in them.

Suffixes: sion

Activity 8 Syllable jigsaw

Clue	Syllables	Word
Sum for sharing things	vi / sion	_____
When something blows up	ex / sion	_____
Ability to see	sion	_____
Everyone can join in	in / sion	_____
Swot for a test	vi / sion	_____
Rust	rro / sion	_____
Gogglebox	le / sion	_____

Support the child to read the words in the box on the left. This is the definition of a word.
Then ask the child to choose which of the words in the box on the right is the accepted spelling of the word, and tick to indicate.

Activity 9 Meaning & spelling   Suffixes: sion

Definition	Which is the accepted spelling?	Tick
The end or final part	conclusion	
	conclussion	
The sense of seeing	vission	
	vision	
In maths, the sharing sum	division	
	divission	
A special event	occassion	
	occasion	

Support the child to read each word. To help the words have been split into chunks of sounds or syllables as indicated by the asterisk * and red, blue and green colour coding.

Direct the child to blend the sounds within the first syllable and say the syllable chunk, then blend the sounds within the second syllable and so on.

Finally push the syllable chunks together to hear the word forming.

At this stage in the programme the child may be meeting vocabulary which is unfamiliar so discuss meaning, as appropriate.

Once the child has read the word, then they can write it on the lines.

For each syllable, encourage the child to say each sound as they write the matching sound spelling and blend the sounds together at the end of each chunk as well as the complete word at the end.

Activity 10 Spelling challenge

Suffixes: sion

vision   v i * sion   _____ * _____

confusion   c o n * f u * sion   _____ * _____ * _____

decision   d e * c i * sion   _____ * _____ * _____

revision   r e * v i * sion   _____ * _____ * _____

television   t e * l e * v i * sion   _____ * _____ * _____ * _____

Answers   Suffixes: sion

Page 371

Activity 2 Syllable split

in / va / sion   te / le / vi / sion
con / fu / sion   o / cca / sion
vi / sion   ex / plo / sion
i / mmer / sion   pre / ci / sion
con / ver / sion   re / vi / sion
con / clu / sion
di / vi / sion
o / cca / sion / al
e / ro / sion
co / rro / sion

pen / sion   'sh' 'u' 'n' suffix reminder
man / sion

Page 372

Activity 3 Advanced word tech

c o n / c l u / sion
t e / l e / v i / sion
r e / v i / sion
v i / sion
c o n / f u / sion
c o / ll i / sion
d e / c i / sion

Page 373

Activity 4 Word strings

television collision decision corrosion

explosion division occasionally confusion

vision invasion conversion occasion

inclusion revision conclusion

Page 375

Activity 8 Syllable jigsaw

di / vi / sion
ex / plo / sion
vi / sion
in / clu / sion
re / vi / sion
co / rro / sion
te / le / vi / sion

Page 376

Activity 9 Meaning & spelling

conclusion

vision

division

occasion

Teacher word list

Suffixes: ture

Advanced sound to sound spelling relationships with schwas

This suffix represents a group of sounds, 'cher'.

2 Syllables		3 Syllables	4 Syllables
ture	ture	ture	ture
capture	structure	adventure	acupuncture
culture	texture	aperture	agriculture
creature	venture	furniture	expenditure
feature	vulture	recapture	manufacture
fixture		signature	temperature
fracture			
future			
gesture			
lecture			
mixture			
moisture			
nature			
nurture			
pasture			
picture			
posture			
rapture			
scripture			
sculpture			
stature			

This set of cards is made up of multisyllable words. The syllables are indicated by an asterisk to aid reading. Copy onto card and cut out. Practise the dynamic blending – syllable by syllable reading strategy, as described in the 'Working through the programme' section, to read the words on these cards.

| Activity 1 Reading multisyllable words highlighted | Suffixes: ture |

c a p * ture
l e c * ture
n a * ture
v u l * ture
f ur * n i * ture
a d * v e n * ture
a * g r i * c u l * ture
m a n * u * f a c * ture

This set of cards is made up of multisyllable words. Copy onto card and cut out.
Practise the dynamic blending – syllable by syllable reading strategy, as described in the 'Working through the programme' section, to read the words on these cards.

Activity 1 Reading multisyllable words	**Suffixes: ture**

culture
creature
fracture
mixture
picture
sculpture
signature
temperature

Support the child to read the words one by one.

Ask the child to say the word again in their head or with their 'thinking voice' and notice how they split up each word into chunks of sounds, or syllables, as they say it.

For each word support the child to draw lines through the word to show where in the word they split it into syllables.

It is useful to discuss how they made their choice.

The first group of words has some sound spellings highlighted to help, and the first one is split as an example.

Activity 2 Syllable split   Suffixes: ture

a d/v e/n ture   l e c ture

p i c ture   f **ur** n i ture

a g r i c u l ture   s i g n a ture

f u ture   s t r u c ture

m a n u f a c ture   c r **ea** ture

Careful, the next ones do not have any sound spellings highlighted:

m i x t u r e

t e m p e r a t u r e

r e c a p t u r e

t e x t u r e

v u l t u r e

s c u l p t u r e

Support the child to read a word. Ask the child to say the word again in their head or with their 'thinking voice' and notice how they split up the word into chunks of sounds, or syllables, as they say it.

Ask the child to show where they split the word up into syllables by drawing lines through it.

Next ask the child to put a ring round each sound spelling or 'ch' 'er' suffix.

Finally ask the child to identify any schwas by highlighting them.

The word is written twice so that the child can refer to an uncluttered version of the word.

Activity 3 Advanced word tech   Suffixes: ture

furniture   furniture

creature   creature

agriculture   agriculture

capture   capture

picture   picture

signature   signature

expenditure   expenditure

mixture   mixture

Ask the child to look at the word strings, each of which contains lots of words written with no gaps between.
Ask the child to track through the string and read each word.
At the end of the string the child writes down how many words are in that string.
Note that strings are written in a variety of styles.

Activity 4 Word strings	Suffixes: ture

signaturefuturetemperatureposturecapture

agriculturefurniturefixturenaturelecture

adventurepicturevulturefracturestature

featurefuturerecapturesculpture

Support the child to read the words by giving information about sounds, supporting blending and syllable splitting, but do not supply the whole word.

Count how many words the child can read in one minute and record on the sheet. Repeat at a later time and see if the child can beat their own record.

Activity 5 Speeding fine   Suffixes: ture

☐ furniture
☐ picture
☐ adventure
☐ temperature
☐ fracture
☐ nature
☐ signature
☐ expenditure
☐ future
☐ sculpture
☐ structure
☐ agriculture
☐ posture
☐ fixture
☐ texture
☐ recapture
☐ lecture
☐ mixture
☐ vulture

Number of words:

1.

2.

3.

Support the child to read the clue on the left and work out what the word is. To help the child, some of the syllables have been written in.

Ask the child to say the word in their head or with their 'thinking voice' and notice how they split up each word into chunks of sounds, or syllables, as they say it.

Support the child to write in the missing syllables, sound by sound, in the appropriate boxes.

Then, covering the boxes, ask the child to write out the word from memory on the line at the end, thinking about the syllables and the sounds in them.

Suffixes: ture

Activity 8 Syllable jigsaw

Exciting journey | re | ven | ture

Catch again | re | | ture

A painting or drawing | | | ture

Related to farming | a | cul | ture

Break a bone | | |

Make something | | u | ture

How something feels | | |

Support the child to read the words in the box on the left. This is the definition of a word.
Then ask the child to choose which of the words in the box on the right is the accepted spelling of the word, and tick to indicate.

Activity 9 Meaning & spelling   Suffixes: ture

Definition	Which is the accepted spelling?	Tick
In a time that hasn't yet happened	futur	
	future	
Your name, written at the end of a letter or document	signiture	
	signature	
Related to farming and growing crops	agriculture	
	agraculture	
To break a bone in the body	fractur	
	fracture	

Support the child to read each word. To help, the words have been split into chunks of sounds, or syllables, as indicated by the asterisk * and red, blue and green colour coding.

Direct the child to blend the sounds within the first syllable chunk, then blend the sounds within the second syllable and so on.

Finally push the syllable chunks together to hear the word forming.

At this stage in the programme the child may be meeting vocabulary which is unfamiliar so discuss meaning, as appropriate.

Once the child has read the word, then they can write it on the lines.

For each syllable, encourage the child to say each sound as they write the matching sound spelling and blend the sounds together at the end of each chunk as well as the complete word at the end.

Activity 10 Spelling challenge   Suffixes: ture

picture   p i c * t u r e   _____ *

future   f u * t u r e   _____ *

adventure   a d * v e n * t u r e _____ * _____ *

furniture   f u r * n i * t u r e _____ * _____ *

agriculture   a * g r i * c u l * t u r e   _____ * _____ * _____ *

Answers

Suffixes: ture

Page 382
Activity 2 Syllable split

ad / ven / ture
pic / ture
a / gri / cul / ture
fu / ture
man / u / fac / ture
mix / ture
tem / per / a / ture
r e / c a p / ture
t e x / ture
v u l / ture
s c u l p / ture

lec / ture
fur / ni / ture
sig / na / ture
struc / ture
crea / ture

Page 383
Activity 3 Advanced word tech

c r ea / ture
a / g r i / c u l / ture
c a p / ture
p i c / ture
s i g / n a / ture
e x / p e n / d i / ture
m i x / ture

Page 384
Activity 4 Word strings

signature future temperature posture capture

agriculture furniture fixture nature lecture

adventure picture vulture fracture stature

feature future recapture sculpture

Page 386
Activity 8 Syllable jigsaw

ad / ven / ture
re / cap / ture
pic / ture
a / gri / cul / ture
frac / ture
man / u / fac / ture
tex / ture

Page 387
Activity 9 Meaning & spelling

future

signature

agriculture

fracture

Teacher word list   Suffixes: sure/zure
Advanced sound to sound spelling relationships with schwas

These suffixes represent a group of sounds, 'zure'.

2 Syllables	3 Syllables

sure   sure

closure   composure
leisure   disclosure
measure   displeasure
pleasure   enclosure
                        erasure
                        exposure
                        leisurely
                        measurement

zure

azure
seizure

This set of cards is made up of multisyllable words. The syllables are indicated by an asterisk to aid reading. Copy onto card and cut out. Practise the dynamic blending – syllable by syllable reading strategy, as described in the 'Working through the programme' section, to read the words on these cards.

Activity 1 Reading multisyllable words highlighted	Suffixes: sure/zure

c l o * sure
m ea * sure
l ei * sure
p l ea * sure
e n * c l o * sure
e x * p o * sure
m ea * sure * m e n t
s ei * zure

This set of cards is made up of multisyllable words. Copy onto card and cut out.
Practise the dynamic blending – syllable by syllable reading strategy, as described in the 'Working through the programme' section, to read the words on these cards.

Activity 1 Reading multisyllable words   Suffixes: sure/zure

leisure
measure
pleasure
composure
disclosure
displeasure
enclosure
seizure

Support the child to read the words one by one.

Ask the child to say the word again in their head or with their 'thinking voice' and notice how they split up each word into chunks of sounds, or syllables, as they say it.

For each word support the child to draw lines through the word to show where in the word they split it into syllables.

It is useful to discuss how they made their choice.

The first group of words has some sound spellings highlighted to help, and the first one is split as an example.

Activity 2 Syllable split	**Suffixes: sure/zure**

d i s/c l o/sure   m **ea** sure

e n c l o sure   m **ea** sure m e n t

s **ei** zure   c o m p o sure

l **ei** sure   p l **ea** sure

e x p o sure   l **ei** sure l y

c l o sure   a zure

Support the child to read a word. Ask the child to say the word again in their head or with their 'thinking voice' and notice how they split up the word into chunks of sounds, or syllables, as they say it.

Ask the child to show where they split the word up into syllables by drawing lines through it.

Next ask the child to put a ring round each sound spelling or 'zj' 'er' suffix.

Finally ask the child to identify any schwas by highlighting them.

The word is written twice so that the child can refer to an uncluttered version of the word.

Activity 3 Advanced word tech   Suffixes: sure/zure

enclosure	
measure	measure
displeasure	displeasure
seizure	seizure
leisure	leisure
measurement	measurement
exposure	exposure

Ask the child to look at the word strings, each of which contains lots of words written with no gaps between.
Ask the child to track through the string and read each word.
At the end of the string the child writes down how many words are in that string.
Note that strings are written in a variety of styles.

Activity 4 Word strings	Suffixes: sure/zure

measurementdisclosureleisurely

pleasureleisureseizureclosure

erasuredispleasureexposure

composurepleasureenclosuremeasure

Support the child to read the words by giving information about sounds, supporting blending and syllable splitting, but do not supply the whole word.

Count how many words the child can read in one minute and record on the sheet. Repeat at a later time and see if the child can beat their own record.

Activity 5 Speeding fine

Suffixes: sure/zure

- ☐ composure
- ☐ enclosure
- ☐ measure
- ☐ exposure
- ☐ disclosure
- ☐ measurement
- ☐ leisure
- ☐ pleasure
- ☐ leisurely
- ☐ closure
- ☐ seizure

Number of words:

1.

2.

3.

Support the child to read the clue on the left and work out what the word is. To help the child, some of the syllables have been written in.

Ask the child to say the word in their head or with their 'thinking voice' and notice how they split up each word into chunks of sounds, or syllables, as they say it.

Support the child to write in the missing syllables, sound by sound, in the appropriate box.

Then, covering the boxes, ask the child to write out the word from memory on the line at the end, thinking about the syllables and the sounds in them.

Suffixes: sure/zure

Activity 8 Syllable jigsaw

Clue				Word line
Reveal something	dis		sure	_____
Open to the weather	ex		sure	_____
Relaxing time			sure	_____
How big or heavy			sure	_____
Enjoyment			sure	_____
Calm		po	sure	_____
Not happy	dis		sure	_____

Support the child to read the words in the box on the left. This is the definition of a word.
Then ask the child to choose which of the words in the box on the right is the accepted spelling of the word and tick to indicate.

Activity 9 Meaning & spelling   Suffixes: sure/zure

Definition	Which is the accepted spelling?	Tick
Free from work	leisure	
	lesure	
Find the quantity or dimensions of something	measure	
	meazure	
A fence or barrier around something	enclozure	
	enclosure	
In control and calm	composure	
	compozure	

Support the child to read each word. To help, the words have been split into chunks of sounds, or syllables, as indicated by the asterisk * and red, blue and green colour coding.

Direct the child to blend the sounds within the first syllable and say the syllable chunk, then blend the sounds within the second syllable and so on.

Finally push the syllable chunks together to hear the word forming.

At this stage in the programme the child may be meeting vocabulary which is unfamiliar so discuss meaning, as appropriate.

Once the child has read the word, then they can write it on the lines.

For each syllable, encourage the child to say each sound as they write the matching sound spelling and blend the sounds together at the end of each chunk as well as the complete word at the end.

Activity 10 Spelling challenge

Suffixes: sure/zure

Word	Chunks			
measure	m ea * sure	___ * ___		
leisure	l ei * sure	___ * ___		
composure	c o m * p o * sure	___ * ___ * ___		
disclosure	d i s * c l o * sure	___ * ___ * ___		
measurement	m ea * sure * m e n t	___ * ___ * ___		

Answers   Suffixes: sure/zure

Page 393
Activity 2 Syllable split

dis / clo / sure	mea / sure
en / clo / sure	mea / sure / ment
sei / zure	com / po / sure
lei / sure	plea / sure
ex / po / sure	lei / sure / ly
cl o / sure	a / zure

Page 394
Activity 3 Advanced word tech

m ea / sure
d i s / p l ea / sure
s ei / zure
l ei / sure
m ea / sure / m e n t
e x / p o / sure

Page 395
Activity 4 Word strings

measurement disclosure leisurely

pleasure leisure seizure closure

erasure displeasure exposure

composure pleasure enclosure measure

Page 397
Activity 8 Syllable jigsaw

dis / clo /sure
ex / po /sure
lei / sure
mea / sure
plea / sure
com / po / sure
dis / plea / sure

Page 398
Activity 9 Meaning & spelling

leisure

measure

enclosure

composure

Teacher word list   Suffixes: cious/scious/tious
Advanced sound to sound spelling relationships with schwas

These suffixes represent a group of sounds, 'shus'.

2 Syllables	3 Syllables	4 Syllables
cious	cious	cious
gracious	atrocious	maliciously
officious	delicious	suspiciously
precious	ferocious	
spacious	graciously	
vicious	malicious	
	suspicious	
	tenacious	
	ungracious	
	vivacious	
	voracious	

scious	scious	scious
conscious	subconscious	subconsciously
luscious	unconscious	unconsciously

tious	tious	
cautious	ambitious	
	cautiously	
	contentious	
	facetious	
	fictitious	
	fractious	
	infectious	
	nutritious	

This set of cards is made up of multisyllable words. The syllables are indicated by an asterisk to aid reading. Copy onto card and cut out. Practise the dynamic blending – syllable by syllable reading strategy, as described in the 'Working through the programme' section, to read the words on these cards.

Activity 1 Reading multisyllable words highlighted	Suffixes: cious/scious/ tious

g r a * cious

f e * r o * cious

m a l * i * cious

u n * c o n * scious

s u b * c o n * scious

i n * f e c * tious

n u * t r i * tious

a m * b i * tious

This set of cards is made up of multisyllable words. Copy onto card and cut out.
Practise the dynamic blending – syllable by syllable reading strategy, as described in the 'Working through the programme' section, to read the words on these cards.

Activity 1 Reading multisyllable words	**Suffixes: cious/ scious/tious**

precious
delicious
suspicious
conscious
luscious
cautious
fictitious
ambitious

Support the child to read the words one by one.

Ask the child to say the word again in their head or with their 'thinking voice' and notice how they split up each word into chunks of sounds, or syllables, as they say it.

For each word support the child to draw lines through the word to show where in the word they split it into syllables.

It is useful to discuss how they made their choice.

The first group of words has some sound spellings highlighted to help, and the first one is split as an example.

Activity 2 Syllable split   Suffixes: cious/scious/tious

m a l/i/cious   g r a cious

c o n scious   c **au** tious

d e l i cious   i n f e c tious

s u s pi cious   n u t r i tious

u n c o n scious   p r e cious

Careful, the next ones do not have any sound spellings highlighted:

luscious

spacious

ambitious

vivacious

vicious

ferocious

Support the child to read a word. Ask the child to say the word again in their head or with their 'thinking voice' and notice how they split up the word into chunks of sounds, or syllables, as they say it.

Ask the child to show where they split the word up into syllables by drawing lines through it.

Next ask the child to put a ring round each sound spelling or 'sh' 'ʊ' 's' suffix.

Finally ask the child to identify any schwas by highlighting them.

The word is written twice so that the child can refer to an uncluttered version of the word.

Activity 3 Advanced word tech	Suffixes: cious/scious/tious
precious	precious
ambitious	ambitious
unconscious	unconscious
suspicious	suspicious
infectious	infectious
spacious	spacious
nutritious	nutritious
maliciously	maliciously

Ask the child to look at the word strings, each of which contains lots of words written with no gaps between.
Ask the child to track through the string and read each word.
At the end of the string the child writes down how many words are in that string.
Note that strings are written in a variety of styles.

Activity 4 Word strings   Suffixes: cious/scious/tious

graciousviciouscautiousconscious

atrociousconsciouspreciousdelicious

maliciousambitiousferociousinfectious

lusciousvivaciousnutritioussuspicious

Support the child to read the words by giving information about sounds, supporting blending and syllable splitting, but do not supply the whole word.

Count how many words the child can read in one minute and record on the sheet. Repeat at a later time and see if the child can beat their own record.

Activity 5 Speeding fine   Suffixes: cious/scious/tious

☐ vicious
☐ ambitious
☐ malicious
☐ cautious
☐ infectious
☐ unconsciously
☐ luscious
☐ precious
☐ graciously
☐ delicious
☐ ferocious
☐ fictitious
☐ spacious
☐ suspicious
☐ nutritious
☐ subconsciously

Number of words:

1.

2.

3.

Support the child to read the clue on the left and work out what the word is. To help the child, some of the syllables have been written in. Ask the child to say the word in their head or with their 'thinking voice' and notice how they split up each word into chunks of sounds, or syllables, as they say it.

Support the child to write in the missing syllables, sound by sound, in the appropriate boxes.

Then, covering the boxes, ask the child to write out the word from memory on the line at the end, thinking about the syllables and the sounds in them.

Activity 8 Syllable jigsaw

Suffixes: cious/scious/tious

Clue	Syllables	Word
Nasty and mean		i	cious	
Keen to do well	am		cious	
Awake and alert	con			
May pass on illness		fec		
Careful	cau			
Really tasty	li			
Very valuable	pre			

Support the child to read the words in the box on the left. This is the definition of a word.
Then ask the child to choose which of the words in the box on the right is the accepted spelling of the word, and tick to indicate.

Activity 9 Meaning & spelling Suffixes: cious/scious/tious

Definition	Which is the accepted spelling?	Tick
Kind and helpful	gracious	
	gratious	
Being careful	cautious	
	causcious	
Of high price or great value	precious	
	prescious	
Tastes lovely	deliscious	
	delicious	

Support the child to read each word. To help the words have been split into chunks of sounds, or syllables, as indicated by the asterisk * and red and blue colour coding.

Direct the child to blend the sounds within the first syllable and say the syllable chunk, then blend the sounds within the second syllable and say the syllable chunk and so on.

Finally push the syllable chunks together to hear the word forming.

At this stage in the programme the child may be meeting vocabulary which is unfamiliar so discuss meaning, as appropriate.

Once the child has read the word, then they can write it on the lines.

For each syllable, encourage the child to say each sound as they write the matching sound spelling and blend the sounds together at the end of each chunk as well as the complete word at the end.

Activity 10 Spelling challenge

Suffixes: cious/scious/tious

gracious	g r a * cious	* ___ ___
precious	p r e * cious	* ___ ___
cautious	c au * tious	* ___ ___
delicious	d e * l i * cious	* * ___ ___
ambitious	a m * b i * tious	* * ___ ___

Answers | Suffixes: cious/scious/tious

Page 404
Activity 2 Syllable split

mal / i / cious	gra / cious
con / scious	cau / tious
de / li / cious	in / fec / tious
su / spi / cious	n u / tri / tious
un / con / scious	pre / cious
lu / scious	
spa / cious	
am / bi / tious	
vi / va / cious	
vi / cious	
fe / ro / cious	

Page 405
Activity 3 Advanced word tech

a m / b i / tious
u n / c o n / scious
s u / s p i / cious
i n / f e c / tious
s p a / cious
n u / t r i / tious
m a l / i / cious / l y

Page 406
Activity 4 Word strings

gracious vicious cautious conscious

atrocious conscious precious delicious

malicious ambitious ferocious infectious

luscious vivacious nutritious suspicious

Page 408
Activity 8 Syllable jigsaw

mal / i / cious
am / bi / tious
con / scious
in / fec / tious
cau / tious
de / li / cious
pre / cious

Page 409
Activity 9 Meaning & spelling

gracious

cautious

precious

delicious

Teacher word list   Suffixes: cial/tial
Advanced sound to sound spelling relationships with schwas

These suffixes represent a group of sounds, 'shul'

2 Syllables	3 Syllables	4 Syllables
cial	cial	cial
crucial	financial	antisocial
facial	judicial	beneficial
racial	official	especially
social	provincial	financially
special	socially	specialism
	socialise	
	specialise	
	specialist	
	unsocial	
tial	tial	tial
martial	credential	differential
partial	essential	influential
spatial	impartial	initialise
	initial	initially
	palatial	residential
	potential	
	sequential	
	substantial	

This set of cards is made up of multisyllable words. The syllables are indicated by an asterisk to aid reading. Copy onto card and cut out. Practise the dynamic blending – syllable by syllable reading strategy, as described in the 'Working through the programme' section, to read the words on these cards.

| **Activity 1 Reading multisyllable words highlighted** | **Suffixes: cial/tial** |

| s p e * cial |
| s o * cial |
| o * ff i * cial |
| b e n * e * f i * cial |
| p ar * tial |
| i n * i * tial |
| e * ss e n * tial |
| re s * i * d e n * tial |

This set of cards is made up of multisyllable words. Copy onto card and cut out.
Practise the syllable by dynamic blending – syllable by syllable reading strategy, as described in the
'Working through the programme' section, to read the words on these cards.

Activity 1 Reading multisyllable words	Suffixes: cial/tial

special
financial
specialist
antisocial
spatial
influential
potential
sequential

Support the child to read the words one by one.
Ask the child to say the word again in their head or with their 'thinking voice' and notice how they split up each word into chunks of sounds, or syllables, as they say it.
For each word support the child to draw lines through the word to show where in the word they split it into syllables.
It is useful to discuss how they made their choice.
The first group of words has some sound spellings highlighted to help, and the first one is split as an example.

Activity 2 Syllable split   Suffixes: cial/tial

f i/n a n/cial   s p e cial

i n f l u e n tial   d i **ff er** e n tial

s p a tial   p o t e n tial

b e n e f i cial   i n i tial

e **ss** e n tial   s e **qu** e n tial

social

official

antisocial

residential

socialise

substantial

415

Support the child to read a word. Ask the child to say the word again in their head or with their 'thinking voice' and notice how they split up the word into chunks of sounds, or syllables, as they say it.

Ask the child to show where they split the word up into syllables by drawing lines through it.

Next ask the child to put a ring round each sound spelling or 'sh' 'u' 'l' suffix.

Finally ask the child to identify any schwas by highlighting them.

The word is written twice so that the child can refer to an uncluttered version of the word.

Activity 3 Advanced word tech	Suffixes: cial/tial

financial	financial
residential	residential
official	official
potential	potential
essential	essential
partial	partial
antisocial	antisocial
specialist	specialist

Ask the child to look at the word strings, each of which contains lots of words written with no gaps between.
Ask the child to track through the string and read each word.
At the end of the string the child writes down how many words are in that string.
Note that strings are written in a variety of styles.

Activity 4 Word strings	Suffixes: cial/tial

officialspecialinitial

socialinfluentialspecialistresidential

financialpartialfacialspecialismofficial

antisocialessentialsequentialsubstantial

Support the child to read the words by giving information about sounds, supporting blending and syllable splitting, but do not supply the whole word.

Count how many words the child can read in one minute and record on the sheet. Repeat at a later time and see if the child can beat their own record.

Activity 5 Speeding fine   Suffixes: cial/tial

☐ crucial
☐ social
☐ financial
☐ essential
☐ initial
☐ residential
☐ beneficial
☐ official
☐ credential
☐ potential
☐ facial
☐ partial
☐ provincial
☐ substantial
☐ differential
☐ sequential

Number of words:
1.
2.
3.

Support the child to read the clue on the left and work out what the word is. To help the child, some of the syllables have been written in.

Ask the child to say the word in their head or with their 'thinking voice' and notice how they split up each word into chunks of sounds, or syllables, as they say it.

Support the child to write in the missing syllables, sound by sound, in the appropriate boxes.

Then, covering the boxes, ask the child to write out the word from memory on the line at the end, thinking about the syllables and the sounds in them.

Suffixes: cial/tial

Activity 8 Syllable jigsaw

Clue			
To do with money	fi		cial
First or beginning	i	ni	
Only partly completed			tial
Friendly			cial
Very important	cru		
One by one	e	quen	
Vital			

Support the child to read the words in the box on the left. This is the definition of a word.
Then ask the child to choose which of the words in the box on the right is the accepted spelling of the word, and tick to indicate.

Activity 9 Meaning & spelling   Suffixes: cial/tial

Definition	Which is the accepted spelling?	Tick
Enjoy the company of people	social	
	sotial	
The first, beginning or start of something	inicial	
	initial	
Really important	crutial	
	crucial	
Unique and valued	spetial	
	special	

Support the child to read each word. To help the words have been split into chunks of sounds or syllables as indicated by the asterisk * and red, blue and green colour coding.

Direct the child to blend the sounds within the first syllable and say the syllable chunk, then blend the sounds within the second syllable and say the syllable chunk and so on.

Finally push the syllable chunks together to hear the word forming.

At this stage in the programme the child may be meeting vocabulary which is unfamiliar so discuss meaning, as appropriate.

Once the child has read the word, then they can write it on the lines.

For each syllable, encourage the child to say each sound as they write the matching sound spelling and blend the sounds together at the end of each chunk as well as the complete word at the end.

Suffixes: cial/tial

Activity 10 Spelling challenge

social	s o * c i a l	* _____ * _____
crucial	c r u * c i a l	* _____ * _____
financial	f i * n a n * c i a l	* _____ * _____ * _____
essential	e * s s e n * t i a l	* _____ * _____ * _____
residential	r e * s i * d e n * t i a l	* _____ * _____ * _____ * _____

Answers

Suffixes: cial/tial

Page 415
Activity 2 Syllable split

fi / nan / cial	spe / cial
in / flu / en / tial	di / ffer / en / tial
spa / tial	po / ten / tial
be / ne / fi / cial	i / ni / tial
e / ssen / tial	se / quen / tial
so / cial	
o / ffi / cial	
an / ti / so / cial	
re / si / den / tial	
so / cial / ise	
sub / stan / tial	

Page 416
Activity 3 Advanced word tech

r e / s i / d e n / tial
o / ff i / cial
p o / t e n / tial
e / ss e n / tial
p ar / tial
a n / t i / s o / cial
s p e / cial / i s t

Page 417
Activity 4 Word strings

official special initial

social influential specialist residential

financial partial facial specialism official

antisocial essential sequential substantial

Page 419
Activity 8 Syllable jigsaw

f i / nan / cial
i / ni / tial
par / tial
so / cial
cru / cial
se / quen / tial
e / ssen / tial

Page 420
Activity 9 Meaning & spelling

social

initial

crucial

special
